Language Modeling for Information Retrieval

THE KLUWER INTERNATIONAL SERIES
ON INFORMATION RETRIEVAL

Series Editor:
W. Bruce Croft
University of Massachusetts, Amherst

Language Modeling for Information Retrieval

Edited by

W. Bruce Croft

*University of Massachusetts,
Amherst U.S.A.*

and

John Lafferty

*Carniege Mellon University,
Pittsburgh, U.S.A.*

KLUWER ACADEMIC PUBLISHERS

DORDRECHT / BOSTON / LONDON

A C.I.P. Catalogue record for this book is available from the Library of Congress.

ISBN 978-90-481-6263-5

Published by Kluwer Academic Publishers,
P.O. Box 17, 3300 AA Dordrecht, The Netherlands.

Sold and distributed in North, Central and South America
by Kluwer Academic Publishers,
101 Philip Drive, Norwell, MA 02061, U.S.A.

In all other countries, sold and distributed
by Kluwer Academic Publishers,
P.O. Box 322, 3300 AH Dordrecht, The Netherlands.

Printed on acid-free paper

Contents

Preface

A statistical language model, or more simply a *language model*, is a prob-abilistic mechanism for generating text. Such a definition is general enough to include an endless variety of schemes. However, a distinction should be made between generative models, which can in principle be used to synthesize artificial text, and discriminative techniques to classify text into predefined categories.

The first statistical language modeler was Claude Shannon. In exploring the application of his newly founded theory of information to human language, Shannon considered language as a statistical source, and measured how well simple n-gram models predicted or, equivalently, compressed natural text. To do this, he estimated the entropy of English through experiments with human subjects, and also estimated the cross-entropy of the n-gram models on natural text.[1] The ability of language models to be quantitatively evaluated in this way is one of their important virtues.

Of course, estimating the true entropy of language is an elusive goal, aiming at many moving targets, since language is so varied and evolves so quickly. Yet fifty years after Shannon's study, language models remain, by all measures, far from the Shannon entropy limit in terms of their predictive power. However, this has not kept them from being useful for a variety of text processing tasks, and moreover can be viewed as encouragement that there is still great room for improvement in statistical language modeling.

In the past several years a new framework for information retrieval has emerged that is based on statistical language modeling. The approach differs from traditional probabilistic approaches in interesting and subtle ways, and is fundamentally different from vector space methods. It is striking that the language modeling approach to information retrieval was not proposed until the late 1990s; however, until recently the information retrieval and language modeling research communities were somewhat isolated. The communities are

---

[1]C. E. Shannon. Prediction and entropy of printed English. *Bell System Technical Journal*, Vol. 30, pp. 51–64, 1951.

now beginning to work more closely together, and research at a number of sites has confirmed that the language modeling approach is an effective and theoretically attractive probabilistic framework for building IR systems. But there is still groundwork to do in understanding the basics of this new approach, and many possibilities exist for further development of the framework.

This book contains a collection of papers that together give an overview of the recent research activity in the area of language modeling for information retrieval. The book grew out of a workshop on this topic that took place at Carnegie Mellon University on May 31 and June 1, 2001, under the support of ARDA. Several of the presentations were extended into the papers that appear here.

The papers reflect the major themes of the workshop, and can be thought of as falling into three broad, overlapping categories. Several papers address the mathematical formulation and interpretation of the language modeling approach. These papers focus on the important but subtle and elusive concept of relevance, which was a recurring theme of the workshop. Another category is the development of the language modeling approach for improving ad hoc retrieval—the problem of finding documents to answer unstructured queries on unrestricted topics. In these papers the focus is on the problems of variance reduction, better estimation of relevance models, improving cross-language retrieval, score normalization and the distribution of scores in relevant and nonrelevant documents. The third category of papers treats the use of language modeling methods in other important application areas within information retrieval, including topic tracking, text classification, and summarization.

The diversity of the papers collected here is an indication of the richness of language modeling methods for approaching information retrieval problems. We believe that the papers provide an interesting cross-section of current work, and hope that they will inspire future research in this rapidly progressing field.

BRUCE CROFT

JOHN LAFFERTY

Contributing Authors

Jamie Callan is an Associate Professor in the School of Computer Science at Carnegie Mellon University. He earned his Ph.D. from the University of Massachusetts, Amherst.

Bruce Croft is a Distinguished Professor in the Department of Computer Science at the University of Massachusetts, Amherst. He received his Ph.D. from the University of Cambridge.

Warren Greiff is a Principal Scientist at The MITRE Corporation. He earned his Ph.D from the University of Massachusetts, Amherst.

David Harper is a Research Professor in the School of Computing at The Robert Gordon University, Aberdeen, Scotland, and Director of the Smart Web Technologies Center.

Wessel Kraaij is a senior researcher and project manager at the department of Multimedia Technology and Statistics of TNO TPD (Netherlands Organization of Applied Scientific Research).

Djoerd Hiemstra wrote his Ph.D. thesis on the use of language models for information retrieval. He is currently an Assistant Professor at the Database Group of the University of Twente.

John Lafferty is an Associate Professor in the Computer Science Department at Carnegie Mellon University. He received his Ph.D. from Princeton University.

Victor Lavrenko is a Research Assistant in the Department of Computer Science at the University of Massachusetts, Amherst.

R. Manmatha is a Research Assistant Professor in the Department of Computer Science at the University of Massachusetts, Amherst. He received his Ph.D. from the University of Massachusetts, Amherst.

Vibhu Mittal is a Senior Scientist at Google corporation and an adjunct faculty member in the School of Computer Science at Carnegie Mellon University. He earned his Ph.D from the University of Southern California.

William Morgan is a Staff Scientist at MITRE Corporation.

Stephen Robertson is a researcher at Microsoft Research Cambridge, and also a Professor at City University, London. For some years, he has contributed to the Okapi system.

Karen Sparck Jones is Professor of Computers and Information at the University of Cambridge, and has worked in language and information processing since the 1950s.

Martjin Spitters is a researcher at the department of Multimedia Technology and Statistics of TNO TPD (Netherlands Organization of Applied Scientific Research).

William Teahan is a lecturer in Computer Science in the School of Informatics at the University of Wales, Bangor. He gained his Ph.D. from the University of Waikato, New Zealand.

Ralph Weischedel is a Principal Scientist at BBN Technologies with a broad range of interests in language processing technologies. He received his Ph.D. from the University of Pennsylvania.

Michael Witbrock is Director, Knowledge Formation & Dialogue, at Cycorp in Austin, TX. He earned his Ph.D in Computer Science from Carnegie Mellon University.

Jinxi Xu is a Scientist at BBN technologies. He earned his Ph.D from the University of Massachusetts, Amherst.

Hugo Zaragoza is a researcher at Microsoft Research Cambridge. He earned his Ph.D. from the University of Paris 6.

ChengXiang Zhai is an Assistant Professor at the University of Illinois at Urbana-Champaign. He received his Ph.D. from Carnegie Mellon University.

Yi Zhang is a Ph.D. candidate in the School of Computer Science at Carnegie Mellon University. She earned her M.S. degree from Carnegie Mellon University and her B.S. degree from Tsinghua University.

Chapter 1

PROBABILISTIC RELEVANCE MODELS BASED ON DOCUMENT AND QUERY GENERATION

John Lafferty
School of Computer Science
Carnegie Mellon University
lafferty@cs.cmu.edu

ChengXiang Zhai
Department of Computer Science
University of Illinois at Urbana-Champaign
czhai@cs.uiuc.edu

Abstract   We give a unified account of the probabilistic semantics underlying the language modeling approach and the traditional probabilistic model for information retrieval, showing that the two approaches can be viewed as being equivalent probabilistically, since they are based on different factorizations of the same generative relevance model. We also discuss how the two approaches lead to different retrieval frameworks in practice, since they involve component models that are estimated quite differently.

Keywords: Language models, relevance models, generative models

1.   Introduction

In the classical probabilistic approach to information retrieval (Robertson and Sparck Jones, 1976), two models are estimated for each query, one modeling relevant documents, the other modeling non-relevant documents.[1] Documents are then ranked according to the posterior probability of relevance. When the document attributes are independent under these relevance models,

---

[1](Sparck Jones et al., 2000) refer to this as *the* probabilistic approach to retrieval.

W.B. Croft and J. Lafferty (eds.), Language Modeling for Information Retrieval, 1–10.
© 2003 *Kluwer Academic Publishers.*

this is simply the naive Bayes model for classification, and has met with considerable empirical success.

In the "language modeling approach" to information retrieval (Ponte and Croft, 1998), a language model is estimated for each document, and the operational procedure for ranking is to order documents by the probability assigned to the input query text according to each document's model. This approach has also enjoyed recent empirical success. However, the underlying semantics of the language model has been unclear, as it appears to ignore the important notion of relevance.

In this paper we give a simple, unified account of both approaches, in which it is shown that an implicit relevance model underlies the language modeling approach. Our derivation shows that the two approaches can be viewed as being equivalent probabilistically, since they are based on different parameterizations of the same joint likelihood. However, as we discuss below, the two approaches are not equivalent from a statistical point of view, since the component models are estimated quite differently.

Our derivation is elementary, and shows that in terms of their underlying probabilistic semantics, the language modeling approach and the traditional probabilistic model are, so to speak, two sides of the same coin. Thus, we provide a simple answer to the question "Where's the relevance?" that has been recently asked of the language modeling approach.

2.   Generative Relevance Models

In our treatment of the probabilistic semantics of relevance models, we follow the presentation of (Sparck Jones et al., 2000), with some minor changes in notation. Thus, the "Basic Question" we are interested in is the following:

What is the probability that *this* document is relevant to *this* query?

To treat the Basic Question in a probabilistic framework, we introduce random variables D and Q to denote a document and query, respectively. In addition, we introduce a binary random variable R to denote relevance.[2] This random variable takes on two values, which we denote as r ("relevant") and $\bar{r}$ ("not relevant"). Here our notation deviates from that of (Sparck Jones et al., 2000), who use L ("liked") and $\bar{L}$ ("not liked") instead of r and $\bar{r}$. We thus adopt the standard notation that denotes random variables using upper case letters and values of random variables using lower case letters. In probabilistic terms, the Basic Question is then equivalent to estimating the probability of

---

[2](Sparck Jones et al., 2000) use R to denote the number of relevant documents.

relevance

$$p(R = r \mid D, Q) \;=\; 1 - p(R = \bar{r} \mid D, Q). \tag{1.1}$$

The justification for using this probability as the basis for ranking comes from the Probability Ranking Principle (Robertson, 1977).

Now, in adopting a *generative* relevance model, the probability of relevance $p(r \mid D, Q)$ is not estimated directly. Rather, it is estimated indirectly by invoking Bayes' rule:

$$p(R = r \mid D, Q) \;=\; \frac{p(D, Q \mid R = r) \, p(R = r)}{p(D, Q)}. \tag{1.2}$$

Equivalently, we may use the following log-odds ratio to rank documents:

$$\log \frac{p(r \mid D, Q)}{p(\bar{r} \mid D, Q)} \;=\; \log \frac{p(D, Q \mid r) \, p(r)}{p(D, Q \mid \bar{r}) \, p(\bar{r})}. \tag{1.3}$$

As we describe next, two statistically different but probabilistically equivalent generative relevance models result from applying the chain rule in different ways to factor the conditional probability $p(D, Q \mid R)$.

2.1   The Robertson-Sparck Jones Model

In the Robertson-Sparck Jones approach (Sparck Jones et al., 2000), the probability $p(D, Q \mid R)$ is factored as $p(D, Q \mid R) = p(Q \mid R) p(D \mid Q, R)$, leading to the following log-odds ratios:

$$\log \frac{p(r \mid D, Q)}{p(\bar{r} \mid D, Q)} \;=\; \log \frac{p(D, Q \mid r) \, p(r)}{p(D, Q \mid \bar{r}) \, p(\bar{r})} \tag{1.4}$$

$$=\; \log \frac{p(D \mid Q, r) \, p(Q \mid r) \, p(r)}{p(D \mid Q, \bar{r}) \, p(Q \mid \bar{r}) \, p(\bar{r})} \tag{1.5}$$

$$=\; \log \frac{p(D \mid Q, r) \, p(r \mid Q)}{p(D \mid Q, \bar{r}) \, p(\bar{r} \mid Q)} \tag{1.6}$$

$$=\; \log \frac{p(D \mid Q, r)}{p(D \mid Q, \bar{r})} + \log \frac{p(r \mid Q)}{p(\bar{r} \mid Q)} \tag{1.7}$$

$$\overset{\text{rank}}{=}\; \log \frac{p(D \mid Q, r)}{p(D \mid Q, \bar{r})}. \tag{1.8}$$

Since the term $\log(p(r \mid Q)/p(\bar{r} \mid Q))$ is independent of D, it can be thought of as a constant bias and can be safely ignored for the purpose of ranking documents; this equivalence is denoted by the symbol $\overset{\text{rank}}{=}$.

Equation (1.7) is precisely the basic ranking formula (1) in (Sparck Jones et al., 2000), although the conditioning on the query Q is implicit there.

In its usual instantiation, the models $p(D \mid Q, r)$ and $p(D \mid Q, r)$ are estimated by assuming that the document is made up of a collection of attributes $D = (A_1, \ldots, A_n)$, such as words, and that these attributes are independent given R and Q:

$$p(D \mid Q, r) \;=\; \prod_{i=1}^{n} p(A_i \mid Q, r) \tag{1.9}$$

$$p(D \mid Q, \bar{r}) \;=\; \prod_{i=1}^{n} p(A_i \mid Q, \bar{r}) \,. \tag{1.10}$$

For a fixed query Q, this is simply the naive Bayes model for classifying documents into the two classes r and $\bar{r}$.

2.2   The Language Modeling Approach

Suppose that we now factor the probability $p(D, Q \mid R)$ as $p(D, Q \mid R) = p(D \mid R) p(Q \mid D, R)$. It is important to note that from a purely probabilistic perspective, nothing has changed; this is simply a different decomposition of the same joint likelihood. Using this factorization, we are led to consider the log-odds ratio in the following *equivalent* form:

$$\log \frac{p(r \mid Q, D)}{p(\bar{r} \mid Q, D)} \;=\; \log \frac{p(D, Q \mid r) p(r)}{p(D, Q \mid \bar{r}) p(\bar{r})} \tag{1.11}$$

$$=\; \log \frac{p(Q \mid D, r) p(D \mid r) p(r)}{p(Q \mid D, \bar{r}) p(D \mid \bar{r}) p(\bar{r})} \tag{1.12}$$

$$=\; \log \frac{p(Q \mid D, r) p(r \mid D)}{p(Q \mid D, \bar{r}) p(\bar{r} \mid D)} \tag{1.13}$$

$$=\; \log \frac{p(Q \mid D, r)}{p(Q \mid D, \bar{r})} + \log \frac{p(r \mid D)}{p(\bar{r} \mid D)} \,. \tag{1.14}$$

The bias term $\log(p(r \mid D)/p(\bar{r} \mid D))$ is now dependent on D, but independent of the query Q, and must, in general, be considered as an integral part of the ranking process. At this point, we have a ranking formula based on generating queries from documents that is equivalent to the ranking formula (1.7) based on generating documents from queries.

Suppose that we now make the assumption that conditioned on the event $R = \bar{r}$, the document D is independent of the query Q; that is:

Assumption 1: $p(D, Q \mid R = \bar{r}) = p(D \mid R = \bar{r}) p(Q \mid R = \bar{r})$

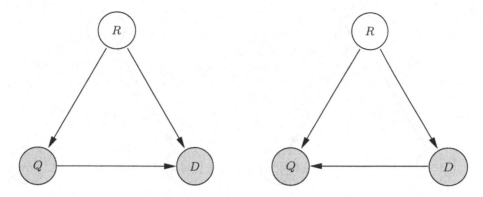

Figure 1.1. Graphical representations of the two factorizations of the joint document-query probability. The factorization $p(D, Q \mid R) = p(D \mid Q, R) p(Q \mid R)$ (left) results in the Robertson-Sparck Jones model, while the factorization $p(D, Q \mid R) = p(Q \mid D, R) p(D \mid R)$ (right) leads to the language modeling approach. Following convention, the document and query nodes are shaded to indicate that they are observed ("this document and this query").

Under this assumption the log-odds ratio becomes

$$\log \frac{p(r \mid Q, D)}{p(\bar{r} \mid Q, D)} = \log \frac{p(Q \mid D, r)}{p(Q \mid \bar{r})} + \log \frac{p(r \mid D)}{p(\bar{r} \mid D)} \qquad (1.15)$$

$$\overset{\text{rank}}{=} \log p(Q \mid D, r) + \log \frac{p(r \mid D)}{p(\bar{r} \mid D)}. \qquad (1.16)$$

This ranking formula has two components, a term involving the query likelihood $p(Q \mid D, r)$, and a bias term that involves the prior probability of relevance for the document, $p(r \mid D)$. Researchers have been referring to the distribution $p(\cdot \mid D, r)$ as a "document language model," or simply as a "language model," which is actually a model of the *queries* to which D would be judged as relevant. Although the Robertson-Sparck Jones approach also makes use of language models, the terminology "language modeling approach" is appropriate for this way of decomposing the document-query probability since many language models are at play, at least one for each document in the database.

If we now make the additional assumption that D and R are independent, the bias term no longer depends on D. That is, under Assumption 1 and

Assumption 2: $p(D, R) = p(D) p(R)$

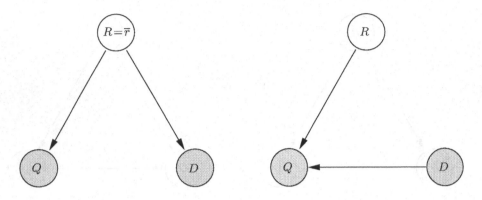

Figure 1.2. Graphical representations of the document-query distribution under Assumption 1 (left), and Assumption 2 (right).

the log-odds ratio becomes

$$\log \frac{p(r \mid Q, D)}{p(\overline{r} \mid Q, D)} \stackrel{\text{rank}}{=} \log p(Q \mid D, r) + \log \frac{p(r)}{p(\overline{r})} \qquad (1.17)$$

$$\stackrel{\text{rank}}{=} \log p(Q \mid D, r). \qquad (1.18)$$

Thus, the ranking of documents is based solely on the probability of the query given the document, under that event that the document is relevant to the query: $p(Q \mid D, r)$. The above assumptions are shown graphically in Figure 1.2.

Equations (1.16) and (1.18) are the basic ranking formulas for the language modeling approach as explored in (Berger and Lafferty, 1999; Miller et al., 1999) and (Ponte and Croft, 1998) respectively.

As in the Robertson-Sparck Jones model, it is expedient to decompose the query into attributes $Q = (A_1, \ldots, A_m)$, typically just the query terms, and to assume that the attributes are independent given R and the document. Thus, under this independence assumption and Assumption 1, the posterior log-odds becomes

$$\log \frac{p(r \mid D, Q)}{p(\overline{r} \mid D, Q)} \stackrel{\text{rank}}{=} \sum_{i=1}^{m} \log p(A_i \mid D, r) + \log \frac{p(r \mid D)}{p(\overline{r} \mid D)}. \qquad (1.19)$$

3.   Discussion

The above derivation shows that the language modeling approach and the traditional probabilistic model can be interpreted within the same probabilistic framework based on a generative relevance model. In this view, the two approaches are simply two sides of the same coin—at the probabilistic level, before independence assumptions are made and without any specification of how the models are actually estimated, they are equivalent.

In previous discussions of the language modeling approach in the literature, an explicit use of a relevance variable has not been made. However, under Assumption 1, which states that $p(D, Q \mid R = \bar{r}) = p(D \mid R = \bar{r}) p(Q \mid R = \bar{r})$, it is seen that introducing an explicit relevance model is operationally of no consequence—the "irrelevant" language model $p(Q \mid \bar{r})$ is irrelevant; it only enters into the bias term, and so can be ignored for ranking. Note that under the same Assumption 1, the log-odds ratios in the Robertson-Sparck Jones approach still involve models for both relevant and non-relevant documents, but now the model for non-relevant documents is simply independent of the query:

$$\log \frac{p(r \mid D, Q)}{p(\bar{r} \mid D, Q)} \overset{\text{rank}}{=} \log \frac{p(D \mid Q, r)}{p(D \mid Q, \bar{r})} = \log \frac{p(D \mid Q, r)}{p(D \mid \bar{r})} . \qquad (1.20)$$

During discussions at the Language Modeling and Information Retrieval Workshop, it became clear that descriptions of the language modeling approach in terms of generative models of queries have caused significant confusion. In particular, such descriptions have led some researchers to claim that the language modeling approach only makes sense if there is exactly one relevant document for each query, and that the model becomes inconsistent in the presence of explicit relevance information from a user. However, as the above presentation makes clear, the underlying probabilistic semantics is the same as for the standard probabilistic model.

While the derivation presented in the previous section clarifies the formalism behind the language modeling approach, it is only formalism. The genius of a statistical approach often lies in the estimation details. Several important differences result from reversing things to generate the query from the document, which make this approach attractive from an estimation perspective.

Perhaps the primary importance of being reversed lies in the fact that by conditioning on the document D, we have a larger foothold for estimating a statistical model. The entire document and, potentially, related documents, can be used to build a language model, and a great deal is known about techniques for estimating such language models from other applications. Intuitively, it is easier to estimate a model for "relevant queries" based on a document than to estimate a model for relevant documents based on a query. Indeed, the Robertson-Sparck Jones model has encountered difficulties in estimating $p(A_i \mid Q, r)$ and $p(A_i \mid Q, \bar{r})$ when no explicit relevance information is available. Typically, $p(A_i \mid Q, r)$ is set to a constant and $p(A_i \mid Q, \bar{r})$ is estimated under the assumption that the entire collection is comprised of non-relevant documents (Croft and Harper, 1979; Robertson and Walker, 1997)—essentially the same as Assumption 1. Recently, a better approach to estimating $p(A_i \mid Q, r)$ is proposed in (Lavrenko and Croft, 2001), in which the query is formally treated as an observation from the model of generating relevant documents, and a set of empirical document language models are exploited to smooth the estimate of $p(A_i \mid Q, r)$. This work can be considered as an example of using language models in the classical probabilistic model.

Another potential advantage lies in the fact that the language modeling approach includes an explicit notion of the importance of a document, represented in the term $\log p(r \mid D)/(1 - p(r \mid D))$, which can be estimated separately. In previous formulations, this role was played by the "document prior" (Berger and Lafferty, 1999; Miller et al., 1999). While to date the document prior has not been significant for TREC-style evaluations, for many real applications its use can be expected to be important. In particular, query-independent scores to assess the importance of documents based on hyperlink analysis have proven to be useful in web search (Brin and Page, 1998).

An additional difference between the two approaches lies in the need for document normalization. In the standard approach, the use of log-odds ratios is essential to account for the fact that different documents have different numbers of terms. Ranking based on document likelihoods $p(D \mid r, Q)$ would not be effective because the procedure is inherently biased against long documents. This observation is symptomatic of a larger problem: by making strong independence assumptions we have an incorrect model of relevant documents. In the language modeling approach, things are reversed to generate the input— the query Q. As a result, competing documents are scored using the same number probabilities $p(A_i \mid D, r)$, and document normalization is not a crucial issue. More generally, incorrect independence assumptions in the model may be mitigated by predicting the input. This advantage of "reverse channel" approaches to statistical natural language processing has been observed in many other applications, notably statistical machine translation (Brown et al., 1990).

Having mentioned some of the advantages of query-generation models, we should add that the Robertson-Sparck Jones model, being based on document-generation, has the advantage of being able to naturally improve the estimation of the component probabilistic models by exploiting explicit relevance information. This is because the relevance judgments from a user provide direct training data for estimating $p(A_i \mid Q, r)$ and $p(A_i \mid Q, \bar{r})$, which can then be applied to *new* documents. The same relevance judgments can also provide direct training data for improving the estimate of $p(A_i \mid D, r)$ in the language modeling approach, but only for the relevant documents that are given judgements. Thus, the directly improved models can *not* be expected to improve our ranking of other unjudged documents. However, such improved models can potentially be beneficial for new queries, a feature that does not apply to document-generation models.

4.   Historical Notes

Interestingly, the very first probabilistic model for information retrieval, namely the Probabilistic Indexing model of Maron and Kuhns (Maron and Kuhns, 1960) is, in fact, based on the idea of "query-generation." Conceptually, the model intends to infer the probability that a document is relevant to a query based on the probability that a user who likes the document would have used this query. However, the formal derivation given in (Maron and Kuhns, 1960) appears to be restricted to queries with only a single term. As a result, the "query-generation" model $p(w \mid D, r)$ essentially provides a probability for each indexing word, and can be used as a basis for assigning indexing terms to the document. Thus, it is referred to as a probabilistic *indexing* model. Possibly due to its restriction to single-term queries and the difficulty of parameter estimation, this model has never been as popular as the Robertson-Sparck Jones model. However conceptually, they can be considered as representing the two major types of classical probabilistic models.

There were some early efforts to unify these two classical probabilistic models (e.g., (Robertson et al., 1982)), but the unification was not completely successful. The difficulty encountered in (Robertson et al., 1982) has to do with using a more restricted event space, namely a space given by the cross product of documents and queries, without the relevance variable. No doubt, this early work already recognizes the symmetry between queries and documents. See (Robertson, 1994) further discussion of this symmetry and objections to it.

The possibility of both document-generation and query-generation decompositions of the same probability of relevance was also recognized at least a decade ago. Indeed, the two different decompositions were already used in (Fuhr, 1992) to derive, respectively, the Robertson-Sparck Jones model and the Binary Independence Indexing (BII) model, which is a variant of the original Maron and Kuhns model that allows multi-word queries.

References

Berger, A. and Lafferty, J. (1999). Information retrieval as statistical translation. In *Proceedings of the 22nd International Conference on Research and Development in Information Retrieval (SIGIR'99)*, pages 222–229.

Brin, S. and Page, L. (1998). Anatomy of a large-scale hypertextual web search engine. In *Proceedings of the 7th International World Wide Web Conference*.

Brown, P. F., Cocke, J., Della Pietra, S. A., Della Pietra, V. J., Jelinek, F., Lafferty, J. D., Mercer, R. L., and Roossin, P. S. (1990). A statistical approach to machine translation. *Computational Linguistics*, 16(2):79–85.

Croft, W. B. and Harper, D. (1979). Using probabilistic models of document retrieval without relevance information. *Journal of Documentation*, 35:285–295.

Fuhr, N. (1992). Probabilistic models in information retrieval. *Computer Journal*, 35:243–255.

Lavrenko, V. and Croft, W. B. (2001). Relevance-based language models. In *24th ACM SIGIR Conference on Research and Development in Information Retrieval*.

Maron, M. and Kuhns, J. (1960). On relevance, probabilistic indexing and information retrieval. *Journal of the ACM*, 7:216–244.

Miller, D., Leek, T., and Schwartz, R. (1999). A hidden Markov model information retrieval system. In *Proceedings of the 22nd International Conference on Research and Development in Information Retrieval (SIGIR'99)*, pages 214–221.

Ponte, J. and Croft, W. B. (1998). A language modeling approach to information retrieval. In *Proceedings of the 21st International Conference on Research and Development in Information Retrieval (SIGIR'98)*, pages 275–281.

Robertson, S. (1977). The probability ranking principle in IR. *Journal of Documentation*, 33:294–304.

Robertson, S. and Sparck Jones, K. (1976). Relevance weighting of search terms. *Journal of the American Society for Information Science*, 27:129–146.

Robertson, S. and Walker, S. (1997). On relevance weights with little relevance information. In *Proceedings of SIGIR'97*, pages 16–24.

Robertson, S. E. (1994). Query-document symmetry and dual models. *Journal of Documentation*, 50(3):233–238.

Robertson, S. E., Maron, M. E., and Cooper, W. S. (1982). Probability of relevance: a unification of two competing models for information retrieval. *Information Technology - Research and Development*, 1:1–21.

Sparck Jones, K., Walker, S., and Robertson, S. E. (2000). A probabilistic model of information retrieval: development and comparative experiments, Part 1. *Information Processing and Management*, 36:779–808.

Chapter 2

RELEVANCE MODELS IN INFORMATION RETRIEVAL

Victor Lavrenko and W. Bruce Croft

Center for Intelligent Information Retrieval
Department of Computer Science
University of Massachusetts
Amherst, MA 01003
{ lavrenko,croft } @cs.umass.edu

Abstract

We develop a simple statistical model, called a relevance model, for capturing the notion of topical relevance in information retrieval. Estimating probabilities of relevance has been an important part of many previous retrieval models, but we show how this estimation can be done in a more principled way based on a generative or language model approach. In particular, we focus on estimating relevance models when training examples (examples of relevant documents) are not available. We describe extensive evaluations of the relevance model approach on the TREC ad-hoc retrieval and cross-language tasks. In both cases, rankings based on relevance models significantly outperform strong baseline approaches.

1. Introduction

The field of information retrieval has been primarily concerned with developing algorithms to identify relevant pieces of information in response to a user's information need. The relevant information may be documents such as medical articles, news stories, or encyclopedia entries, or it may consist of small parts or passages in the documents. The notion of relevance is central to information retrieval, and much research in the area has focused on developing formal models of relevance, often using a probabilistic framework (Robertson, 1977; Robertson et al., 1982; Robertson and Walker, 1994; Robertson and Sparck Jones, 1976; Turtle and Croft, 1991). One of the most popular models, introduced by Robertson and Sparck Jones (Robertson and Sparck Jones, 1976), ranks documents by their likelihood of belonging to the relevant class

W.B. Croft and J. Lafferty (eds.), Language Modeling for Information Retrieval, 11–56.
© 2003 *Kluwer Academic Publishers.*

of documents for a query, based on the estimated word occurrence character-
istics of those classes. This is expressed as $P(D|R)/P(D|N)$ where R is
the relevant class of documents, N is the non-relevant class, and $P(D|R)$ is
the probability that a document D is observed in the relevant class. One of
the main challenges to applying this retrieval model is the estimation of the
characteristics of the relevant class without any training data, in the form of
user-identified examples of relevant documents.

Other approaches to modeling the retrieval process have taken a somewhat
different approach to relevance. Van Rijsbergen's logical implication model
(van Rijsbergen, 1986) viewed relevant documents as those from which the
query Q could be inferred using a probabilistic logic (written $D \rightarrow Q$). The
inference network model, implemented in the INQUERY system (Turtle, 1990;
Turtle and Croft, 1991), took a similar approach in that it is based on calcu-
lating $P(I|D)$, the probability that an information need I is satisfied given
a document. Although the inference network framework did more explicitly
acknowledge that the information need is not the same as the query, neither
model mentioned relevance explicitly. More recently, in the language modeling approach (Ponte and Croft, 1998; Berger and Lafferty, 1999; Miller et al.,
1999; Song and Croft, 1999; Hiemstra, 2001), the retrieval process was described as an i.i.d. random sampling of the query from some unknown doc-
ument model. In other words, documents are ranked by $P(Q|D)$, the proba-
bility of generating a query text Q given an estimated language model for the
document D. The advantage of this approach was to shift from developing
heuristic $tf.idf$ weights for representing term importance to instead focus on
estimation techniques for the document model. Subsequent work on this model
has introduced refinements in the estimation techniques used for the language
models and techniques for other important IR features such as multi-word features (Song and Croft, 1999), query expansion (Ponte, 1998), and crosslingual
retrieval (Hiemstra and de Jong, 1999; Xu et al., 2001). The simple language
modeling approach is very similar to the logical implication and inference network models, and all of these retrieval models, despite their successes, have a
common problem in directly using training data (examples of relevant documents).

In this work, we develop a formal model of relevance which represents an
integration of the *classical* probabilistic model of retrieval with the recent developments in estimation techniques. This integration results in a retrieval
model that combines the advantages of the language modeling approach with
the ability to directly use training data about relevance. We discuss how we can
estimate relevance models in a typical IR setting and describe how they can be
applied to two IR tasks studied in TREC: ad-hoc retrieval and cross-lingual
retrieval.

The remainder of this chapter is structured as follows. In section 2, we propose a formal definition of a relevance model and describe how this relates to the classical probabilistic retrieval model. In section 3, we describe how relevance models can be estimated in various settings. In particular, in section 3.2 and 3.3, we introduce novel techniques for estimating relevance models without training examples in monolingual and crosslingual retrieval settings. Section 4 focuses on applications of relevance models to the ad-hoc and crosslingual tasks. Special attention is given to the question of ranking using relevance models and we demonstrate that a common way of applying the probability ranking principle leads to sub-optimal performance. Sections 4.3 and 4.7 provide extensive evaluations of relevance models on the two retrieval tasks.

1.1 Related Work

There are two directions of information retrieval research that provide a theoretical foundation for our model: the now classic work on probabilistic models of relevance, and the recent developments in language modeling techniques for IR. To the former we owe the concept of a relevance model: a language model representative of a class of relevant documents. To the latter we credit the methods of modeling and specific estimation techniques. In this section we give a brief survey of several developments in both of these directions, highlighting interesting connections between the two. We also provide an overview of language-modeling approaches to cross-language retrieval, which form the baseline for our evaluations.

1.1.1 Classical Probabilistic Approaches. Underlying most research on probabilistic models of information retrieval is the *probability ranking principle*, advocated by Robertson in (Robertson, 1977), which suggests ranking the documents D by the odds of their being observed in the relevant class: $P(D|R)/P(D|N)$. Robertson argued that ranking determined by the probability ratio would be optimal with respect to a number of important metrics. In order to apply this principle, we need to be able to estimate the probability $P(D|R)$ associated with the relevant class (estimating $P(D|N)$ is considerably easier, as we show in section 4.4). Following Robertson, a number of researchers proposed different models for estimating the probability $P(D|R)$. The Binary Independence Model (Robertson and Sparck Jones, 1976; van Rijsbergen, 1977) treats each document as a binary vector over the vocabulary space, ignoring word frequencies. {inxxRobertson-Sparck Jones model The 2-Poisson Model (Robertson and Walker, 1994) goes a step further in modeling term frequencies in documents according to a mixture of two Poisson distributions. The Inference Network Model (Turtle and Croft, 1991) treats R as a feed-forward Bayesian belief network model, with parameters estimated in a heuristic manner. In a typical retrieval setting no relevant examples are available, so most of the models we mentioned rely on heuristic approximations.

1.1.2   Language Modeling Approaches.   Recent work in conceptual models of information retrieval shifted away from modeling the probability of relevance $P(D|R)$, and focused on viewing documents themselves as models and queries as strings of text randomly sampled from these models. Most of these approaches rank the documents in the collection by the probability that a query Q would be observed during repeated random sampling from the model of document D: $P(Q|D)$. The calculation of the above probability differs significantly from model to model. For example, Ponte and Croft (Ponte and Croft, 1998), treat the query Q as a binary vector over the entire vocabulary, leading to a *multiple-Bernoulli* view of model. Miller et al. (Miller et al., 1999), Song and Croft (Song and Croft, 1999), and Hiemstra (Hiemstra, 2001) choose to treat the query Q as a *sequence* of independent words, rather than a binary vector, leading to a *multinomial* view of the document model. Berger and Lafferty (Berger and Lafferty, 1999) view the query Q as a potential *translation* of the document D, and use powerful estimation techniques detailed in (Brown et al., 1993) and synthetic training data to compute $P(Q|M_D)$. A major drawback to a wide acceptance of the translation model is its requirement for training data and the complexity of parameter estimation. A common theme in these approaches is their shift away from trying to model relevance and towards careful estimation of the sampling probabilities. This shift allowed researchers to avoid the use of heuristics and apply powerful statistical estimation techniques. Accurate estimation of the model became possible because we have an example document D, which we can use to construct its model.

1.1.3   Cross-language Approaches.   Language-modeling approaches have been extended to cross-language retrieval by Hiemstra and de Jong (Hiemstra and de Jong, 1999) and Xu *et al.* (Xu et al., 2001; Xu and Weischedel, 2000). The model proposed by Berger and Lafferty (Berger and Lafferty, 1999) applies to the "translation" of a document into a query in a monolingual environment, but it can readily accommodate a bilingual environment. The three approaches above all make use of translation probabilities attached to pairs of words. The pairs of words and their corresponding probabilities are often obtained from a bilingual dictionary by assigning the same probability to all the translations of a word. When a parallel corpus or a pseudo-parallel corpus (where parallel documents are produced by an MT system) is available, the required translations and probabilities can be obtained by applying Brown *et al.*'s approach to machine translation (Brown et al., 1990) (or some related technique (Hiemstra et al., 1997)). Xu *et al.* (Xu and Weischedel, 2000) showed that combining statistics from various lexical resources can help correct problems of coverage and lead to significant improvements.

2. Relevance Models

2.1 Mathematical Formalism

Suppose $\mathcal{V}$ is a vocabulary in some language, and let $\mathcal{C}$ be some large collection of documents (strings over that vocabulary). We define the **relevant class** R to be the subset of documents in $\mathcal{C}$, which are relevant to some particular information need. The underlying information need may be a TREC-style query, a TDT topic, or even a broader category. The only requirement is that there exists a subset of documents $R \subset \mathcal{C}$, which satisfies that particular information need. We define a **relevance model** to be the probability distribution $P(w|R)$. For every word $w \in \mathcal{V}$, the relevance model gives the probability that we would observe w if we randomly selected some document D from the relevant class R and then picked a random word from D.

Our definition of a relevance model represents a convergence of ideas from the classical probabilistic approaches and the language modeling approaches. From the classical standpoint, we described a model that can be used for computing the probability of relevance, since we explicitly model the class R of relevant documents. From the language modeling perspective, we described a unigram generative model for a set of text samples. We can assume that documents in the relevant set R are random samples from the relevance model $P(w|R)$.

Unigram language models ignore any short-range interactions between the words in a sample of text, so a relevance model cannot distinguish between well-formed (grammatical) sentences and their nonsensical re-orderings. For many areas of Natural Language Processing grammaticality is a critical issue. For example, in the field of Speech Recognition it is very important that a language model focus its probability mass on well-formed sentences. To that end researchers make frequent use of higher order language models, such as trigram or grammar-based models. In Information Retrieval we are not trying to actually *generate* new samples of text, so our models don't have to distinguish between grammatical and non-grammatical samples of text. The important issue in IR is capturing the topic discussed in a sample of text, and to that end unigram models fare quite well. To date, virtually all applications of language modeling framework to IR relied on unigram models. The attempts to use higher-order models were few and did not lead to noticeable improvements (Song and Croft, 1999). Experiments in section 4 will suggest that an accurate relevance model can be quite effective in discerning the topical content of a piece of text, or its relevance to a particular information need. The choice of estimation techniques has a particularly strong influence on the quality of relevance models. We devote Section 3 to the detailed discussion of estimation techniques that could be applied in various settings.

2.2   Document Retrieval with Relevance Models

The primary goal of Information Retrieval systems is to identify a set of documents $R \subset C$ relevant to some query Q. This is usually accomplished by ranking all the documents in the collection, and presenting the resulting ranked list to the user for examination. In this section we outline how relevance models could be used to produce a reasonable document ranking. For the purpose of this section, we assume that we have already estimated a relevance model (the set of probabilities $P(w|R)$ for every word w in the vocabulary). We discuss two approaches to document ranking the *probability ratio*, advocated by the classical probabilistic models of IR, and *cross-entropy*, based on recent applications of language-modeling ideas to Information Retrieval. We briefly discuss the details of each method. A thorough empirical comparison of the two approaches is provided in section 4.4 and is followed by a short theoretical discussion of the differences.

2.2.1   Probability Ratio.   In his now classical work, Robertson (Robertson, 1977) introduced the *Probability Ranking Principle*, which has become the starting point for most probabilistic models of Information Retrieval. Suppose we have a probabilistic model $P(D|R)$ which assigns the probability to observing a given document D in the relevant class R. Similarly, let $P(D|N)$ be the corresponding probabilistic model for the non-relevant class N. The probability ranking principle suggests that we should rank the documents $D \in C$ in order of decreasing probability ratio: $\frac{P(D|R)}{P(D|N)}$. Robertson (Robertson, 1977) demonstrates that the resulting document ranking will be optimal with respect to a number of important measures of performance, including average precision. If we assume a document D to be a sequence independent words: $d_1 \ldots d_n$, the probability ranking principle may be expressed as a product of the ratios:

$$\frac{P(d_1 \ldots d_n|R)}{P(d_1 \ldots d_n|N)} = \prod_{i=1}^{n} \frac{P(d_i|R)}{P(d_i|N)} \qquad (2.1)$$

Documents that have a higher probability under the relevance model are more likely to be relevant, so we rank the documents in order of *decreasing* probability ratio. The probabilities $P(d_i|N)$ can be easily approximated by setting them equal to background probabilities $P(d_i|C)$. The approximation holds because for most queries, the majority of the documents in the collection C are non-relevant. Relevant documents are so few that they are unlikely to affect word probabilities in any significant way. On the other hand, finding accurate estimates for the probabilities $P(d_i|R)$ associated with the relevant class has been a major area of research in probabilistic Information Retrieval. In section 3 we will suggest a number of techniques for estimating relevance-based probabilities $P(d_i|R)$, both from the set of training examples and from the query alone. Mono-lingual techniques developed in section 3.2 will allow us to use equation 2.1 for ranking the documents in ad-hoc retrieval. Similarly, cross-lingual methods detailed in section 3.3 are directly applicable to ranking documents in a different language than the query.

2.2.2   Cross-Entropy.   Cross-entropy is a ranking measure inspired by the recent successes of language-modeling (Ponte and Croft, 1998; Hiemstra, 2001; Song and Croft, 1999; Miller et al., 1999) approaches to Information Retrieval. Let $P(w|R)$ denote the language model of the relevant class, and for every document D let $P(w|D)$ denote the corresponding *document* language model (document language models will be discussed in section 3.1). Cross-entropy is a natural measure of divergence between two language models, defined as:

$$H(R||D) = -\sum_{w \subset \mathcal{V}} P(w|R) \log P(w|D) \qquad (2.2)$$

Intuitively, documents with smaller cross-entropy from the relevance model are more likely to be relevant, so we rank the documents by *increasing* cross-entropy. Note that summation in equation (2.2) is performed over all the words w in the vocabulary. However, we can always exclude the terms for which $P(w|R)$ is zero, since they don't affect the value. Cross-entropy enjoys a number of attractive theoretical properties, most of which are beyond the scope of our discussion. One property is of particular importance: suppose we estimate $P(w|R)$ as the relative frequency of the word w in the user query Q. In this case ranking the documents based on cross-entropy is **equivalent** to ranking by the query-likelihood, popular in the language-modeling approaches to IR. Accordingly, approaches based on query-likelihood represent a special case of entropy-based approaches. The entropy-based view (equation 2.2) is more general, since it allows us to estimate $P(w|R)$ in any fashion, including the methods based on training examples, or sparse estimation techniques that will be developed in sections 3.2 and 3.3. It is worth noting that ranking the documents D by the cross-entropy $H(R||D)$ is also equivalent to ranking by the Kullback-Leibler divergence $KL(R||D)$, which was originally proposed by Croft in (Croft, 2000) and then used by Zhai in the development of the general risk-minimization retrieval framework (Zhai, 2002).

3.   Estimating a Relevance Model

In this section we discuss a set of techniques that could be used to estimate the set of probabilities $P(w|R)$. We address the following estimation problems:

1   **Estimation from a set of examples.** We start with the simple case when we have full information about the set R of relevant documents. Then we briefly address the case when the set R is not known, but we have a representative subset $S \subset R$. Special attention is given to smoothing methods.

2   **Estimation without examples.** The main focus of the section is the case when we have no examples from which we could estimate $P(w|R)$ directly. We introduce a powerful formalism that allows us to estimate the set of probabilities $P(w|R)$ starting with extremely short strings consisting of as little as 2-3 words, such as user queries or questions.

3   **Cross-lingual estimation**. In Section 3.3 we address the problem of estimating relevance models in a cross-lingual environment, where, for instance, we may start with a question or a query in English and attempt to derive the corresponding relevance model in Chinese.

4   **Making estimation tractable**. Finally, we address an important issue of computational complexity of our estimation methods and discuss a way of speeding up the computation.

3.1   Estimation from a Set of Examples

We start with the simplest case where we have perfect knowledge of the entire relevant class R. Recall that R is the set of documents D considered relevant to some information need. Our goal is to estimate the relevance model of R, i.e. a probability distribution $P(w|R)$ over the words w in our vocabulary, which tells us how frequently we expect to see each word in relevant documents. Formally, $P(w|R)$ is the probability that a randomly picked word from a random document $D \in R$ will be the word w. Since we know the entire set R, the estimation is extremely simple and proceeds as follows. Let $p(D|R)$ denote the probability of randomly picking document D from the relevant set R. We assume each relevant document is equally likely to be picked at random, so the estimate is:

$$p(D|R) = \left\{ \begin{array}{ll} 1/|R| & \text{if } D \in R \\ 0 & \text{otherwise} \end{array} \right. \tag{2.3}$$

Here $|R|$ represents the total number of documents in R. Once we fix a document D, the probability of observing a word w if we randomly pick some word from D is simply the relative frequency of w in D:

$$P_{ml}(w|D) = \frac{\#(w, D)}{|D|} \qquad (2.4)$$

In the equation above $\#(w, D)$ denotes the number of times the word w occurs in some relevant document D, and $|D|$ designates the length of document D. It is important to note that equation (2.4) defines a *document language model*, (Ponte and Croft, 1998; Berger and Lafferty, 1999; Miller et al., 1999; Song and Croft, 1999; Hiemstra, 2001). Specifically, equation (2.4) represents an unsmoothed maximum-likelihood language model of D. Combining the estimates from equations (2.3) and (2.4), the probability of randomly picking a document D and then observing the word w is:

$$P(w, D|R) = P_{ml}(w|D)p(D|R) \qquad (2.5)$$

In deriving equation (2.5), we assumed that the document model of D completely determines word probabilities, i.e. once we fix D, the probability of observing w is independent of the relevant class R and only depends on D. The overall probability of observing the word w in the relevant class is therefore just the expectation of equation (2.5) over all the documents in our collection $\mathcal{C}$:

$$P(w|R) = \sum_{D \in \mathcal{C}} P(w|D)p(D|R) \qquad (2.6)$$

Here $P(w|D)$ and $p(D|R)$ are given by equations (2.4) and (2.3) respectively. We don't have to restrict the sum in equation (2.6) to the relevant documents, since the prior probability $p(D|R)$ is zero for documents not in R. Equation (2.6) makes is explicit that every relevance model is simply a linear mixture of relevant document models. Hence, the universe of all possible relevance models is a discrete collection of mixtures, corresponding to all possible relevant sets $R \subset \mathcal{C}$. Most of the estimation techniques in this work can be re-formulated in terms of equation (2.6), with different estimates for the prior distribution $p(D|R)$.

3.1.1 Incomplete Set of Examples.

Until this point we concerned ourselves only with the case where we had perfect knowledge of the relevant class R. Now suppose we have a sufficiently large, but incomplete subset of examples $S \subset R$, and would like to estimate the relevance model $P(w|R)$. This situation arises frequently in the field of text categorization, and sometimes in information routing and filtering. If the set S is sufficiently large, we can simply use equation (2.6), substituting the incomplete set of samples S in place of the full relevant set R. The hypothesis here is that estimated probabilities $P(w|S)$ will be sufficiently close to the actual probabilities $P(w|R)$. Indeed, the resulting estimator $P(w|S)$ has a number of interesting properties[1]:

1. $P(w|S)$ is an *unbiased* estimator of $P(w|R)$ for a random subset $S \subset R$. This means that over a large number of random subsets $S \subset R$, the expected value of $P(w|S)$ will converge to $P(w|R)$ for every word w.

2. $P(w|S)$ is the *maximum-likelihood* estimator with respect to the set of examples S. This means that if we consider the simplex $I\!\!P^{\mathcal{V}}$ of all possible probability distributions over $\mathcal{V}$, the distribution $P(w|S)$ will assign the highest probability to the set of strings S.

3. $P(w|S)$ is the *maximum-entropy* probability distribution constrained by S. This means that out of all statistical models that mimic the word frequencies observed in S, the model $P(w|S)$ is the most "random", or has the highest entropy.

Despite these attractive properties, using S as a substitute for R leads to a significant problem of estimator variance. Since $P(w|S)$ is an unbiased estimator, we know that *on average* it will be correct. However, for different subsets of examples $S \subset R$, the estimated probabilities $P(w|S)$ may be quite different from each other, and may vary significantly around $P(w|R)$. In particular, the estimator $P(w|S)$ may contain a lot of zero probabilities where $P(w|R)$ is non-zero. This will happen because of the sparse nature of word occurrences – most words occur in very few documents, and many will occur in the relevant documents which are not in S. The problem of zero frequencies becomes particularly acute when the set of examples S is small compared to the full relevant class R.

3.1.2   The role of smoothing.

A popular way to counter the the problem of high variance in maximum-likelihood estimators is through a technique called *smoothing*. Most smoothing methods center around a fairly simple idea: they take some probability mass away from the maximum-likelihood estimator $P(w|S)$ and distribute it among the words that have zero frequency in the set S of examples. This results in a more stable estimator: the word probabilities do not vary as much with different subsets $S \subset R$ because they include a component that is independent of S. Usually, smoothing is achieved by interpolating the maximum-likelihood probability $P_{ml}(w|D)$ from equation (2.4), with some background distribution $P(w)$ over the vocabulary:

---

[1] Formal proofs of these properties are omitted from this work, but (1) can be proved from the *law of large numbers* by assuming a uniform prior on subsets $S \subset R$, (2) is a simple application of *Jensen's* inequality, to the log-likelihood ratio, and (3) follows from the duality of maximum-entropy in constrained models and maximum-likelihood in *exponential* models.

$$P_{smooth}(w|D) = \lambda_D P_{ml}(w|D) + (1 - \lambda_D)P(w) \qquad (2.7)$$

Here λ_D is a parameter that controls the degree of smoothing. $P(w)$ is the background probability of observing w, usually interpreted as the probability of observing the word in any sample of text, irrespective of topic. $P(w)$ is commonly estimated by averaging the maximum-likelihood probabilities $P_{ml}(w|D)$ over all the documents D in the collection C. At this point we can make an important connection between the background probability $P(w)$ and relevance models. According to equation (2.6), the background model is the same as a relevance model corresponding to the whole collection C. This connection allows us to interpret *smoothing* as a way of selecting a different prior distribution $p(D|S)$. The smoothing effect of equation (2.7) is equivalent to adjusting equation (2.3) as follows:

$$p_{smooth}(D|S) = \begin{cases} (1 - \lambda_D)/|\mathcal{C}| + \lambda_D/|S| & \text{if } D \in S \\ (1 - \lambda_D)/|\mathcal{C}| & \text{otherwise} \end{cases} \qquad (2.8)$$

Observe that this prior is always non-zero, so the resulting relevance model includes a little bit of every document in the collection. However, the relevance model still assigns the bulk of its probability mass to the set of examples S. By varying the smoothing parameters λ_D, we can control the amount of variance in the resulting estimator. For large values of λ_D we get estimators that are more focused on the set of examples, but exhibit a high degree of variance. By driving λ_D towards smaller values we can significantly reduce the variance, but there is a price to pay for that reduction: our estimator will no longer be un-biased with respect to $P(w|R)$. The optimal selection of λ_D is usually achieved through experimentation and varies from application to application.

3.1.3 Application to Relevance Feedback.

One of the major disadvantages of the established language modeling framework for Information Retrieval is the difficulty of incorporating the results of user interaction. Recall that in the standard language modeling framework (Ponte and Croft, 1998; Ponte, 1998) we treat the query as a fixed random sample and focus on accurate estimation of document language models. Now suppose we are operating in an interactive environment, and the user provides some form of feedback to the system, perhaps in the form of documents she considers relevant to the query in question. These examples could be very valuable in estimating word statistics in the relevant class $P(w|R)$. However, in the standard LM framework we explicitly avoid any discussion of the relevant class, and the only type of distributions we estimate are of the form $P(w|D)$. Accordingly, there is no formal mechanism to incorporate user relevance judgments into the language modeling framework.

In his dissertation Ponte (Ponte, 1998) proposed a limited way to deal with this problem: we can think of example relevant documents as examples of what the query might have been, and re-sample (or expand) the query by adding highly descriptive words from the documents that were judged relevant. In particular, if R' is the subset of relevant documents marked by the user, Ponte proposed adding some number k words that have the highest average log-ratio in the set of relevant examples:

$$\sum_{D \in R'} \log \frac{P(w|D)}{P(w)} \qquad (2.9)$$

Here $P(w|D)$ is the maximum-likelihood probability of observing word w in document D and $P(w)$ is the background probability of observing the word in the collection. The approach proposed by Ponte is effective but has little formal justification. It does not lend itself to the standard statistical estimation methods, since we are not refining the model but changing the sample.

Within the framework of relevance models, incorporating user feedback is considerably easier and more intuitive. Recall that a relevance model is the probability distribution $P(w|R)$, and we can directly apply the methods from the above sections to refine our estimate based on examples labeled relevant by the user. Specifically, if R' is a set of labeled examples, the estimated relevance model would be given by:

$$P(w|R') = \frac{1}{|R'|} \sum_{D \in R'} P(w|D) \qquad (2.10)$$

where $P(w|D)$ is either the maximum-likelihood estimate given by equation (2.4), or the smoothed-out estimate from equation (2.7) and $|R'|$ is the number of relevant examples. Note that this formulation does not make any use of the original query and only considers example documents. The original query is essentially discarded. We are actively working on new ways to combine this estimate with the sparse estimation techniques that will be discussed in Section 3.2 below. A brief evaluation of the simple relevance feedback approach is provided in Section 4.6.

3.1.4   Summary: estimation from a set of examples.   This section addressed the case where we had access to a set of example documents – either the full relevant set R or the subset $S \subset R$. We described how we can estimate relevance models as mixtures of individual document models, and demonstrated how smoothing can be interpreted in terms of mixture models. To support our hypothesis that we can get a reasonable approximation to $P(w|R)$ even if we only have a small subset $S \subset R$, we performed the following experiment. We have constructed relevance model estimates $P(w|S)$

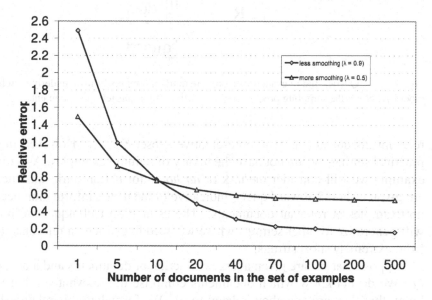

Figure 2.1. Relevance Models constructed from a subset $S \subset R$ quickly converge to models constructed from the whole relevant class R. The rate of convergence, and the achievable minimum depends on the value of the smoothing parameter λ_D in equations (2.7) and (2.8).

from random subsets $S \subset R$ and measured the relative entropy between these estimates and the relevance model constructed from the full relevant class R. Figure 2.1 shows that these estimates are reasonably close to $P(w|R)$ for as few as 20 documents in S. This is encouraging, since in many applications only a small portion of the relevant set is available for training. Note that the value of the smoothing parameter λ has a strong effect on the entropy. When the set of examples S is very small (1-10 documents) the estimator $P(w|S)$ will exhibit very high variance, and smoothing is essential. When we consider larger subsets $S \subset R$, less smoothing is preferable, since the variance is lower to begin with, and smoothing introduces a significant bias in the estimates.

3.2 Estimation without Examples

We now turn our attention to a more challenging problem: estimation of relevance models when virtually no training examples are available. Recall that what we want to estimate is the set of probabilities $P(w|R)$ which give the relative frequency with which we expect to see any word w during repeated independent random sampling of words from the relevant documents. The previous section outlined estimation of $P(w|R)$ when we know the class of

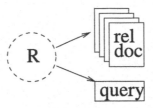

Figure 2.2.   Queries and relevant documents are random samples from an underlying relevance model R. Note: the sampling process could be different for queries and documents.

relevant documents R, or a representative subset $S \subset R$. However, in many practical settings we do not have the luxury of training examples. As a running example we will consider the task of *ad-hoc* information retrieval, where we are given a short 2-3 word query, indicative of the user's information need and no examples of relevant documents. The estimation techniques we propose will generalize to other settings where we need to estimate a relevance model from extremely short strings.

Suppose that we are given a large collection of documents and a user query Q. We do not know which documents comprise the relevant set, but we do know that they are somehow related to Q. We formalize this relationship as follows. We assume that for every information need there exists an underlying relevance model R, which assigns the probabilities $P(w|R)$ to the word occurrence in the relevant documents. The relevance model also assigns probabilities $P(Q|R)$ to the various queries that might be issued by the user for that specific information need. Figure 2.2 shows the relationship graphically: we assume that the relevant documents are random samples from the distribution $P(w|R)$. The query Q is also a sample from R. However, we would like to stress that the sampling process that generates the queries does not have to be the same as the process that generates the words in the relevant documents. In other words, the probability of a one-word query "w" under R need not be the same as the probability of observing w in a random relevant document.

Our assumptions about query generation are similar to the assumptions made in (Ponte and Croft, 1998; Song and Croft, 1999; Miller et al., 1999; Berger and Lafferty, 1999), but there is a crucial distinction: we don't assume that the query is a sample from any specific document model. Instead we assume that both the query and the relevant documents are samples from an unknown relevance model R. In the remainder of this section we show how we can leverage the fact that Q is a random sample from R to learn the parameters of R.

Let $Q = q_1...q_k$. Suppose we play the following game. We have an unknown process R, a black box, from which we can repeatedly sample words. After sampling k times we observe the words $q_1...q_k$. What is the probability that the next word we pull out of R will be w? The only information we have is that we just observed $q_1...q_k$, so our best bet is to relate the probability of w to the conditional probability of observing w given that we just observed $q_1...q_k$:

$$P(w|R) \approx P(w|q_1 \ldots q_k) \tag{2.11}$$

Equation (2.11) can be thought of as a probability of "translating" the query Q into the word w, similarly to (Berger and Lafferty, 1999). Note that we are "translating" a set of words into a single word. By definition, we can express the conditional probability in terms of the joint probability of observing w with the query words $q_1 \ldots q_k$:

$$P(w|R) \approx \frac{P(w, q_1 \ldots q_k)}{P(q_1 \ldots q_k)} \tag{2.12}$$

The challenge now lies in estimating the joint probability of observing the word w together with the query words $q_1 \ldots q_k$. We present two methods for estimating this probability. The first method is conceptually simpler, and assumes that w was sampled in the same way as the query words. The second method assumes that w and the query words were sampled using two different mechanisms. The two methods differ in the independence assumptions that are being made, and we try to highlight this in the derivations. We contrast the performance of these two methods in section 4.5.

3.2.1   Method 1: i.i.d. sampling.   Let's assume that the query words $q_1 \ldots q_k$ and the words w in relevant documents are sampled identically and independently from a unigram distribution $P(w|R)$. Let $\mathcal{C}$ represent some finite universe of unigram distributions from which we could sample. The sampling process proceeds as follows: we pick a distribution $D \in \mathcal{C}$ with probability $p(D)$, and sample from it $k+1$ times. Then the total probability of observing w together with $q_1 \ldots q_k$ is:

$$P(w, q_1 \ldots q_k) = \sum_{D \in \mathcal{C}} p(D) P(w, q_1 \ldots q_k|D) \tag{2.13}$$

Because we assumed that w and all q_i are sampled independently and identically to each other, we can express their joint probability as the product of the marginals:

$$P(w, q_1 \ldots q_k|D) = P(w|D) \prod_{i=1}^{k} P(q_i|D) \tag{2.14}$$

When we substitute equation (2.14) into equation (2.13), we get the following final estimate for the joint probability of w and $q_1 \ldots q_k$:

$$P(w, q_1 \ldots q_k) = \sum_{D \in \mathcal{C}} p(D) P(w|D) \prod_{i=1}^{k} P(q_i|D) \qquad (2.15)$$

Note that in the course of this derivation we made a very strong independence assumption: in equation (2.14) we assumed that w and $q_1 \ldots q_k$ are mutually independent once we pick a distribution D. A graphical diagram of the dependencies between the variables involved in the derivation is shown on the left side of Figure (2.3).

3.2.2   Method 2: conditional sampling.

Now let's consider a different approach to sampling. We fix a value of w according to some prior $P(w)$. Then perform the following process k times: pick a distribution $D_i \in \mathcal{C}$ according to $p(D_i|w)$, the sample the query word q_i from D_i with probability $P(q_i|D_i)$. A graphical diagram of the sampling process is given on the right side of Figure (2.3).

The effect of this sampling strategy is that we assume the query words $q_1 \ldots q_k$ to be independent of each other, but we keep their dependence on w:

$$P(w, q_1 \ldots q_k) = P(w) \prod_{i=1}^{k} P(q_i|w) \qquad (2.16)$$

To estimate the conditional probabilities $P(q_i|w)$ we compute the expectation over the universe $\mathcal{C}$ of our unigram models.

$$P(q_i|w) = \sum_{D \in \mathcal{C}} P(q_i|D_i) P(D_i|w) \qquad (2.17)$$

Note that we made an additional assumption that q_i is independent of w once we picked a distribution D_i. When we substitute the result of equation (2.17) into equation (2.16), we get the following final estimate for the joint probability of w and $q_1 \ldots q_k$:

$$P(w, q_1 \ldots q_k) = P(w) \prod_{i=1}^{k} \left(\sum_{D_i \in \mathcal{C}} P(q_i|D_i) P(D_i|w) \right) \qquad (2.18)$$

3.2.3   Final Estimation Details.

This section provides the final details for estimating relevance models without examples, using either Method 1 or Method 2. The estimation choices in this section are either dictated by the axioms of probability theory, or represent techniques that are well-known and accepted by the language modeling community. To ensure proper additivity of our model, we set the query prior $P(q_1 \ldots q_k)$ in equation (2.12) to be:

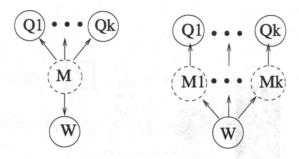

Figure 2.3. Dependence networks for two methods of estimating the joint probability $P(w, q_1 \ldots q_k)$. Left: i.i.d. sampling (method 1). Right: conditional sampling (method 2).

$$P(q_1 \ldots q_k) = \sum_{w \in \mathcal{V}} P(w, q_1 \ldots q_k) \qquad (2.19)$$

where the joint probability $P(w, q_1 \ldots q_k)$ is computed according to equations (2.15) and (2.18) for Method 1 and Method 2 respectively. The summation is performed over all words w in the vocabulary $\mathcal{V}$. We set the word prior $P(w)$ to be:

$$P(w) = \sum_{D \in \mathcal{C}} P(w|D)P(D) \qquad (2.20)$$

Word probabilities $P(w|D)$ are computed according to equation (2.4), and smoothed according to equation (2.7). Smoothing parameters λ_D are tuned empirically. For Method 1 we arbitrarily choose to use uniform priors $P(D)$. For Method 2, we choose to estimate the conditional probabilities of picking a distribution D_i based on w as follows:

$$P(D_i|w) = P(w|D_i)P(w)/P(D_i) \qquad (2.21)$$

Here $P(w|D_i)$ is calculated according to equations (2.4) and (2.7), $P(w)$ is computed as in equation (2.20), and $P(D_i)$ is kept uniform over all the documents in $\mathcal{C}$.

3.2.4   Summary: estimation without examples.   In this section we presented a novel technique for estimating probabilities of words in the unknown set of documents relevant to the query $q_1 \ldots q_k$. In a nutshell, we approximate the probability of observing the word w in the relevant set by the probability of co-occurrence between w and the query. $P(w|R)$ is what we ultimately want to estimate. We argue that $P(w|q_1 \ldots q_k)$ is the best possible approximation in the absence of any training data. We present two formal derivations of this probability of co-occurrence. We use widely accepted

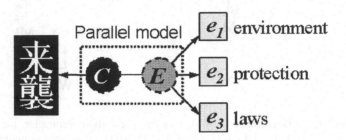

Figure 2.4.   Graphical representation of cross-lingual relevance models. The model consists of a set of paired Chinese / English distributions. English queries are random samples from some English distribution from the paired set. Relevant Chinese documents are random samples from the corresponding Chinese distribution. Paired distributions could be estimated from a parallel corpus.

estimation techniques. Evaluation of the model will be covered in detail in Section 4.

3.3   Cross-lingual Estimation

In many practical applications it may be desirable to extend the estimation methods from previous section to the cross-lingual setting. Typically, we would be given a short sample of words in the source language, such as a query or a question. Our goal is to estimate the relevance model in some target language, different from the language of the query. As an example, we could start with an English query and guess what words might occur in a Chinese document relevant to that query. Despite its odd appearance, cross-lingual estimation has many practical applications in cross-language information retrieval, question answering, summarization, and may be applicable to machine translation.

Let $Q_S = s_1 \ldots s_k$ be the query in the source language and let R_T be the unknown set of target documents that are relevant to that query. We would like to estimate the relevance model corresponding to R_T, i.e. the probability distribution $P(t|R_T)$ for every word t in the vocabulary of the target language. Since the relevant class R_T is unknown and we are not provided with any examples, we follow the argument in Section 3.2 and suggest that a reasonable way to approximate the probability of seeing t in the relevant class R_T is by the conditional probability of observing the word t given we have observed sample words $s_1 \ldots s_k$:

$$P(t|R_T) \approx P(t|s_1 \ldots s_k) = \frac{P(t, s_1 \ldots s_k)}{P(s_1 \ldots s_k)} \tag{2.22}$$

An implicit assumption behind equation (2.22) is that there exists a joint probabilistic model $P_{S \times T}$ from which we can compute the joint probability $P(t, s_1 \ldots s_k)$. The estimation is complicated by the fact that $s_1 \ldots s_k$ and t represent words from different languages, and so will not naturally occur in the same documents. In the following sections we discuss two estimation strategies, one based on a parallel corpus of documents, and one based on a statistical lexicon.

3.3.1   Estimation with a parallel corpus.   Suppose we have at our disposal a parallel corpus $\mathcal{C}$, a collection of document pairs $\{D_S, D_T\}$, where D_S is an document in the source language, and D_T is a document in the target language discussing the same topic as D_S. Using estimation Method 1 from equation (2.15), we can estimate the joint probability of observing the word t together with $s_1 \ldots s_k$ as:

$$P(t, s_1 \ldots s_k) = \sum_{\{D_S, D_T\} \in \mathcal{C}} P(\{D_S, D_T\}) \left(P(t|D_T) \prod_{i=1}^{k} P(s_i|D_S) \right) \tag{2.23}$$

Similarly, if we wish to use Method 2 from equation (2.18), the joint probability may be estimated as:

$$P(t, s_1 \ldots s_k) = P(t) \prod_{i=1}^{k} \left(\sum_{\{D_S, D_T\} \in \mathcal{C}} P(s_i|D_S) P(D_T|t) \right) \tag{2.24}$$

In both bases the prior probability $P(\{D_S, D_T\})$ can be kept uniform. Language model probabilities $P(t|D_T)$ and $P(s_i|D_S)$ are calculated according to equations (2.4) and (2.7), but each in its own language. The posterior distribution $P(D_T|t)$ can be computed as $P(t|D_T)P(D_T)/P(t)$ with the uniform prior $P(D_T)$. The target-word prior probability $P(t)$, which arises twice in equation (2.24), can be estimated according to equation (2.20).

3.3.2   Estimation with a statistical lexicon.   As we demonstrated above, a parallel corpus allows for elegant estimation of joint probabilities $P(t, s_1 \ldots s_k)$ across two different languages. However, parallel corpora are often difficult to obtain, while estimation of joint probabilities is very desirable. In the cases when a parallel corpus is not available, it is still possible to estimate the joint probability $P(t, s_1 \ldots s_k)$ if we have a statistical lexicon. A

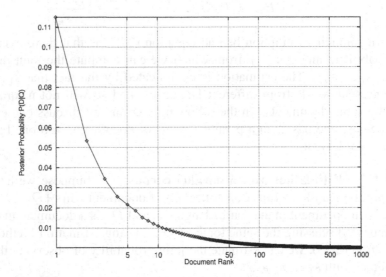

Figure 2.5.   Posterior probabilities $P(D|q_1 \ldots q_k)$ rapidly decrease with the rank of the retrieved document. Documents which are not in the top 100 will have a negligible contribution to overall Relevance Model. Posterior probabilities are averaged over 100 TREC queries on the AP dataset.

statistical lexicon is special dictionary which gives the translation probability $p(s_i|t)$ for every source word s_i and every target word t.   Note that any bilingual dictionary can be turned into a statistical lexicon by simply assigning uniform translation probabilities to all source translations s of a given target word t. While the quality of this lexicon may be inferior, it will still serve the purpose. In this case we let $\mathcal{C}$ be the set of target documents D_T. Now $P(t|D_T)$ can be computed directly from equations (2.4) and (2.7). In order to compute $P(s_i|D_T)$ for a source word s_i in a target document D_T, we can use the translation model, advocated by Berger and Lafferty (Berger and Lafferty, 1999) and recently used in cross-lingual setting by (Xu et al., 2001; Hiemstra and de Jong, 1999). According to (Xu et al., 2001):

$$P(s_i|D_T) = (1 - \lambda)P(s_i) + \lambda \sum_t p(s_i|t)P_{ml}(t|D_T) \qquad (2.25)$$

Here the summation goes over all the target words t in the vocabulary, $p(s_i|t)$ is the translation probability from the statistical lexicon, and $P_{ml}(t|D_T)$ is given by equation (2.4). $P(s_i)$ is the background probability of s_i, computed according to equation (2.20).

3.4 Complexity of Estimation

Sections 3.2 and 3.3 discussed the problem of estimating a relevance model $P(w|R)$ in the case where the relevant set is unknown R. The estimation techniques involve computing expectations over every document D (or every document pair $\{D_S, D_T\}$) in a large collection $\mathcal{C}$. That computation has to be repeated for every word w in the target vocabulary, which makes the estimation extremely expensive. For estimation Method 1, it is possible to re-write the equations in a form that will allow us to make some shortcuts during the estimation process. If we expand the probability of the query as $P(q_1 \ldots q_k) = \sum_w P(w, q_1 \ldots q_k)$, and substitute equation (2.15) for the joint probability $P(w, q_1 \ldots q_k)$, it becomes possible to estimate the probability of observing w in the set of relevant documents R as:

$$P(w|R) = \sum_{D \in \mathcal{C}} P(w|D)P(D|q_1 \ldots q_k) \qquad (2.26)$$

When expressed like this, it becomes obvious that a relevance model (under estimation Method 1) is a linear mixture of documents from $\mathcal{C}$, where each distribution D is "weighted" by its posterior probability of generation the query: $P(D|q_1 \ldots q_k)$. In our model, the posterior probability is expressed as:

$$P(D|q_1 \ldots q_k) = \frac{P(D) \prod_i P(q_i|D)}{\sum_D P(D) \prod_i P(q_i|D)} \qquad (2.27)$$

In practice, because of the product in the numerator, this posterior has near-zero values for all but a few documents D in a given collection $\mathcal{C}$. These documents are precisely the ones that rank highest when the query $q_1 \ldots q_k$ is issued against the collection $\mathcal{C}$. Figure 2.5 shows how the posterior probabilities in equation (2.27) quickly decay with the rank of the retrieved documents. Accordingly, instead of computing equation (2.15) over the entire collection, we can compute equation (2.26) over some number n of top-ranked models retrieved by $q_1 \ldots q_k$. The result is a very significant speedup of the estimation process. The same optimization may be applied to the case of cross-lingual estimation with Method 1.

4. Experimental Results

In this section we turn our attention to evaluating the performance of the proposed techniques for estimating relevance models. We consider two important Information Retrieval tasks: *adhoc* retrieval and *cross-language* retrieval. In both problems we start with a short user query Q and a large collection of documents $\mathcal{C}$. The goal is to identify the set of relevant documents $R \subset \mathcal{C}$. We approach the problem by estimating a relevance model $P(w|R)$ using the query Q as a short sample and leveraging the techniques we developed in sections 3.2 and 3.3 respectively. Once a relevance model $P(w|R)$ is computed, we rank all documents $D \in C$ by how well they match the model.

The remainder of this section is organized as follows. We start by describing the evaluation metrics and the corpora which were used in our experiments. In section 4.2 we provide examples of relevance models that could be estimated from a short 2-3 word query. Section 4.3 presents experimental results obtained on the adhoc retrieval task. In section 4.4 we address an important question of how we could rank the documents in the collection using a relevance model. Section 4.5 contrasts the two proposed methods of estimating the joint probability $P(w, Q)$. Section 4.6 demonstrates how we can use relevance models when limited user feedback is available. We conclude by discussing cross-language retrieval results in section 4.7.

4.1   Experimental Setup

4.1.1   Evaluation Paradigm.   The primary goal of many Information Retrieval applications lies in identifying a set $R \subset C$ of documents relevant to some information need. This is a set-based decision task, but in practice most retrieval systems are evaluated by how well they can *rank* the documents in the collection. Let D_1, D_2, $\ldots$ D_N denote some ordering of the documents in the collection. Then, for every rank k, we can compute *recall* as the fraction of relevant documents that were observed in the set $\{D_1 \ldots D_k\}$. Similarly, *precision* is defined as the fraction of documents $\{D_1 \ldots D_k\}$ which are in fact relevant. System performance is evaluated by comparing precision at different levels of recall, either in a form of a table (e.g. Table 2.6), or as a graph (e.g. Figure 2.7). A common objective is to increase precision at all levels of recall. For applications that require interaction with a user, it is common to consider precision at specific ranks, e.g. after 5 or 10 retrieved documents. When one desires a single number as a measure of performance, a popular choice is *average precision* defined as an arithmetic average of precision at different ranks. Another possible choice is R-precision, precision that is achieved when at rank R, where R is the number of relevant documents in the dataset. In all of these measures, precision values are usually averaged across a large set of queries with known relevant sets.

We will adopt average precision as the primary evaluation measure for all the experiments in this paper. In most cases we will also report precision at different recall levels, or precision at specific ranks. When possible, we will report the results of statistical significance tests.

4.1.2   English Resources.   We use five different datasets in our evaluation of adhoc retrieval effectiveness in section 4.3. Table 2.1 provides detailed information for each dataset. All five datasets contain news releases, the ma-

Name	Sources	Years	#Docs	#Terms	dl	cf	Queries	ql
AP	Associated Press	89-90	242,918	315,539	273	210	51-150	4.32
FT	Financial Times	91-94	210,158	443,395	237	112	251-400	2.95
LA	Los Angeles Times	89-90	131,896	326,609	290	117	301-400	2.52
WSJ	Wall Street Journal	87-92	173,252	185,903	265	247	1-200	4.86
TDT2	AP, NYT, CNN, ABC, PRI, VOA	1998	62,596	122,189	167	85	TDT	3.02

Table 2.1. Information for the corpora used in ad-hoc retrieval experiments. *dl* denotes average document length, *cf* stands for average collection frequency of a word, and *ql* represents average number of words per query.

jority of them printed, although TDT2 corpus contains a significant broadcast component. The datasets vary in size, time frame, and word statistics. All datasets except TDT2 are homogeneous, i.e. they contain documents from a single source. For each dataset there is an associated set of topics, along with human relevance judgements. For TDT2 dataset the judgements are exhaustive, meaning that every document has been manually labeled as either relevant or non-relevant for every topic. The other four datasets contain *pooled* judgements, i.e. only top-ranked documents from a set of retrieval systems were judged with respect to each topic. TREC topic come in the form of queries, containing title, description and narrative portions. We used only the titles, resulting in queries which are 3-4 words in length. TDT topics are defined by a set of examples and do not have associated queries. However, short titles were assigned to them by annotators, and we used these titles as queries.

4.1.3   English processing.
Prior to any experiments, each dataset was processed as follows. Both documents and queries were tokenized on whitespace and punctuation characters. Tokens with fewer than two characters were discarded. Tokens were then lower-cased and reduced to their root form by using the Krovetz (Allan et al., 2001) stemmer, which combines morphological rules with a large dictionary of special cases and exceptions. After stemming, 418 stop-words from the standard InQuery (Allan et al., 2001) stop-list were removed. All of the remaining tokens were used for indexing, and no other form of processing was used on either the queries or the documents.

4.1.4   Chinese Resources.
All of our cross-language experiments were performed on the dataset used in the TREC9 cross-lingual evaluation. The dataset consists of 127,938 Chinese documents, totaling around 100 million characters. We used the official set of 25 queries. We used two query representations: *short* queries used only the title field, while *long* queries used title, description and narrative fields.

	LDC	CETA	HK News	Combined
English terms	86,000	35,000	21,000	104,997
Chinese terms	137,000	202,000	75,000	305,103

Table 2.2. Composition of the BBN bilingual lexicon

	HK News	TDT	HK News + TDT
Document pairs	18,147	46,692	64,839
English terms	28,806	67,542	83,152
Chinese terms	49,218	111,547	132,453

Table 2.3. Composition of the parallel corpus used in our experiments.

Experiments involving a bilingual dictionary used the statistical lexicon created by Xu et.al (Xu et al., 2001). The lexicon was assembled from three parts: the LDC dictionary, the CETA dictionary, and the statistical dictionary, learned from the Hong-Kong News corpus by applying the GIZA machine translation toolkit. Table 2.2 provides a summary of the dictionary components.

In the experiments that made use of the parallel corpus, we used the Hong-Kong News parallel dataset, which contains 18,147 news stories in English and Chinese. Because it is so small, the Hong-Kong parallel corpus has a significant word coverage problem. In order to alleviate the problem, we augmented the corpus with the TDT2 and TDT3 (Cieri et al.,) pseudo-parallel datasets. These corpora contain 46,692 Chinese news stories along with their SYSTRAN translations into English. Since the documents are translated by software, we do not expect the quality of the TDT corpus to be as high as Hong-Kong News. We discuss the impact of adding the TDT corpus in section 4.7. The composition of the parallel corpus is detailed in Table 2.3.

4.1.5   Chinese processing.   The pre-processing performed on the Chinese part of the corpus was very crude, due to our limited knowledge of the language. The entire dataset, along with the Chinese queries was converted into the simplified encoding (GB). We carried out separate experiments with three forms of tokenization: (i) single Chinese characters (unigrams), (ii) half-overlapping adjacent pairs of Chinese characters (bigrams), and (iii) Chinese "words", obtained by running a simple dictionary-based segmenter, developed by F. F. Feng at the University of Massachusetts. In section 4.7 we report separate figures for all three forms of tokenization, as well as a linear combination of them. We did not remove any stop-words, or any punctuation characters from either Chinese documents or queries. This results in some spurious matches and also in these characters figuring prominently in the relevance models we constructed.

"Monica Lewinsky"		"Rats in Space"		"John Glenn"		"Unabomber"	
$P(w\|R)$	w	$P(w\|R)$	w	$P(w\|R)$	w	$P(w\|R)$	w
0.041	lewinsky	0.062	rat	0.032	glenn	0.046	kaczynski
0.038	monica	0.030	space	0.030	space	0.046	unabomber
0.027	jury	0.020	shuttle	0.026	john	0.019	ted
0.026	grand	0.018	columbia	0.016	senate	0.017	judge
0.019	confidant	0.014	brain	0.015	shuttle	0.016	trial
0.016	talk	0.012	mission	0.011	seventy	0.013	say
0.015	case	0.012	two	0.011	america	0.012	theodore
0.014	president	0.011	seven	0.011	old	0.012	today
0.013	clinton	0.010	system	0.010	october	0.011	decide
0.010	starr	0.010	nervous	0.010	say	0.011	guilty

Table 2.4. Examples of mono-lingual relevance models for the TDT2 topics. Probabilities are estimated using techniques from section 3.2, starting with just the topic title. For each topic we show 10 words with highest estimated probabilities under the relevance model.

Q = "environmental protection laws" 环境保护法		
P(word|Q)	word	meaning
0.061	，	[punctuation]
0.036	的	[possessive suffix]
0.027	。	[punctuation]
0.017	和	and
0.016	、	[punctuation]
0.009	环境	environment
0.009	了	[end of sentence]
0.008	海洋	sea
0.008	法	law
0.008	资源	resource
0.007	全国	whole country
0.007	在	in
0.006	保护	protect
0.006	污染	pollution
0.006	胶	rubber
0.006	发泡	defects in plastic
0.005	与	and
0.005	中国	china
0.005	产品	product
0.005	法律	law

Figure 2.6. Example of a cross-lingual relevance model, estimated from query number 58 of the CLIR task of TREC-9. Shown are the 20 tokens with highest probabilities under the cross-lingual relevance model.

4.2 Examples of Relevance Models

Table 2.4 provides five examples of mono-lingual relevance models constructed from extremely short samples. We used estimation techniques from section 3.2 to construct relevance models from the titles of several TDT topics.

The titles are shown at the top of each column, and below them we show 10 words that get the highest probabilities under the relevance model. For every topic, we can see a lot of words which are highly-related to the topic, but also a few general words, perhaps unrelated to the particular topic. This is not surprising, since a relevance model is the probability distribution over all words in the relevant documents, and as such will certainly include common words. Recall that stop-words (very frequent words, such as "of", "the", etc.) were excluded from the computation. We used estimation Method 2 (section 3.2.2) for computing the probabilities.

In Figure 2.6 we provide an example of a cross-lingual relevance model. In this case we started with an English query and used methods from section 3.3 to estimate a relevance model for Chinese documents. We used query number 58 from the cross-language retrieval task of TREC-9. The English query was: *"environmental protection laws"*. We show 20 tokens with highest probability under the model. It is evident that many stop-words and punctuation characters are assigned high probabilities. This is not surprising, since these characters were not removed during pre-processing, and we naturally expect these characters to occur frequently in the documents that discuss any topic. However, the model also assigns high probabilities to words that one would consider highly relevant to the topic of environmental protection. Note that we did not perform any morphological analysis of Chinese and did not remove any stop-words. Cross-lingual estimation Method 1 was used for computing the probabilities.

4.3   Ad-hoc Retrieval Experiments

The problem of *ad-hoc* retrieval is the most fundamental problem in the field of Information Retrieval. We are given a query $Q = q_1 \ldots q_k$, representative of some user's information need, and a large collection of documents C. The goal is to identify documents which are relevant to a given information need. In our experiments we compare four established baselines against an approach that uses relevance models:

tf.idf Our first baseline represents one of the most widely-used and success-
ful approaches to adhoc retrieval. We use the InQuery (Allan et al., 2001) modification of the popular Okapi *BM25* (Robertson et al., 1998) weighting scheme. Given a query $Q = q_1 \ldots q_k$, the documents D are ranked by the following formula:

$$S(Q, D) = \sum_{q \in Q} \frac{\#(q, D)}{\#(q, D) + 0.5 + 1.5 \frac{dl}{avg.dl}} \frac{\log\left(0.5 + N/df(q)\right)}{\log\left(1.0 + \log N\right)}$$

$$(2.28)$$

Here $\#(q, D)$ is the number of times query word q occurs in document D, dl is the length of document D, $df(q)$ denotes the number of documents containing word q, and N stands for the total number of documents in the collection. Equation (2.28) represents a heuristic extension of the classical probabilistic models of IR. The formula is remarkable for its consistently good performance in yearly TREC evaluations.

LCA In section 4.5 we mentioned that relevance models can be viewed as a technique for massive query expansion. To provide a fair comparison, we describe performance of a popular heuristic query expansion technique: Local Context Analysis (LCA) (Xu and Croft, 1996). LCA is a technique for adding highly-related words to the query, in the hope of handling synonymy and reducing ambiguity. Given a query $Q = q_1 \ldots q_k$, and a set of retrieved documents R, LCA ranks all words w in the vocabulary by the following formula:

$$Bel(w; Q) = \prod_{q \in Q} \left(0.1 + \frac{1/\log n}{1/idf_w} \log \sum_{D \in R} D_q D_w \right)^{idf_q} \quad (2.29)$$

Here n is the size of the retrieved set, idf_w is the inverse document frequency of the word w (Robertson and Sparck Jones, 1976), D_q and D_w represent frequencies of words w and q in document D. To perform query expansion, we add m highest-ranking words to the original query $q_1 \ldots q_k$, and perform retrieval using **tf.idf** method described above. n and m represent parameters that can be tuned to optimize performance. Based on preliminary experiments, we set $n = 10$ and $m = 20$.

LM Language-modeling approaches have recently enjoyed significant interest for their success in adhoc and cross-language retrieval tasks. The approaches were pioneered by Ponte and Croft (Ponte and Croft, 1998) and further developed by a number of other researchers (Song and Croft, 1999; Hiemstra, 2001; Miller et al., 1999). In the language-modeling framework, the query $Q = q_1 \ldots q_k$ is viewed as an i.i.d. random sample from some unknown document model. Documents D are ranked by the probability that $q_1 \ldots q_k$ would be observed during random sampling from the model of D:

$$S(Q, D) = \prod_{q \in Q} \left(\lambda_D \frac{\#(q, D)}{dl} + (1 - \lambda_D) P(q) \right) \quad (2.30)$$

Here $\#(q, D)$ and dl are as above, and $P(q)$ is the background probability of the query word q, computed over the entire corpus. The smoothing parameter λ_D was set to the Dirichlet(Zhai, 2002) estimate $\lambda_D = \frac{dl}{dl+\mu}$. Based on previous experiments, μ was set to 1000 for all TREC corpora and to 100 for the TDT2 corpus.

Recall from section 4.4 that this method of ranking is equivalent to using cross-entropy where the relevance model $P(w|R)$ was replaced with the query Q.

LM+X Most language-modeling approaches do not automatically include a query expansion component. In his thesis, Ponte (Ponte, 1998) developed a heuristic query expansion approach that demonstrated respectable performance when combined with the ranking formula described above. Given the set of documents R, retrieved in response to the original query, we rank all the words w by the following formula:

$$Bel(w; R) = \sum_{D \in R} log \left(\frac{P(w|D)}{P(w)} \right) \qquad (2.31)$$

Here $P(w|D)$ is computed according to equation 2.7 and $P(w)$ is the background probability of w. m highest-ranking words are added to the original query $q_1 \ldots q_k$, and retrieval was performed according to the **LM** method described above. Based on prior experiments, we added $m = 5$ words from the retrieved set of size $n = 5$.

RM Relevance models are immediately applicable to the adhoc retrieval task. We use techniques from section 3.2 to estimate a relevance model from the query $q_1 \ldots q_k$. We opt for estimation method 1 (section 3.2.1) because of its superior performance (section 4.5) and lower computational demands (see section 3.4). Once the relevance model is estimated, we use cross-entropy (section 4.4) to rank the documents in the collection.

Table 2.5 presents the performance of five systems on the Wall-Street Journal (WSJ) dataset with TREC title queries 1 - 200. We observe that in general, language-modeling approaches (**LM** and **LM+X**) are slightly superior to their heuristic counterparts. Query expansion techniques lead to significant improvements at high recall. Relevance models (**RM**) noticeably outperform all four baselines at all levels of recall, and also in terms of average precision and R-precision (precision at the number of relevant documents). Improvements over **tf.idf** are all statistically significant at the 95% confidence level according to the Wilcoxon(Walpole and Myers, 1989) signed-rank test.

In Table 2.6 we show the performance on the remaining four datasets: AP, FT, LA and TDT2. We compare relevance models (**RM**) with two of the four baselines: **tf.idf** and **LM**. As before, we notice that language modeling approach (**LM**) is somewhat better than the heuristic **tf.idf** ranking. However,

WSJ: TREC queries 1-200 (title)

	tf.idf	LCA	%chg	LM	%chg	LM+X	%chg	RM	%chg
Rel	20982	20982		20982		20982		20982	
Rret	11798	12384	4.97*	12025	1.92*	12766	8.20*	13845	17.35*
0.00	0.634	0.666	4.9	0.683	7.6*	0.653	3.0	0.686	8.1*
0.10	0.457	0.465	1.8	0.474	3.8	0.481	5.4	0.533	16.8*
0.20	0.383	0.380	-0.8	0.395	3.0	0.403	5.1	0.463	20.7*
0.30	0.334	0.333	-0.3	0.340	1.8	0.352	5.3	0.403	20.6*
0.40	0.287	0.283	-1.4	0.288	0.2	0.307	6.7	0.350	21.9*
0.50	0.240	0.240	0.1	0.246	2.7	0.270	12.6*	0.304	26.6*
0.60	0.191	0.195	2.3	0.203	6.5	0.226	18.5*	0.254	33.0*
0.70	0.138	0.153	11.1*	0.158	14.7*	0.178	29.0*	0.196	42.2*
0.80	0.088	0.108	22.8*	0.110	24.9*	0.133	50.7*	0.146	66.1*
0.90	0.049	0.061	25.3*	0.074	51.8*	0.080	64.2*	0.085	73.3*
1.00	0.011	0.013	25.4	0.017	55.6*	0.022	104.3*	0.022	99.7*
Avg	0.238	0.244	2.89	0.253	6.61*	0.265	11.46*	0.301	26.51*

Table 2.5. Comparison of Relevance Models (**RM**) to the baseline systems: (**tf.idf**) Okapi / InQuery weighted sum, (**LCA**) tf.idf with Local Context Analysis, (**LM**) language model with Dirichlet smoothing, (**LM+X**) language model with Ponte expansion. Relevance Models noticeably outperform all baseline systems. Stars indicate statistically significant differences in performance with a 95% confidence according to the Wilcoxon test. Significance tests are performed against the **tf.idf** baseline.

the improvements are not always consistent, and rarely significant. Relevance models demonstrate consistent improvements over both baselines on all four datasets. Compared to **tf.idf**, overall recall of relevance models is higher by 12% - 25%, and average precision is up by 15% - 25%. Improvements are statistically significant with 95% confidence according to the Wilcoxon test.

4.4 Comparison of Ranking Methods

In section 2.2 we described two ways of ranking documents with a relevance model. In this section we provide empirical comparison of effectiveness for the two ranking methods. We will also provide a brief argument of why the methods differ in effectiveness.

Specifically, we would like to compare the effectiveness of document ranking using equations (2.1) and (2.2). In this comparison, we want to factor out the effects of what method we use for estimating the probabilities $P(w|R)$. We start by estimating $P(w|R)$ from a set of 1, 5 or 10 training documents. In each case we construct smoothed maximum-likelihood models as described in section 3.1. Smoothing parameters were tuned individually to maximize performance. The quality of the resulting rankings are shown in the top portion of Figure 2.7. Solid lines reflect the performance of rankings based on cross-entropy, dashed lines correspond to the probability ranking principle. We ob-

AP: TREC queries 51-150 (title)

	tf.idf	LM	%chg	RM	%chg
Rel	21809	21809		21809	
Rret	10115	10137	0.2	12525	23.8*
0.00	0.644	0.643	-0.1	0.632	-1.8
0.10	0.442	0.436	-1.4	0.484	9.4*
0.20	0.359	0.349	-2.8	0.425	18.4*
0.30	0.308	0.299	-3.0*	0.379	23.1*
0.40	0.255	0.246	-3.5	0.333	30.8*
0.50	0.212	0.209	-1.4	0.289	35.9*
0.60	0.176	0.170	-3.6*	0.246	39.8*
0.70	0.128	0.130	1.3	0.184	43.9*
0.80	0.084	0.086	2.8	0.128	52.0*
0.90	0.042	0.048	14.9	0.071	70.8*
1.00	0.016	0.022	38.8*	0.018	10.5
Avg	0.222	0.219	-1.4	0.277	25.0*

FT: TREC queries 251-400 (title)

	tf.idf	LM	%chg	RM	%chg
Rel	4816	4816		4816	
Rret	2541	2593	2.0*	3197	25.8*
0.00	0.531	0.561	5.5	0.535	0.8
0.10	0.415	0.421	1.4	0.430	3.7
0.20	0.353	0.355	0.4	0.368	4.4
0.30	0.291	0.303	4.3	0.316	8.8*
0.40	0.249	0.258	3.6	0.282	13.3*
0.50	0.213	0.230	7.8	0.256	20.0*
0.60	0.158	0.187	17.9*	0.210	32.6*
0.70	0.108	0.137	26.4*	0.160	47.3*
0.80	0.078	0.102	30.6*	0.128	63.3*
0.90	0.058	0.078	32.9*	0.089	53.0*
1.00	0.042	0.066	56.5*	0.059	40.1*
Avg	0.211	0.230	8.8*	0.246	16.7*

LA: TREC queries 301-400 (title)

	tf.idf	LM	%chg	RM	%chg
Rel	2350	2350		2350	
Rret	1581	1626	2.9	1838	16.3*
0.00	0.586	0.619	5.7	0.566	-3.5
0.10	0.450	0.486	8.2*	0.474	5.5
0.20	0.356	0.362	1.9	0.384	8.1
0.30	0.295	0.316	7.0*	0.332	12.5*
0.40	0.247	0.273	10.4	0.286	15.6*
0.50	0.217	0.238	9.8	0.264	21.7*
0.60	0.164	0.197	19.7	0.206	25.5*
0.70	0.129	0.159	23.0*	0.174	34.9*
0.80	0.100	0.123	23.1	0.138	37.5*
0.90	0.050	0.074	47.0	0.085	69.4*
1.00	0.042	0.059	41.5*	0.056	32.6*
Avg	0.223	0.247	10.6*	0.258	15.6*

TDT2: TDT topics 1-100 (title)

	tf.idf	LM	%chg	RM	%chg
Rel	7994	7994		7994	
Rret	5770	5399	-6.4	6472	12.2*
0.00	0.846	0.843	-0.4	0.854	0.9
0.10	0.794	0.797	0.4	0.831	4.5*
0.20	0.755	0.748	-0.9	0.806	6.8*
0.30	0.711	0.705	-0.9	0.785	10.3*
0.40	0.663	0.669	0.8	0.766	15.5*
0.50	0.614	0.616	0.3	0.742	20.9*
0.60	0.565	0.563	-0.5	0.704	24.6*
0.70	0.528	0.517	-2.1	0.675	27.8*
0.80	0.485	0.477	-1.5*	0.648	33.6*
0.90	0.397	0.394	-0.7*	0.587	48.0*
1.00	0.297	0.307	-3.5	0.477	60.4*
Avg	0.596	0.592	-0.6	0.709	18.9*

Table 2.6. Comparison of Relevance Models (**RM**) to the InQuery (**tf.idf**) and language-modeling (**LM**) systems. Relevance Model significantly outperms both baselines. Stars indicate statistically significant differences in performance with a 95% confidence according to the Wilcoxon test. Significance is against the **tf.idf** baseline.

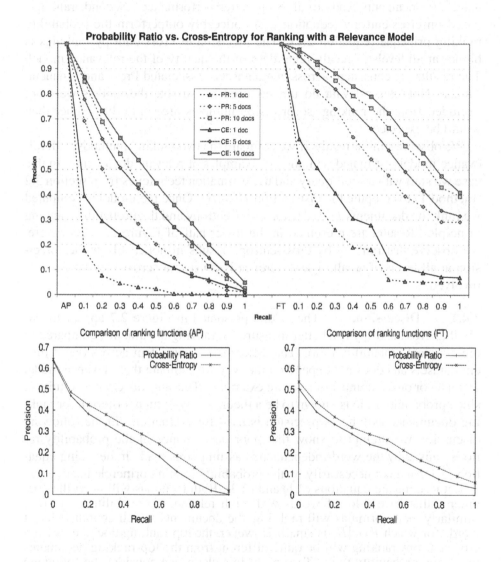

Figure 2.7. Comparing the effectiveness of two ranking functions: Probability Ratio (**PR**) and Cross-Entropy (**CE**). We show results for two datasets: (**AP**) on the left side and (**FT**) on the right. Using cross-entropy leads to noticeably higher precision at all levels of recall. The difference is consistent for relevance models of different quality: 1, 5 or 10 training documents (top) as well as relevance models estimated from the words in the query using Method 1 (bottom).

serve two consistent effects. First, as expected, more training documents trans-
lates to better performance. Relevance models estimated from 5 documents
exhibit higher precision than models constructed from 1 relevant document,
using 10 documents leads to an even better performance. Second, rankings
based on cross-entropy (equation 2.2) noticeably outperform the probability
ranking principle (equation 2.1). The precision of cross-entropy rankings is
higher at all levels of recall, regardless of the quality of the relevance model.
The results are consistent across two datasets: Associated Press and Financial
Times. Note that relevant documents used to estimate the models were not
excluded from the ranking, so precision numbers are somewhat higher than
would be expected.

We observe similar results if we compare the two ranking methods with relevance models estimated without any examples of relevant documents. In this
case we start with a short query and use estimation techniques from section 3.2
(method 1) to compute the distribution $P(w|R)$. Once the model is computed
we rank the documents $D \in C$ using cross-entropy and the probability ranking
principle. Results are presented in the lower half of Figure 2.7. As before,
we observe that ranking by cross-entropy results in noticeably higher precision at all levels of recall. The difference is consistent across the two datasets
involved.

4.4.1   Discussion.   The results presented in Figure 2.7 appear to imply that cross-entropy is a better measure for ranking documents, compared to
the classical probability ratio. The difference is consistent across two different datasets and does not depend on the way we estimate the relevance model
$P(w|R)$ or on the number of relevant examples. This appears counter-intuitive,
since probability ratio is known to be a theoretically optimal criterion for ranking documents, as long as precision is used for evaluation. In the following
discussion we attempt to show that poor performance of the probability ratio is caused by the word-independence assumptions made in deducing equation (2.1), and not necessarily by the probability ranking principle itself.

Let us compare equations (2.1) and (2.2). Both formulas will favor the doc-
uments that have a lot of words with high relevance probabilities $P(w|R)$.
Similarly, both formulas will rank low the documents which contain a lot of
words for which $P(w|R)$ is small. However, the top-ranking documents from
cross-entropy ranking will be quite different from the top-ranking documents
under the probability ratio. To support this claim, we consider the following
question:

> *Out of all possible documents, which document would be ranked highest by each
> method?*

First, consider the probability ratio. In mathematical terms, we would like
to find the string $D_{PR} = d_1 \ldots d_n$ of a given length n, which would maximize
equation (2.1):

$$D_{PR} = \arg\max_{d_1 \ldots d_n} \left\{ \frac{P(d_1 \ldots d_n | R)}{P(d_1 \ldots d_n | N)} \right\}$$

$$= \arg\max_{d_1 \ldots d_n} \left\{ \prod_{i=1}^{n} \frac{P(d_i | R)}{P(d_i | N)} \right\}$$

$$= \arg\prod_{i=1}^{n} \max_{d_i} \left\{ \frac{P(d_i | R)}{P(d_i | N)} \right\}$$

$$= \underbrace{ww \ldots w}_{n \text{ times}} : \text{such that } w \text{ maximizes } \frac{P(w|R)}{P(w|N)} \qquad (2.32)$$

The first step of the derivation is a direct consequence of assuming word independence in equation (2.1). The second step comes from simple intuition: if we want to maximize the product of n independent terms, we can maximize each term individually, since they don't affect each other. Since the maximization of all terms is done over the same vocabulary, each term will be driven towards the same word w, which has the highest ratio $\frac{P(w|R)}{P(w|N)}$ out of all the other words in the vocabulary. In other words the consequence of equation (2.32) is this: the document D_{PR} that would be ranked highest by the probability ratio would contain a single word w, repeated multiple times. That word w would be the one that best discriminates between the relevant class R and non-relevant class N. In practical applications, documents that contain a single word do not occur very often. However, the implication of our argument is this:

The probability ratio will favor documents that contain many occurrences of a few words with highest $\frac{P(w|R)}{P(w|N)}$.

As we shall demonstrate below, cross-entropy will favor a very different type of document. As before, we task ourselves with finding the string $D_{CE} = d_1 \ldots d_n$ that will minimize equation (2.2).

$$D_{CE} = \arg\min_{D} \left\{ \sum_{w} P(w|R) \log P(w|D) \right\}$$

$$= \arg\max_{D} \left\{ \sum_{w} P(w|R) \log \left(\lambda_D \frac{\#(w, D)}{n} + (1 - \lambda_D) P(w) \right) \right\}$$

$$= D : \text{such that } \#(w, D) \approx n P(w|R) \text{ for all } w \qquad (2.33)$$

Here $\#(w, D)$ denotes the number of times a word w occurs in the document D. The first step in equation (2.33) comes from the definition of a smoothed document model, equation (2.7). The second step can be verified by showing that cross-entropy $H(R||D)$ is always bounded below by the entropy

$H(R||R)$ (an application of Jensen's inequality to logarithms), and further by convergence of relative frequencies to probabilities. Equation (2.33) implies that highest-ranked document would have all words w occurring with frequencies that would be predicted by the relevance model for a document of length n. In practice, such documents may not exist, since relevance models are constructed from a set of documents, but the general implication is this:

> *Cross-entropy will favor documents that contain many of the words for which*
> $P(w|R)$ *is non-zero.*

Consequently, cross-entropy will tend to produce different rankings than the probability ratio. Without experimental evidence, it would be difficult to guess which ranking principle would perform better. Is it preferable to favor a few highly-relevant words, as done by the probability ratio, or many possibly-relevant words, as favored by cross-entropy? Experiments in Figure 2.7 suggest that rankings based on cross-entropy are noticeably better. However, it is important to realize that our experiments do not contradict the arguments of Robertson (Robertson, 1977), and do not diminish the importance of the probability ranking principle. The key step in the derivation of equation (2.32) was the assumption of word independence. While it is prevalent in all but a few approaches to Information Retrieval, it is by no means a part of the probability ranking principle. What we demonstrated is that assuming word independence leads to sub-optimality of the probability ranking principle, and that cross-entropy provides a better ranking principle. Following this finding, we will use cross-entropy to rank the documents in all of the remaining experiments.

4.5   Comparison of Estimation Methods 1 and 2

In Section 3.2 we presented two different ways of estimating the joint probability $P(w, q_1 \ldots q_k)$ which is the core step in estimating a relevance model. Specifically, in Section 3.2.1 we introduced a method based on i.i.d. sampling, and in Section 3.2.2 we relaxed the assumption of mutual independence and considered conditional sampling. In this section we provide a brief contrastive evaluation of the two methods, and then discuss the theoretical differences between them and their relation to two popular heuristic query expansion heuristics.

Figure 2.7 shows an empirical comparison of the two estimation methods on four different datasets. We compare performance of the methods both for the Probability Ranking Principle (PRP) and the Cross-entropy ranking. With PRP there no significant difference between the two estimation methods. Method 2 is slightly worse for three of the five datasets and slightly better for the other two. Interestingly, when we cross-entropy to rank the documents, the results are different. Method 1 is consistently better than Method 2 on all 5 datasets, and the difference is substantial on two datasets (FT and WSJ).

Corpus	Probability Ranking Principle			Cross-entropy		
	Method 1	Method 2	%chg	Method 1	Method 2	%chg
AP	0.228	0.216	-5.3	0.272	0.259	-4.8
FT	0.212	0.211	-0.5	0.244	0.203	-16.8
LA	0.226	0.229	+1.3	0.254	0.239	-6.0
WSJ	0.195	0.202	+3.6	0.300	0.255	-15.0
TDT	0.621	0.613	-1.3	0.712	0.638	-10.4

Table 2.7. Contrasting performance of relevance models with estimation methods 1 and 2. Method 1 noticeably outperforms method 2 when cross-entropy is used to rank documents in the collection. We show un-interpolated average precision and relative change in going from Method 1 to Method 2.

4.5.1   Discussion.   By Bayes' rule, Method 1 can be viewed as sampling of $q_1 \ldots q_k$ conditioned on w, similarly to Method 2. However, for Method 1, this would add an additional constraint that all query words q_i are sampled from the same distribution M, whereas in Method 2 we are free to pick a separate M_i for every q_i. This distinction is graphically illustrated by the dependence networks on the left and the right sides of Figure 2.3. We believe that Method 1 makes a stronger mutual independence assumption in equation (2.14), compared to a series of pairwise independence assumptions made by Method 2 in equation (2.17).

From the viewpoint of traditional Information Retrieval, relevance models represent a technique for massive *query expansion* (indeed, we "expand" the original query by all words in the vocabulary). The two proposed methods of estimation can be related to two heuristic query expansion techniques popular in IR. Method 1 is functionally similar to the modification of Rocchio's formula (Rocchio, 1971) for *pseudo relevance feedback*. The modified Rocchio's formula computes the following weight for a given word w:

$$R_w = \alpha Q_w + \beta \sum_{D \in R} \frac{1}{|R|} D_w \qquad (2.34)$$

Here Q_w represents the weight of the word in the original query, D_w is the weight of the word in document D. R denotes the set of *pseudo-relevant* documents, which is usually taken to be the set of top-ranked documents retrieved in response to the query Q. α and β represent tunable parameters. Note that equation (2.34) is functionally very similar to equation (2.6), if we set $\alpha = 0$, $\beta = 1$ and interpret document-model probabilities $P(w|D)$ as document weights D_w. It turns out that estimation Method 1 (equation (2.15)) is also functionally similar to equation (2.34). However, there is a very important difference. Rocchio's formula is essentially an *un-weighted* linear combination of document vectors, since the contribution of every document $D \in R$

is weighted by a constant $\frac{1}{|R|}$. Estimation Method 1 uses posterior document probabilities $P(D \mid q_1 \ldots q_k)$ to weigh the contributions of different document models. Weighted linear combinations are less sensitive to the selection of the pseudo-relevant set R, since document contributions decay slowly with the posterior probabilities, as opposed to the abrupt drop from $\frac{1}{|R|}$ to 0, which happens at the cut-off in the ranking.

Estimation Method 2 also has an important parallel among heuristic query-expansion techniques. It is functionally similar to the technique of Local Context Analysis (LCA) (Xu and Croft, 1996). The LCA formula was empirically derived by Xu, and is one of the most robust query expansion techniques available today. In LCA, the words and noun phrases w are ranked with respect to a query Q by the following formula:

$$ Bel(w; Q) = \prod_{q \in Q} \left(0.1 + \frac{1/\log n}{1/idf_w} \log \sum_{D \in R} D_q D_w \right)^{idf_q} \quad (2.35) $$

Here R refers to the set of top-ranked documents or passages retrieved by the query Q, n is the number of top-ranked documents used, D_q and D_w are the respective frequencies of the words q and w in a document D, and idf_q and idf_w are the inverse document frequencies, as in (Robertson and Sparck Jones, 1976). The LCA formula in equation 2.35 is functionally similar to estimation Method 2 (equation 2.18).

While our estimation methods are similar to LCA and Rocchio in appearance, they are fundamentally different both in theory and in performance. Our estimation techniques produce probabilities that are interpretable and can be tightly integrated with probabilistic approaches to retrieval, while the weights obtained from LCA and Rocchio are heuristic in nature and difficult to interpret. Also, the distributions obtained from Method 1 and Method 2 are often quite different from the top-ranked words produced by LCA and Rocchio.

4.6   Relevance Feedback

In this section we will briefly report experimental results for very simple applications of user feedback in the framework of relevance models. The focus of this work is on estimation of relevance models from extremely small samples (such as queries), a detailed study of relevance feedback methods requires a separate investigation. In the experiments that follow we assumed a very simplistic feedback setting. We assume that along with the query $Q = q_1 \ldots q_k$ we get a set R' of 5 relevant documents, chosen chronologically from the beginning of the collection. We compare the following retrieval algorithms:

1 **Language Model Baseline.** Use just the original query Q, perform retrieval using the standard language-modeling approach with smoothing

based on the Dirichlet prior (Zhai and Lafferty, 2001), and the smoothing parameter set to $\mu = 1000$.

2 **Language Model Feedback.** Use Ponte's formulation of relevance feedback for language models (Ponte, 1998). Apply equation (2.9) to the provided set of relevant documents R'. Select 5 words $w_1 \ldots w_5$ with the highest average log-likelihood ration. Add these words to the original query to form the expanded query $Q^{exp} = q_1 \ldots q_k, w_1 \ldots w_5$. Use the expanded query to perform standard language model retrieval, using Jelinek-Mercer smoothing (Zhai and Lafferty, 2001) with the smoothing parameter set to $\lambda = 0.9$.

3 **Relevance Model Feedback.** Estimate a relevance model from the incomplete set of examples: apply equation (2.10) to the provided set R'. Rank the documents using cross-entropy between the estimated relevance model and the document model, equation (2.2). We used Jelinek-Mercer smoothing and the parameter λ was set to 0.1 for the document language model. For the purposes of ranking the smoothing parameter on the relevance model can be set to any value. Note that the original query $q_1 \ldots q_k$ was completely ignored.

All smoothing parameters listed in the table above were selected to provide best possible performance for each method. Parameters were selected on the test data. Figure 2.8 shows the standard 11-point recall-precision curves for the above three algorithms. Experiments were performed on three datasets: Associated Press (AP), Financial Times (FT) and Los-Angeles Times (LA), refer to Table 2.1 for details. Five documents used for feedback were removed from evaluation in all cases.

We observe that on all three datasets both of the feedback algorithms noticeably outperform the strong language-modeling baseline. Precision is better at all levels of recall, and average precision is improved by 20-25%, which is considered standard for relevance feedback. Differences are statistically significant. If we compare the two feedback algorithms to each other, we see that their performance is almost identical. The differences are very small and not statistically significant. Note that algorithm using relevance models completely ignored the original query, whereas Ponte's feedback used it as a basis for the expanded query. We believe performance of the relevance modeling algorithm can be further improved by retaining the query and making use of the sparse estimation techniques developed in Section 3.2.

4.7 Cross-Lingual Experiments

The problem of cross-language information retrieval mirrors the problem of adhoc retrieval with one important distinction: the query $Q = s_1 \ldots s_k$ is given

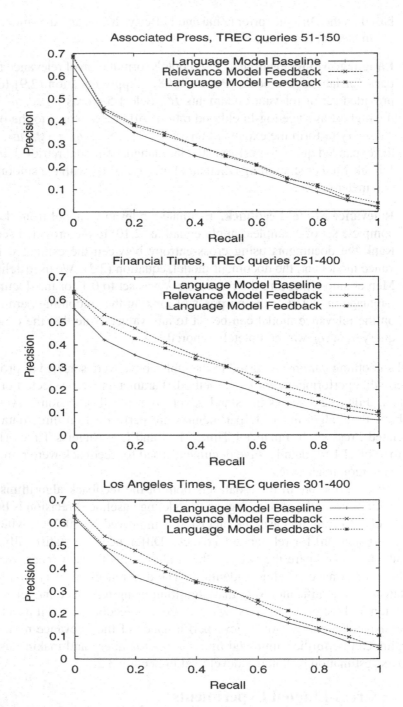

Figure 2.8.   Relevance Feedback: Relevance Models perform as well as the feedback mechanism proposed by Ponte. Both feedback methods significantly outperform a strong baseline.

in a language that is different from the collection of documents C. In section 3.3 we discussed how we can use a parallel corpus or a statistical dictionary to estimate the relevance model $P(t|R)$ in the target language. Once a relevance model is computed, we can directly use ranking methods from section 4.4 to retrieve relevant documents from the collection C. In this section we carry out an evaluation of this approach on the cross-language (English - Chinese) retrieval task of TREC9. We compare retrieval performance of the following models:

LM Mono-lingual baseline. We use the basic language modeling system, which was reported as a baseline in a number of recent publications (Xu et al., 2001; Voorhees and Harman, 2000). The system is identical to the **LM** system described in section 4.3. Chinese documents D are ranked according to the probability that a Chinese query $c_1 \dots c_k$ was generated from the language model of document D. Word probabilities are estimated according to equation (2.7).

RM Mono-lingual Relevance Model. This system is included as an alternative mono-lingual baseline, and to demonstrate the degree to which Relevance Models degrade, when estimated in a cross-lingual setting. The system is identical to the **RM** system from section 4.3. Given a Chinese query $c_1 \dots c_k$, we compute a Relevance Model using estimation method 1 from section 3.2.1. We use cross-entropy as the ranking function.

TM Probabilistic Translation Model. As a cross-lingual baseline, we report the performance of our implementation of the system used by Xu et.al. (Xu et al., 2001). The translation model was originally proposed by Berger and Lafferty (Berger and Lafferty, 1999) and Hiemstra and de Jong (Hiemstra and de Jong, 1999). We used the formulation advocated by Xu et al. (Xu et al., 2001). We used the same statistical lexicon and the same system parameters that were reported in (Xu et al., 2001).

pRM Cross-lingual Relevance Model (parallel). Given an English query $e_1 \dots e_k$, we estimate a Relevance Model in Chinese using techniques suggested in section 3.3.1. We use the combined parallel corpus for estimating the probabilities in equation (2.23). The Chinese documents are then ranked by their cross-entropy with respect to the relevance model.

dRM Cross-lingual Relevance Model (dictionary). We estimate the cross-lingual relevance model as suggested in section 3.3.2. Equation (2.25) is used to compute the probability of an English word s_i given a Chinese document D_T. We use the lexicon reported in (Xu et al., 2001) for translation probabilities $P(s_i|t)$. Cross-entropy is used as the ranking method.

In all cases we performed separate experiments on the three representations of Chinese: unigrams, bigrams and "words". Refer to section 4.1.5 for details. The smoothing parameters λ_D were tuned separately for each representation as we found that smoothing affects unigrams and bigrams very differently. The results from the three representations were then linearly combined. The weights attached to each representation were set separately for every model, in order to show best results. As an exception, the Probabilistic Translation Model was evaluated on the same representation that was used by Xu et.al. (Xu et al., 2001). Due to the absence of the training corpus, the tuning of all parameters was performed on the testing data using a brute-force hill-climbing approach. The small number of queries in the testing dataset precluded the use of any statistical significance tests.

4.7.1   Baseline Results.   Table 2.8 shows the retrieval performance, of the described models on the TREC9 cross-language retrieval task. We use non-interpolated average precision as a performance measure. Percentage numbers indicate the difference from the mono-lingual baseline. We show results for both short and long versions of the queries. Our monolingual results form a strong baseline, competitive with the results reported by (Voorhees and Harman, 2000; Xu et al., 2001). This is somewhat surprising, since our processing of Chinese queries was very simplistic, and a lot of spurious matches were caused by punctuation and stop-words in the queries. We attribute the strong performance to the careful selection of smoothing parameters and combination of multiple representations. Monolingual Relevance Model provides an even higher baseline for both short and long queries.

The Probabilistic Translation Model achieves around 85% - 90% percent of the mono-lingual baseline. Xu et.al. in (Xu et al., 2001) report the performance of the same model to be somewhat higher than our implementation (0.3100 for long queries). We attribute the differences to the different form of pre-processing used by Xu et.al, since we used the same bilingual lexicon and the same model parameters as (Xu et al., 2001).

4.7.2   Cross-lingual Relevance Model Results.   Table 2.8 shows that Cross-lingual Relevance Models perform very well, achieving 93% - 98% of the mono-lingual baseline on the combined representation. This performance is better than most previously-reported results (Voorhees and Harman, 2000; Xu et al., 2001), which is somewhat surprising, given our poor pre-processing of Chinese. Our model noticeably outperforms the Probabilistic Translation Model on both long and short queries (see figure 2.9). It is also encouraging to see that Cross-lingual Relevance Models perform very well on different representations of Chinese, even though they do not gain as much from the combination as the baselines.

Note that Relevance Models estimated using a bilingual lexicon perform better than the models estimated from the parallel corpus. We believe this is due to the fact that our parallel corpus has an acute coverage problem. The bilingual dictionary we used (Xu et al., 2001) covers a significantly larger number of both English and Chinese words. In addition, two thirds of our parallel corpus was obtained using automatic machine translation software, which uses a limited vocabulary. It is also worth noting that the remaining part of our parallel corpus, Hong-Kong News, was also used by Xu et al. (Xu et al., 2001) in the construction of their bilingual dictionary.

Table 2.10 illustrates just how serious the coverage problem is. We show performance of Relevance Models estimated using just the Hong-Kong News portion of the corpus, versus performance with the full corpus. We observe tremendous improvements of over 100% which were achieved by adding the TDT data, even though this data was automatically generated using SYS-TRAN.

4.7.3   High-precision performance.   Average precision is one of the most frequently reported metrics in cross-language retrieval. This metric is excellent for research purposes, but it is also important to consider user-oriented metrics. Table 2.9 shows precision at different ranks in the ranked list of documents. Precision at 5 or 10 documents is what affects a typical user in the web-search setting. We observe that Cross-lingual Relevance Models exhibit exceptionally good performance in this high-precision area. Models estimated using the parallel corpus are particularly impressive, outperforming the monolingual baseline by 20% at 5 retrieved documents. Models estimated from the bilingual dictionary perform somewhat worse, though still outperforming mono-lingual performance at 5 documents. Both estimation methods outperform the Probabilistic Translation Model. We consider these results to be extremely encouraging, since they suggest that Cross-lingual Relevance Models perform very well in the important high-precision area.

5.   Conclusions

In this work we introduced a formal framework for modeling the notion of relevance in Information Retrieval. We defined a **relevance model** to be the language model that reflects word frequencies in the class of documents that are relevant to some given information need. We assumed that a unigram language model is sufficient for accurately discerning the relevance of a sample of text, and hypothesized that higher-order models may not necessarily improve the accuracy.

In section 3 we discussed an ensemble of techniques for estimating relevance models in various settings. We started by reviewing the popular maximum likelihood techniques that are suitable when we have sufficient training

	Unigrams		Bigrams		Words		Combination	
Short Queries								
LM (mono)	0.2447		0.2375		0.2604		0.2874	
RM (mono)	0.2404	-2%	0.2524	+6%	0.3072	+18%	0.3100	+8%
TM	——		——		——		0.2549	-11%
dRM (dictionary)	0.2776	+13%	0.2684	+13%	0.2779	+7%	0.2807	-2%
pRM (parallel)	0.2258	-8%	0.2519	+6%	0.2493	-4%	0.2670	-7%
Long Queries								
LM (mono)	0.2750		0.3090		0.2837		0.3302	
RM (mono)	0.2835	+3%	0.3414	+10%	0.3240	+14%	0.3767	+14%
TM	——		——		——		0.2768	-16%
dRM (dictionary)	0.3002	+9%	0.3074	-1%	0.3178	+12%	0.3182	-4%

Table 2.8.   Average Precision on the TREC9 cross-language retrieval task. Cross-lingual Relevance Models perform around 95% of the strong mono-lingual baseline

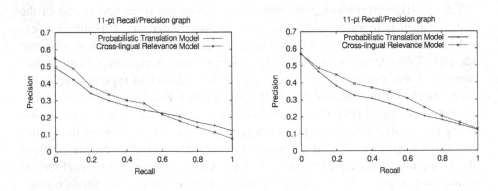

Figure 2.9.   Cross-lingual Relevance Models outperform the Probabilistic Translation Model on both the short (left) and long (right) queries.

Prec.	LM	RM		TM		dRM		pRM	
5 docs	0.2880	0.3360	+17%	0.2560	-11%	0.3200	+11%	0.3520	+22%
10 docs	0.2600	0.2880	+11%	0.2120	-19%	0.2320	-11%	0.2880	+11%
15 docs	0.2240	0.2427	+8%	0.1867	-17%	0.2080	-7%	0.2453	+10%
20 docs	0.2120	0.2220	+5%	0.1700	-20%	0.1960	-8%	0.2080	-2%
30 docs	0.1867	0.1907	+2%	0.1440	-23%	0.1693	-9%	0.1827	-2%

Table 2.9.   Initial precision on the TREC9 CLIR task. Cross-lingual Relevance Models noticeably outperform the mono-lingual baselines.

Average Precision	HK News	HK News + TDT	
Unigrams	0.1070	0.2258	+111%
Bigrams	0.1130	0.2519	+123%
"Words"	0.1210	0.2493	+106%

Table 2.10. Parallel corpus size has a very significant effect on the quality of Cross-lingual Relevance Models. Adding the pseudo-parallel TDT corpus more than doubled the average precision.

data. In section 3.2 we developed a novel framework for estimating relevance models when no training examples are available. These techniques carry particular importance for Information Retrieval applications, since they allows us to estimate formal models of relevance starting with just the query. In section 3.3 we show how our estimation techniques can be carried over into the cross-lingual setting, making it possible to directly estimate relevance models in the target language. This leads us to a novel model of cross-language retrieval, where we don't have to perform word-for-word query translation.

The question of how to use relevance models for effective retrieval is in some sense orthogonal to the problem of estimation. The probability ranking principle, advocated by Robertson (Robertson, 1977) appears to be an obvious choice. In section 4.4 we suggested that the likelihood ratio may not be optimal if we make the common assumption of word independence. In fact, cross-entropy provides a better measure for ranking the documents, both theoretically and empirically. We supported our arguments with experiments performed with relevance models of different quality.

In section 4 we presented a thorough evaluation of our methods on two problems in Information Retrieval: adhoc retrieval task and cross-language retrieval task. In our experiments, relevance models exhibit excellent performance on both tasks. On the adhoc retrieval task, the model substantially outperformed four strong baseline algorithms. We observed 15% - 25% improvements in average precision, which were statistically significant with 95% confidence. The results are consistent across five different datasets with an aggregate of 500 different queries.

Our experiments with the cross-language retrieval task demonstrate that performance of relevance model is as good as or better than that of previously reported models. The model performs around 90% - 95% of the strong mono-lingual baseline in terms of average precision. In terms of initial precision, the model outperforms the mono-lingual baseline by 20%. We discussed how Cross-Lingual Relevance Models can be estimated using either a parallel/comparable corpus, or a bilingual dictionary. Our experiments show that coverage is an extremely important aspect of the resources. We have been able to use a commercial MT system to increase the coverage of our corpus.

6.   Acknowledgments

We would like to thank Djoerd Hiemstra, and James Allan for valuable comments during the early stages of this work, Jinxi Xu for providing us with the bilingual dictionary and Fang-Fang Feng for providing the Chinese segmenter and other resources. Thanks to Martin Choquette for implementing the Probabilistic Translation Model. This work was supported in part by the Center for Intelligent Information Retrieval, and in part by SPAWARSYSCEN-SD grant number N66001-99-1-8912. Any opinions, findings and conclusions or recommendations expressed in this material are the author(s) and do not necessarily reflect those of the sponsor.

References

Allan, J., Connell, M. E., Croft, W. B., Feng, F.-F., Fisher, D., and Li, X. (2001). INQUERY and TREC-9. In *Proceedings of the Ninth Text REtrieval Conference (TREC-9)*, pages 551–562.

Berger, A. and Lafferty, J. (1999). Information retrieval as statistical translation. In (Hearst et al., 1999), pages 222–229.

Brown, P. F., Cocke, J., Della Pietra, S. A., Della Pietra, V. J., Jelinek, F., Lafferty, J. D., Mercer, R. L., and Roossin, P. S. (1990). A statistical approach to machine translation. *Computational Linguistics*, 16(2):79–85.

Brown, P. F., Della Pietra, S. A., Della Pietra, V. J., and Mercer, R. L. (1993). The mathematics of machine translation: Parameter estimation. *Computational Linguistics*, 19(2):263–311.

Cieri, C., Strassel, S., Graff, D., Martey, N., Rennert, K., and Liberman, M. Corpora for topic detection and tracking. pages 33–66.

Croft, W. B., editor (2000). *Advances in Information Retrieval — Recent Research from the Center for Intelligent Information Retrieval*, volume 7 of *The Kluwer international series on information retrieval*. Kluwer Academic Publishers, Boston, MA.

Croft, W. B., Harper, D. J., Kraft, D. H., and Zobel, J., editors (2001). *Proceedings of the Twenty-Fourth Annual International ACM-SIGIR Conference on Research and Development in Information Retrieval*, New Orleans, LA. ACM Press.

Hearst, M., Gey, F., and Tong, R., editors (1999). *Proceedings of the Twenty-Second Annual International ACM-SIGIR Conference on Research and Development in Information Retrieval*, Berkeley, CA. ACM Press.

Hiemstra, D. (2001). *Using Language Models for Information Retrieval*. PhD dissertation, University of Twente, Enschede, The Netherlands.

Hiemstra, D. and de Jong, F. (1999). Disambiguation strategies for cross-language information retrieval. In Abiteboul, S. and Vercoustre, A.-M., editors, *Proceedings of the Third European Conference on Research and Advanced*

Technology for Digital Libaries, ECDL'99, volume 1696 of *Lecture Notes in Computer Science*, pages 274–293. Springer-Verlag, Paris.

Hiemstra, D., de Jong, F., and Kraaij, W. (1997). A domain specific lexicon acquisition tool for cross-language information retrieval. In Devroye, L. and Chrisment, C., editors, *Proceedings of the Fifth RIAO International Conference*, pages 255–270, Montreal, Canada. Centre de Hautes Études Internationales d'Informatique Documentaire (C.I.D).

Miller, D. R. H., Leek, T., and Schwartz, R. M. (1999). A hidden markov model information retrieval system. In (Hearst et al., 1999), pages 214–221.

Ponte, J. M. (1998). *A language modeling approach to information retrieval*. Phd dissertation, University of Massachusets, Amherst, MA.

Ponte, J. M. and Croft, W. B. (1998). A language modeling approach to information retrieval. In Croft, W. B., Moffat, A., van Rijsbergen, C. J., Wilkinson, R., and Zobel, J., editors, *Proceedings of the Twenty-First Annual International ACM-SIGIR Conference on Research and Development in Information Retrieval*, pages 275–281, Melbourne, Australia. ACM Press.

Robertson, S. E. (1977). The probability ranking principle in IR. *Journal of Documentation*, 33:294–304. Reprinted in (Sparck Jones and Willett, 1997).

Robertson, S. E., Maron, M. E., and Cooper, W. S. (1982). Probability of relevance: a unification of two competing models for document retrieval. *Information Technology: Research and Development*, 1:1–21.

Robertson, S. E. and Sparck Jones, K. (1976). Relevance weighting of search terms. *Journal of the American Society for Information Science*, 27:129–146. Reprinted in (Willett, 1988).

Robertson, S. E. and Walker, S. (1994). Some simple effective approximations to the 2–poisson model for probabilistic weighted retrieval. In Croft, W. B. and van Rijsbergen, C. J., editors, *Proceedings of the Seventeenth Annual International ACM-SIGIR Conference on Research and Development in Information Retrieval*, pages 232–241, Dublin, Ireland. Springer-Verlag.

Robertson, S. E., Walker, S., and Beaulieu, M. M. (1998). Okapi at TREC-7: automatic ad hoc, filtering, VLC and interactive track. In Voorhees, E. M. and Harman, D. K., editors, *Proceedings of the Seventh Text REtrieval Conference (TREC-7)*, pages 253–264, Gaithersburg, MD. National Institute of Standards and Technology (NIST) and Defense Advanced Research Projects Agency (DARPA), Department of Commerce, National Institute of Standards and Technology.

Rocchio, J. (1971). *Relevance feedback in information retrieval*, pages 313–323. Prentice-Hall Publishing, New Jersey.

Song, F. and Croft, W. B. (1999). A general language model for information retrieval. In (Hearst et al., 1999), pages 279–280.

Sparck Jones, K. and Willett, P., editors (1997). *Readings in information retrieval*. Multimedia Information and Systems. Morgan Kaufmann, San Francisco, CA.

Turtle, H. R. (1990). *Inference Network for Document Retrieval*. PhD dissertation, University of Massachusets, Amherst, MA.

Turtle, H. R. and Croft, W. B. (1991). Evaluation of an inference network-based retrieval model. *ACM Transactions on Information Systems*, 9(3):187–222.

van Rijsbergen, C. J. (1977). A theoretical basis for the use of co-occurrence data in information retrieval. *Journal of Documentation*, 33:106–119.

van Rijsbergen, C. J. (1986). A non-classical logic for information retrieval. *The Computer Journal*, 29(6):481–485.

Voorhees, E. M. and Harman, D. K., editors (2000). *Proceedings of the Ninth Text REtrieval Conference (TREC-9)*, Gaithersburg, MD. Department of Commerce, National Institute of Standards and Technology.

Walpole, R. E. and Myers, R. H. (1989). *Probability and Statistics for Engineers and Scientists*, pages 108–109. MacMillan Publishing Company, New York.

Willett, P., editor (1988). *Document Retrieval Systems*, volume 3 of *Foundations of Information Science*. Taylor Graham, London, UK.

Xu, J. and Croft, W. B. (1996). Query expansion using local and global document analysis. In Frei, H.-P., Harman, D., Schauble, P., and Wilkinson, R., editors, *Proceedings of the Nineteenth Annual International ACM-SIGIR Conference on Research and Development in Information Retrieval*, pages 4–11, Zurich, Switzerland. ACM Press.

Xu, J. and Weischedel, R. (2000). TREC-9 cross-lingual retrieval at BBN. In (Voorhees and Harman, 2000), pages 106–116.

Xu, J., Weischedel, R., and Nguyen, C. (2001). Evaluating a probabilistic model for cross-lingual information retrieval. In (Croft et al., 2001), pages 105–110.

Zhai, C. (2002). *Risk Minimization and Language Modeling in Text Retrieval*. PhD dissertation, Carnegie Mellon University, Pittsburgh, PA.

Zhai, C. and Lafferty, J. (2001). A study of smoothing methods for language models applied to ad hoc information retrieval. In (Croft et al., 2001), pages 334–342.

Chapter 3

LANGUAGE MODELING AND RELEVANCE

Karen Sparck Jones
University of Cambridge
Cambridge, UK
ksj@cl.cam.ac.uk

Stephen Robertson
Microsoft Research
Cambridge, UK
ser@microsoft.com

Djoerd Hiemstra
University of Twente
Enschede, The Netherlands
hiemstra@cs.utwente.nl

Hugo Zaragoza
Microsoft Research
Cambridge, UK
hugoz@microsoft.com

Abstract   Relevance is a basic concept in information retrieval, but its role in the language modeling approach to retrieval is not completely straightforward. We examine the issues involved, especially in dealing with multiple relevant documents and in applying relevance feedback, and consider various strategies for developing the language modeling approach to accommodate multiple, rather than single, relevant documents in a theoretically principled way.

W.B. Croft and J. Lafferty (eds.), Language Modeling for Information Retrieval, 57–71.
© 2003 *Kluwer Academic Publishers.*

1. Introduction

This paper addresses three questions about the Language Modeling (LM) approach to information retrieval. These questions are about LM and relevance. They arise because relevance has always been taken as fundamental to information retrieval (see, e.g. Saracevic, 1975, or Mizzaro, 1997). Thus from the standpoint of retrieval theory, the presumption has been that as relevance is the key notion in retrieval (for how could it not be?), this should be explicitly recognized in any formal model of retrieval. The Probabilistic Model (PM) of retrieval does this very clearly. Turtle and Croft (Turtle and Croft, 1990; Croft and Turtle, 1992) present the INQUERY network model as a probabilistic classifier testing for whether the hypothesis of relevance holds given the evidence supplied by document and query. The Vector Space Model assumes that some of the points in the multidimensional information space of a retrieval system represent relevant documents. But the LM account of what retrieval is about seems quite different: relevance does not formally figure in it at all.

A retrieval model that does not mention relevance appears paradoxical. But the form in which the LM account is expressed immediately provokes the question:

1 What about relevance?

and as a natural consequence, in the face of retrieval realities:

2 What about multiple relevant documents?

and hence, for the design of retrieval systems:

3 What about relevance feedback?

In this paper, we consider these questions in more detail. We examine the status of relevance itself in the LM view, and its implications for multiple relevant documents and relevance feedback. We present the problems we see and outline some possible solutions to them. The paper generally takes an informal approach; little mathematical detail is presented. The aim is to explore the concepts behind the models rather than the mechanics of modelling.

For our present purpose we will treat LM as developed by Croft and his colleagues at the University of Massachusetts, Amherst and later at Mitre Corporation, by Hiemstra and others at University of Twente, by Lafferty and others at Carnegie Mellon University, and at Bolt, Beranek and Newman (see references under Section 2), as representing a single theory, unless specific distinctions are required. We will develop our arguments by contrasting Language Modelling with Probabilistic Modelling (PM) as formulated by Robertson and his colleagues, taking Sparck Jones et al., 2000, as a convenient default reference point for this. Moreover, though LM is well established for speech processing and has been explored for translation and summarizing, for instance, these other tasks – with the possible exception of topic detection and tracking (see Walls et al., 1999) – do not have the particular properties of document/text retrieval on which we wish to focus, and we will therefore confine ourselves to the retrieval case.

2.   Relevance in LM

2.1   The status of relevance

LM approaches the relation between a document and a request by asking: how probable is it that this document generated the request? More strictly the question is: how probable is it that the document, as represented by its index description, generated the request as represented by its indexing description, i.e. the search query? There is no explicit reference to relevance here. However the presumption is that if it is highly probable that the document generated the request, then the document's content is relevant to the information need underlying the user's request. A good match on index keys implies relevance, though relevance is never mentioned in the model.

PM asks a quite different question: how probable is it that the document is relevant to the request? More properly the question is: how probable is it that the document content is relevant to the user's need? Then since both content and need are unobservables, it is necessary to provide an argument for taking index descriptions as levers in deriving the operational equivalent of probability of relevance. The PM approach thus leads to the same position as the LM one: a good match on index keys implies relevance. However, in contrast to the LM approach, relevance figures explicitly in the PM model.

This stems from the fact that, strictly, LM assumes there is just one document, the 'source' document, that generates the request and that the user knows (or correctly guesses) something about this document. Even if the system does not deliver this document first, the user recognizes it as the generating document when they see it. One view of this account is that as there is only one document that matters in the file, whether it is called a generating document or a relevant document is just a matter of labelling.[1]

This does not seem wholly satisfactory. However the only way of saving relevance as an independent notion within the source document framework is to say that the user has an ideal document in mind, i.e. some notional relevant document, and judges a particular document (the erstwhile generating document) as relevant if it comes close to this ideal (see Ponte, 2000, and Miller et al., 1999). But this compromises a key LM advantage. The LM approach is quite explicit about the form of the measure of association or similarity

---

[1]We are aware that Lafferty and Zhai, in a paper in the present volume, argue that no such assumption is required for the usual language model for IR. We believe that the matter is not yet fully resolved.

between document and request. LM, like PM, eschews the vague notion of similarity that characterizes many other approaches and works with a measure that follows from the model assumptions. In the LM case this applies only if the assumption is made that there is a specific precursor document, i.e. the measure of similarity is the probability that a particular document is the generator. Invoking a notional ideal document implies another, and weaker, notion of similarity between a specific document and this ideal one.

But does this difference between the formal models matter when their operational interpretations, and hence manifestation for the user, are the same? The LM approach might seem to have the advantage that it does not deal directly in unobservables, since even if it allows for different forms of index description these are still derived from observable initial documents and requests. However a more honest view is to accept that LM is being applied to retrieval, which deals in content and need, so this surface distinction between LM and PM is somewhat spurious. It is possible to *apply* LM as an effective retrieval tool, without bothering about the prior reasoning which led to its design, much as one can find that one saw cuts wood rather better than another without having to know what the functional explanation for this is. Thus LM can be seen (and has been used) simply as a good way of scoring document-query matches and hence of organizing system output. But as the analogy with saws suggests, such an uncritical use of a tool may have its dangers: anyone using a power saw for the first time is well advised to read the instruction book, and especially the safety page.

2.2   Multiple relevant documents

In all ordinary experience of retrieval, it is a fact of life that there may be more than one relevant document for a request; indeed there are normally several, and with large files there may be hundreds.

Formally, LM takes each document D and, using its individual model $P(T_i|D)$ in conjunction or comparison with a generic model $P(T_i)$ (the file model), asks how likely it is that this document generated the request, by assuming that query terms T_i are conditionally independent given the document. The basic formula used in several of the papers which take a language modeling approach to IR can be written as follows:

$$P(T_1, \cdots, T_n|D) = \prod_{i=1}^{n}((1 - \lambda)P(T_i) + \lambda P(T_i|D)) \qquad (3.1)$$

The outcome is different values for documents. This conveniently leads to a ranking, and for practical purposes the comparison output is treated like that for any other retrieval method that induces a ranking, i.e. as delivering multiple relevant documents if these exist. System performance can also be measured using rank-based methods. However as just mentioned, the principle underlying the model is that it is identifying *the* document that generated *the* request. This document ought to be the one with the highest value, but since the base for estimating value is not perfect, the generating (i.e. relevant) document could be another one. However once this relevant document is recovered, i.e. is encountered going down the ranking, retrieval stops.

The way the LM approach is applied in practice, that is, subtly changes its meaning. As long as documents are really different, they should generate different requests. The actual request may not be the best they could generate (indeed, will obviously not be), but that's tough and incidental. Similarly if the document index descriptions used for generation are impoverished, e.g. consist of two or three subject headings as opposed to full text, several documents could be deemed equally likely to have generated a given request. Or if the indexing language is restricted, different requests could be represented by the same search query. But this again simply implies that the base for determining the real relative status of different documents vis-a-vis a request is weak, not that there are no real differences of status.

Thus if we now consider the situation where we recognize the empirical fact that there may be several documents relevant to the user's information need, and where we also have some particular expression of that need as a request, what does this imply for the formal LM account of retrieval?

We exclude, for the moment, the use of feedback. We assume batch searching (and also that whatever means the user has exploited to develop their request are outside the retrieval system proper). Then the LM approach most obviously works as follows. We determine how probable it is that each document generated the request. Then since each relevant document has to be viewed as independent of every other and, further, in assuming that this document generated the request we have formally to treat all the other relevant documents as non-relevant, we notionally conduct a series of R independent searches for each relevant document D_j $(1 \leq j \leq R)$ alone. The logic is the same as if we actually had several needs each with its own single relevant document and its own request, but the requests just incidentally happen to be worded in the same way. Then we might seek to find the set of documents which maximizes the probability:

$$P(T_1, \cdots, T_n | D_1, \cdots, D_R) = \prod_{j=1}^{R} \prod_{i=1}^{n} ((1 - \lambda)P(T_i) + \lambda P(T_i | D_j)) \quad (3.2)$$

In practice, we might economize and simplify the set selection process, and emerge with the same single ranking of documents as in conventional systems, but this would be vulgar practice, not proper principle.

Unfortunately, this way of saving the theory is not convincing as a way of capturing empirical facts: real users can, of their own accord, accept several documents as relevant to their need. At least, more fieldwork is needed to establish that they are always *really* working with a family of needs and, more especially, with a sequence of needs when accepting documents while assessing a sequence of documents.

However if we try to incorporate the reality that there may be several documents relevant to the need into the model, this formally implies not that we look for the single document that generated the request, but that we look for the *set* of documents that generated the request. That is, the relevant document set is the set of documents that most probably generated the request. But of course this way madness lies, or at least we have a large combinatorial challenge.

Formally, we have the exact same situation as in Equation 3.1 considering the set of documents $\tilde{d}$, but here the relevant subset of documents is acting as a hidden variable. As such, it can be disposed of by marginalizing it, at the cost of having to consider all its possible values, in this case, all possible subsets of the document collection, denoted as D^*.

$$P(T_1, \cdots, T_n | D) = \sum_{\tilde{d} \in D^*} P(T_1, \cdots, T_n | \tilde{D} = \tilde{d}) P(\tilde{D} = \tilde{d} | D) \qquad (3.3)$$

This might not be felt to be too much of a problem, given modern machines and some smart mathematical analysis. But there is a more important difficulty about the strategy. This is that given that the information available to determine the set is only the initial request, the chance that the most probable set will coincide with the relevant set is rather low.

An interesting way out of the multiple relevant documents problem is to reverse the language models: instead of assuming that queries are generated from documents, we assume that documents are generated from a request model, or perhaps more generally, from a *relevance model*. This approach has been adopted by some authors for the topic detection and tracking task (Jin et al., 1999; Spitters and Kraaij, 2000), where the request actually consists of a known relevant document. However, some LM authors working with the traditional IR task have also attempted to develop relevance models.

Lavrenko and Croft, 2001, who start with the aim of combining ideas from PM and LM, consider a model in which the query terms are generated from a mixture of single-document models. Lafferty and Zhai, 2001, consider not only document models, but also a language model based on the request, first a simple one involving query terms only, and then a more complex one in which the user is assumed to choose the query terms from a succession of documents found in the course of a search. However, in both cases they find it necessary to make an assumption similar to that mentioned earlier involving an idealized relevant document, about some user measure of similarity (not specified by the model) between the relevance model and the document models of the relevant documents.

Both approaches lead to a two-stage retrieval process which is very much like so-called pseudo-relevance feedback. In the first stage, a query term is used to rank the documents (just as in 'normal retrieval'). In the second stage, the probabilities of the top ranked documents are used to infer a relevance model, and the documents are ranked by the probability that they were generated by this relevance model. Lafferty and Zhai also indicate that their approach could be used for real relevance feedback, though they do not test this possibility.

Clearly, the multiple relevant document problem is of particular concern if we wish to make use of real relevance feedback. Thus there are good reasons for asking how relevance feedback fits the LM approach. As the LM approach, like the PM one, benefits from having more information for estimating probabilities, it is rational to ask how knowing about some relevant documents can improve estimation, and hence retrieval, for others.

2.3   Relevance feedback

In the pure LM approach, with a single generating document, there is of course no motivation for relevance feedback proper. Indeed while the probabilities assigned to all the documents in the collection should change, in an appropriately consistent way, as the user inspects proffered documents, once the user has found the generating document, the only but otiose form that feedback could take would be to be negative. What, however, are the implications for the LM approach if we try to accommodate multiple relevant documents?

Suppose that we do our first search and find our first relevant document, i.e. the document that generated our initial request. If we modify the request, say by adding terms taken from the document, the LM approach strictly requires that we now treat this as a new request and find the document that most probably generated it. But of course since the new request has been explicitly built from a document - in the limiting case we might just have adopted that document's description as the new request - we have to withhold that document in the search or we will simply go round in circles. We thus change the file (if only infinitesimally) as well as the request, i.e. change the component of the situation that the LM assumes will remain the same: even if the status of the documents in the file alters, the presumption is that the membership of the file is constant over the user's search session.

It is nevertheless clearly possible to continue on the one by one basis. But it has to be accepted that if there is no reference to an underlying need and a process that is intended to improve the expression of that need so as to increase the chance of identifying all the documents relevant to it, the LM approach is dealing with a succession of needs and corresponding requests. The real life analogue is routing rather than adhoc retrieval. Moreover, the one-by-one model of retrieval that is entrenched in the LM approach naturally implies a step-wise modification (i.e. replacement) of the last version of the request. This does not necessarily lead to the same eventual request for retrieving the last relevant document as when requests are modified (or replaced) using the information supplied by a set of relevant documents all taken together.

Hiemstra's (Hiemstra, 2002) proposed solution to the multiple relevant documents problem is to assume that each relevant document independently generated the request as stated in Equation 3.2, and to give the standard LM approach a slightly different justification. The usual justification for Equation 3.2 is a form of 'smoothing': the model for a specific document is smoothed by the generic model for the collection as a whole in order to avoid certain extremes such as zero probabilities assigned to some terms. Hiemstra's basic assumption is the same (the user is assumed to have a specific document in mind and a request and then search query is generated on the basis of this document); but instead of smoothing, the generation process is assumed to assign a binary importance value to each term position in the query. The position for an important term is filled with a term from the document; a non-important one is filled with a general language term. If we define $\lambda_i = P$(term position i is important), we get:

$$P(T_1, \cdots, T_n|D) = \prod_{i=1}^{n}((1 - \lambda_i)P(T_i) + \lambda_i P(T_i|D)) \qquad (3.4)$$

Then in feedback each known relevant document provides evidence for the importance of each query term, and the evidence across the known documents is accumulated to provide estimates of importance for the different query terms. However, this strategy assumes that each query term has a (general or average) importance status which is independent of particular documents, and this is incompatible with the generation process on which the LM approach is founded. For example, if a term does not occur in a document it must have been *un*important when the request was generated, but may nevertheless now be deemed important. This clearly subverts the whole LM idea.

Relevance feedback in general allows for either or both of query reweighting and query expansion. Hiemstra's strategy is only for reweighting. Ponte, 2000, addresses expansion. He combines LM information with other more conventional data about term value in order to produce an enlarged query. This is treated as a new query for which the generating probabilities for the file documents that have not already been inspected are computed. But in fact, the rationale for the new part of the query lies in the set of documents already seen, not in the unseen putative generating set, while at the same time the values for the old part have already been computed for all the documents in the file and exploited as the base for the user's past assessments. This is not a consistent, principled interpretation of LM for relevance feedback.

Neither Hiemstra nor Ponte, therefore, provide a fully convincing way of handling feedback within the LM framework, and specifically a proper account of model training on relevance data. It may be that such an account can be found in the more recent models of Lafferty and Zhai, 2001, and Lavrenko and Croft, 2001, discussed in the previous section, though they have not been developed in this direction.

Overall, LM in its classical form emerges as a minimalist theory about the information that can be drawn from multiple relevant documents, that they supply about one another, and hence can jointly supply to leverage a query that best retrieves them all. PM responds to this situation in a more wholehearted way.

3. A possible LM approach: parsimonious models

What would a proper LM approach to the multiple-relevant-documents case look like?

One suggestion is that there should be an explicit model which generates the *set* of relevant documents, i.e. that relevance sets should be built into the model from the start rather than in the 'brute force' fashion sketched in 2.2 above. In this way relevant documents could be seen in the LM approach to have some similarity, different from the whole collection, which would in principle allow some form of relevance feedback. But such a model would seem to have considerable difficulties.

The LM approach at present allows for $N + 1$ language models, where N is the collection size. The additional one is the general language model. The relationship between this last and the individual document models does not seem to have been examined for the aggressively generative theoretical stance on LM for retrieval being examined here. Thus how can a document be generated from one language model when the entire collection is generated from a different one? There is an issue here for LM in itself, but there is clearly much more of a problem when we start looking at models for sets of relevant documents.

Is there any mechanism within the LM field to support some kind of global-and-local model structure for the sets case? One possible mechanism is the one with which we are familiar: the mixture model. However, the mixture model implies a curious view of the interaction between the various parts – *two* distinct (in this case unigram) language models with unrelated probabilities for the same event, *and* a combination model for deciding which of these to use.

This view would seem to bear little relation to any real authorship process. The language that we use in writing a paper on a specialist subject is basically the same language we use when talking to our families, with only some parts modified by the particular contexts. It seems that what we need is a general model for some large accumulation of text, which is modified (not replaced) by a local model for some smaller part of the same corpus. This is resorting to a perfectly conventional account of language use as underspecified or highly abstracted in the large, but involving specific form (and content) variations in text type (register, etc.) in any individual situation. In the present case, where we are dealing with simple index terms, this local variation is in the uses of or selections from the language vocabulary.

But having just a two-level account, covering a whole-collection model and a single local model, is not enough when we have a set of relevant documents rather than a single one. Although we are considering documents that are all relevant to the same one request, this cannot be taken to imply, unrealistically, that these documents are identical, or are generated by a single model. We have to allow for the fact that requests as topic specifiers can be selective on the normally much richer topic content of documents, especially when the necessary variation in topic granularity is factored in. Even if the presumption is that (the whole of) a (highly) relevant document is *about* the request topic, this does not imply that the document has just one topic. Documents are multi-topic, can be relevant to more than one different request, and can resemble other different documents in different ways.

Then if we accept, as we have to, that documents are multi-topic, and that relevance to a request topic in the retrieval sense is only one topic relationship for a multi-topic document, we actually need not a two-level but a three-level LM structure:

1 A whole-collection or generic model...

2 ... modified by a relevant-documents model...

3 ... modified by an individual document model.

The third model includes all the special aspects of a particular document that are specific to topics other than the topic of this particular user request. It would play something like the role of the error or residual term in a regression or ANOVA model – "all the variance not explained by the above". All of these distinct models appear to be necessary for a proper application of LM in the retrieval context without making the unsatisfactory assumption that all relevant documents are the same.

Before describing in a little more detail in section 3.2 how such a system of models might be applied in the retrieval context, we need to discuss the notion of *parsimonious* models. This is a necessary feature of a structure with models at more than one level.

In what follows, the concepts of 'explanation', 'generation' and 'prediction' are taken as more or less equivalent: saying a model *explains* a piece of text is the same as saying it *generates* it (in the language model sense), or that it *predicts* it.

3.1 The need for parsimony

One difficulty with the multi-level approach suggested above lies in comparing different models for their explanatory power concerning a piece of text. If a model can incorporate as many parameters as it wants, then it can fit any fixed set of data to any degree of accuracy. In principle, a document-specific model can explain a document completely (or rather, explain it within the limits of the basic LM approach, e.g. bigram, being applied), and has no need to appeal to a higher-level model of a collection of documents. The only sense in which such a higher-level model might contribute is in the sense of explaining the data more parsimoniously. Thus we may have a generic collection model to cover all the documents taken together, along with individual document models that need only a few parameters to distinguish each document from the others. So although there are two levels of model, their combined complexity is less than that implied by having a complete set of full individual document models all on the same level.

For example, consider the usual LM approach, represented by Equation 3.2, $[\lambda P(T|D) + (1 - \lambda) P(T)]$. This formula defines a mixture of a generic collection model and a specific document model, controlled by the parameter λ. From a maximum likelihood perspective, and without any constraints on parsimony, $P(T|D)$ is always preferable to $P(T)$, since it will best explain the observable data. From this perspective λ should be close to 1, so (unfortunately) the least parsimonious explanation is obtained.

On the other hand, parsimony would clearly prefer a probability estimate for T similar to $P(T)$ for most terms, that is:

$$[\lambda P(T|D) + (1 - \lambda) P(T)] \approx P(T)$$

We see that this is only possible if: i) $\lambda \approx 0$, in which case all words have the same probability of emission regardless of the document they belong to, or ii) $P(T|D) \approx P(T)$, that is the term T appears in the document with exactly the same distribution as it appears in the corpus, which would certainly not apply to the terms and documents we are particularly interested in.

Since λ is independent of T in the LM approach of Equation 3.1, we could not 'zoom-in' or 'explain-away' the behavior of certain terms only under this framework – we would have to do so *for all terms* in the same degree. What we would need for parsimony is for λ to be equal to zero *for most terms and for most documents*, similar to the separate λ for each query term suggested by

Equation 3.4. But in this case λ would have to depend on T and D. We would need to select or *fit* lambda values for each term in each document.

So, for example, a generic unigram model for the collection as a whole, accompanied at some lower level by a small number of specific unigram models, each of which had parameters for only a small number of terms with distinctive document behavior, would be a very parsimonious model for a collection of documents. These lower-level models might be at the level of individual documents, or of individual topics, for example. For this whole strategy to work, the way any of these models, whether individually or in combination, are fitted must reward parsimony. There are approaches to statistical model fitting, particularly some Bayesian and maximum entropy ones, which do reward parsimony. But as far as we know no such model has been used in connection with LM and retrieval.

3.2   A 3-level model again

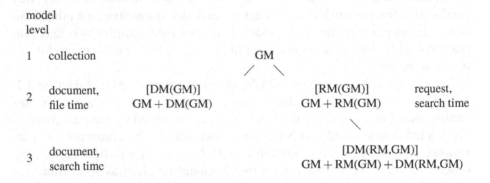

Figure 3.1.   Scope and relations of language models for document retrieval. [] denotes residual.

Assume, then, that we have an approach to language modelling which (a) rewards parsimony, and (b) allows a more specialist model to be built at a lower level than a more general one. We suppose that every document is generated by a general language or collection model, denoted GM, accompanied by some unknown set of special models relating to topics that occur in the document (and also perhaps in other documents). We will assume that these various topic models can all be rolled into a single individual-document model, denoted DM(GM), which represents the residual: everything in that document that cannot be described by the GM. The complete individual document model thus becomes GM+DM(GM), as illustrated on the left hand side of Figure 3.1. Further (though not shown in the figure), if we had a model for a specific topic that occurs in the document, this particular topic model would take over part of DM(GM) – potentially more parsimoniously because it is applicable to all documents in which this topic is appears, and because it makes the remaining genuinely-individual document model yet more parsimonious.

We can now express the relevance hypothesis as follows: A request is generated from a specific topic, i.e. relevance, model as usual, to accompany the generic collection model: call this relevance model RM(GM) (so by analogy with the previous case, the full model for relevance is GM+RM(GM)). Then if and only if a document is relevant to the request, the RM(GM) component will apply to this document – that is, it will replace part of DM(GM) in explaining the document. So for a relevant document, we should have a new residual model for all the unexplained parts, DM(GM,RM), and a new complete model GM+RM(GM)+DM(GM,RM), as shown on the right hand side of Figure 3.1. In this complete model, the RM(GM) component would relate to that part or aspect of the document that makes it relevant to the request.

Thus the probability of relevance of a document is the probability that the complete model just introduced explains the document; more specifically, this is the probability that the GM+RM(GM)+DM(GM,RM) combination is better than the GM+DM(GM) combination. Another way of expressing the relevance hypothesis is as follows: there is a null hypothesis about each document, expressed by the GM+DM(GM) combination; and there is an alternative (relevance) hypothesis, expressed by GM+RM(GM)+DM(GM,RM). We have to test whether the latter explains the document better than the former (where 'better' includes a reward for parsimony); in the usual retrieval fashion, we may express this test by assigning a probability or likelihood to the relevance hypothesis against the null hypothesis.

Now a document that has already been judged relevant provides us with independent evidence, additional to the query, about RM(GM). Thus the multi-level account of the retrieval situation that we have just introduced accommodates the notion of relevance feedback quite naturally. An interesting observation is that the multi-level account actually requires (in principle) that there is more than one relevant document – we can only achieve parsimony if RM(GM) is shared between two or more documents. This is not, however, a practical constraint – any retrieval rule which we could derive from the model would have to be useful in the first stage when we know no relevant documents, and in early feedback when we might have only one; if it subsequently turns out that there is only one or even none in the collection, this will not affect the application of the rule.

The foregoing is clearly only a sketch, but one which suggests some requirements to be met for a comprehensive LM account of retrieval. However, an interesting observation can be made about the approach even at this stage. The process of developing a DM(GM) model for an individual document in the GM+DM(GM) case is independent of any request, and is essentially a file-indexing process: it asks the question "How does the language of this document differ from that of the whole collection?". It looks as if answering this question should deal automatically with stopwords as well as with tf and idf (which one might expect LM to do). Stopwords (or at least some of them) would be words for which the general language model is sufficient, and which therefore do not figure at all in the residual DM(GM) model for an individual document.

4.   Concluding comment

This paper was inspired by the desire to make sense of the relationship between traditional probabilistic models of retrieval and the newer language modelling approach. But this led us to address the role of relevance in the LM approach, which in turn raises issues about the way the LM account of retrieval, when considered from the theoretical rather than the practical point of view, can handle the fact that a request may have any number of relevant documents.

The ideas we have presented are an informal indication of what a suitable LM account of retrieval, i.e. one that recognizes the realities, has to be like. It is evident that such an account, implying multiple levels of model, is a good deal more complicated than the attractive basic notion of a (relevant) document generating a request suggests. Our informal analysis clearly needs proper formal development. But it is complicated - indeed disagreeably complex - enough to make doing this quite a difficult enterprise. However it is only when the formal version has been developed that a fair comparison between the LM and PM approaches, as theoretical views of IR, can be properly made. Or, to put the point another way, if both LM and PM are bringing relevance onto the stage in the role of hidden variable, how elegant is her costume, and how convincing are her lines?

References

W. B. Croft and H. R. Turtle. Text retrieval and inference. In P. Jacobs, editor, *Text-based Intelligent Systems*, pages 127–156. Hillsdale, NJ: Lawrence Erlbaum, 1992.

D. Hiemstra. *Term-Specific Smoothing for the Language Modeling Approach to Information Retrieval: The Importance of a Query Term. Proceedings of the 25th ACM SIGIR Conference on Research and Development in Information Retrieval (SIGIR'02)*, 2002.

H. Jin, R. Schwartz, S. Sista, and F. Walls. Topic tracking for radio, tv broadcast, and newswire. In *Proceedings, Eurospeech 99*, Vol. VI, pages 2439-2442, 1999.

J. Lafferty and C. Zhai. Document language models, query models, and risk minimization. *Proceedings of the 24th ACM SIGIR Conference on Research and Development in Information Retrieval (SIGIR'01)*, pages 111–119, 2001.

V. Lavrenko and W. B. Croft. Relevance-based language models. *Proceedings of the 24th ACM SIGIR Conference on Research and Development in Information Retrieval (SIGIR'01)*, pages 120–128, 2001.

D. R. H. Miller, T. Leek, and R. M. Schwartz. A hidden Markov model information retrieval system. *Proceedings of the 22nd ACM SIGIR Conference on Research and Development in Information Retrieval (SIGIR'99)*, pages 214–221, 1999.

S. Mizzaro. Relevance: The whole story. *Journal of the American Society for Information Science*, 48(9), pages 810–832, 1997.

J. M. Ponte and W. B. Croft. A language modeling approach to information retrieval. *Proceedings of the 21st ACM SIGIR Conference on Research and Development in Information Retrieval (SIGIR'98)*, pages 275–281, 1998.

J. M. Ponte. Language models for relevance feedback. In W.B. Croft, editor, *Advances in information retrieval : recent research from the Center for Intelligent Information Retrieval*, pages 73–95. Dordrecht: Kluwer, 2000.

T. Saracevic. Relevance: A review of and a framework for the thinking on the notion in information science. *Journal of the American Society for Information Science*, 26, pages 321–343, 1975.

K. Sparck-Jones, S. Walker, and S. E. Robertson. A probabilistic model of information retrieval: Development and comparative experiments. Parts 1 and 2). *Information Processing & Management*, 36(6), pages 779–840, 2000.

M. Spitters and W. Kraaij. A language modeling approach to tracking news events. *Proceedings of the DARPA Topic Detection and Tracking Evaluation Workshop*, 2000.

H. R. Turtle and W. B. Croft. Inference networks for document retrieval. *Proceedings of the 13th Annual International ACM SIGIR Conference on Research and Development in Information Retrieval (SIGIR'01)*, pages 1-24, 1990.

F. Walls, H. Jin, S. Sista and R. Schwartz. Probabilistic models for topic detection and tracking. *Proceedings, ICASSP 99*, 1999.

Chapter 4

CONTRIBUTIONS OF LANGUAGE MODELING TO THE THEORY AND PRACTICE OF INFORMATION RETRIEVAL

Warren R. Greiff and William T. Morgan

The MITRE Corporation

202 Burlington Road, Bedford, MA

greiff@mitre.org, wmorgan@mitre.org

Abstract   This paper presents an analysis of what *language modeling* (LM) is in the context of information retrieval (IR). We argue that there are two principal contributions of the language modeling approach. First, that it brings the thinking, theory, and practical knowledge of research in related fields to bear on the retrieval problem. Second, that it makes patent that parameter estimation is important for probabilistic IR approaches. In particular, it has brought to the attention of the IR community the idea that explicit consideration needs to be given to variance reduction in the design of statistical estimators. We describe a simulation environment which has been developed for the study of theoretical issues in information retrieval. Results obtained from the simulation are presented, which show quantitatively how variance reduction techniques applied to parameter estimation can improve performance for the ad-hoc retrieval task.

Keywords: Language model, document ranking, statistical modeling, parameter estimation, variance reduction, shrinkage estimator, bias-variance tradeoff.

1.   Introduction

In recent years, a new thrust has emerged in information retrieval (IR) research. In a clear and unquestionably beneficial example of cross-fertilization across research communities, what has come to be called *language modeling* in IR (LMIR) has developed as an area of research, borrowing directly from the use of language models (LM) in other areas of human language technology (HLT).

W.B. Croft and J. Lafferty (eds.), Language Modeling for Information Retrieval, 73–93.
© 2003 *Kluwer Academic Publishers.*

Language models have a well-developed research history. For more than twenty-five years, language models have played a central role in speech recognition research and system development (Jelinek, 1998). Based on a model of how a given language, such as English, is produced, a speech recognition system is able to choose among competing hypotheses of what was spoken. The language model assigns a probability to each utterance that can occur in English discourse. The recognizer then compares the probabilities assigned to each hypothesis in conjunction with other factors, and chooses the transcription hypothesis most likely to correspond to the speech signal being analyzed.

Language models have also played a central role in statistical machine translation (Brown et al., 1990). To translate French to English, a statistical translation system treats the input text as if it were a result of the transmission of what was originally English across a *noisy channel*. The task of the translator is conceptualized as determining the original English text that resulted in the French at the receiving end of the channel. As with speech recognition, a previously trained language model is a component of the decision procedure invoked to choose among competing hypotheses.

Numerous other areas of textual language processing have also experimented with the language modeling approach, especially with the application of hidden Markov models (Rabiner et al., 1983). This includes part-of-speech tagging (Cutting et al., 1992), named-entity identification (Burger et al., 1998), topic segmentation (Greiff et al., 2001; Yamron et al., 1998), and selectional preference (Abney and Light, 1999).

An important factor in all technologies that use language modeling is that the model is learned. Statistical characteristics of the language of interest are extracted from a *training corpus*. From these statistics, parameters of the language model are estimated. The far from trivial problem of parameter estimation is a major focus of all work on language modeling.

It was Ponte who first saw that the theoretical results and practical techniques produced in work with language models in HLT are relevant to information retrieval (Ponte, 1998). In the intervening four years many other researchers have made important contributions to this area. As is to be expected, different researchers, coming from different backgrounds, brought with them different perspectives and focused on different aspects of the problem, ultimately contributing in different ways. There is no doubt that LM research has brought with it fresh ideas and new energy and has made valuable contributions to the field. It is the position of this paper that this is a good moment in the evolution of LMIR to take a step back, analyze what language modeling has come to mean in the context of information retrieval research, and attempt to identify with clarity which aspects of the approach best account for its success.

We claim in this paper that the most significant contribution of language modeling in information retrieval is that it has brought with it an awareness of the role of statistical estimation in probabilistic approaches to IR. In 1977, Robertson published a statement of the *Probability Ranking Principle* (PRP) (Robertson, 1977).[1] Frequently cited, this principle states that documents are to be ranked "in order of decreasing probability of usefulness to the user". Less frequently noted is that the PRP also councils that the probabilities are to be "estimated as accurately as possible on the basis of whatever data has been made available to the system for this purpose". Since the publication of the PRP, many researchers have grappled with the challenge of developing adequate probabilistic models of the information retrieval problem. The question of how best to go about estimating the probabilities and what precisely should be understood by "as accurately as possible" have received less attention. With the advent of LMIR, this is changing.

In this paper, we argue that much of the statistical estimation work in language modeling can be understood as confronting what is often phrased as the *bias-variance tradeoff*. We describe what it means to trade off increased estimation bias for reduced estimation variance. We claim that recognition of the role of variance reduction in obtaining optimal retrieval performance must be a central component in all attempts to understand the retrieval problem or design retrieval systems within a probabilistic framework.

Although credit goes to the LMIR research area for bringing recognition of variance reduction issues to our field, we believe it is important to recognize that the importance of variance reduction is not limited to just the LM approach. To this end, we describe simulation experiments we have conducted with the goal of demonstrating how variance reduction can be used to improve the performance of a probabilistic IR algorithm. The probabilistic model we adopt has been motivated by the use of additive *tf-idf* ranking formulae used in current state-of-the-art retrieval systems. It has been designed to reflect traditional probabilistic thinking in IR, and to draw attention to the importance of statistical estimation in all probabilistic approaches, not just those involving language models.

In the following sections we analyze what LM has been in IR. After setting the stage with a strict interpretation, we evaluate what LM is in practice, and review the four years of work in LMIR. We argue for the importance of statistical estimation in general, and variance reduction in particular, which leads us to demonstrate the validity of our claim through the use of simulation studies. We describe the simulation environment we have developed and present results that support our principal position — that variance reduction must receive explicit attention in any probabilistic theory of information retrieval.

---

[1] Robertson credits the original formulation of *Probability Ranking Principle* to Cooper.

2.   What is Language Modeling in IR

In this section we analyze the term *language modeling* as it has come to be used in the field of information retrieval over the last few years. As a point of departure, we begin with the formal definition of the term, and consider what a strict interpretation would entail. We go on to contrast this with the way the term is actually being used in current IR literature. We analyze the various facets of the language modeling approach to IR and our view of the importance of each to IR research. We conclude with a brief review of the major contributions to LM research in IR, relating this work to our view of what language modeling is, and why it is important.

2.1   LM in IR: A Strict Interpretation

A language model is a probability distribution over a set of strings. More formally, given a vocabulary, V, the set of strings over V is given by:

$$V^* = \{\sigma \mid \text{for some } n; \ v_1, \ldots, v_n \in V : \sigma = < v_1, \ldots, v_n >\},$$

and a probability distribution over V^* is a mapping:

$$p : V^* \to [0, 1] \qquad \text{such that:} \quad \sum_{\sigma \in V^*} p(\sigma) = 1.$$

It would be reasonable then to understand a language modeling approach to information retrieval as any approach to IR for which:

   1 a language model is estimated;

   2 the probability distributions of (one or more) language models enter into the calculations that are used to compare two arbitrary documents, relative to a specified information need.

If we restrict our understanding of language modeling to a definition such as this, then the following would not, strictly speaking, be sufficient for an approach to be considered an LM approach:

   1 probabilistic modeling;

   2 explicit recognition of the role of estimation;

   3 document scoring in terms of the probability of the query, $p(q|d)$.

We note also that, under this view, neither of the last two conditions would be strictly necessary for an approach to be considered an LM approach.

2.2   LM in IR: In practice

While it will be useful to keep a strict interpretation of language modeling in mind, it is important as well to attempt to identify what, more informally, results in certain research directions being understood as LM approaches. We propose that IR language modeling approaches share some combination of the following characteristics:

1 a language model is estimated, and plays an essential role in the assignment of Retrieval Status Values (RSV's);

2 document scoring is in terms of the probability of the query, $p(q|d)$;

3 parallels are drawn to, and ideas are adapted from, language modeling as a paradigm in other areas of human language technology;

4 the role of estimation is recognized.

2.2.1   Estimation of a language models.   One would think that estimation of a language model and its use in ranking documents would be an essential component of a language modeling approach, and it is.   But, we believe it is a mistake to assume that this is one of the main contributions of language modeling approaches to IR. Language models are by no means new. There is a long history of taking term frequency (*tf*) as the probability of a word appearing in a document. Typically, a Poisson distribution is assumed, with the two-Poisson model (Bookstein and Swanson, 1975; Harter, 1975a; Harter, 1975b) being, perhaps, the best known. It is not treatment of term frequency as the probability of word occurrence is not what is novel. It is conscious attention to *tf* as the manifestation of an underlying probability distribution rather than *tf* as the probability itself, and the concomitant concern for the question of estimation, that distinguishes recent work on language modeling from earlier research.

This is not to equate all previous probabilistic approaches to information retrieval with language modeling. The inference networks approach uses Bayesian reasoning to calculate the probability that a user's information need will be met by a given document (Turtle and Croft, 1990). As part of its computational mechanism the framework provides for calculating the probability that a set of documents will satisfy an information need; for probabilistic interpretation of complex query operators; and for marginalizing over latent variables. Information theoretic approaches have also been proposed (Wong and Yao, 1992). These too are based on probabilistic concepts. Neither of these research veins, however, can properly be classified as language modeling. Generative models of language are not considered and the role of parameter estimation in the application of these models has not been explicitly addressed. Work based on

logistic regression is also probabilistic and is more closely associated with recent language modeling work in that explicit attention is given to the issues
of statistical estimation (Cooper et al., 1992). However, the parameters to be
estimated are limited to coefficients in a generalized linear model of the probability of relevance conditioned on features of a document-query pair. The
probabilistic framework in this case is also not based in any direct sense on
what can be considered language models.

2.2.2   Probability of the query.   Much of the LMIR work views query
production as a stochastic process and takes the stand that ranking should be
based on the probability that the given query would have been produced, conditioned in some way on the document. This represents a departure from the classical probabilistic perspective. Traditional probabilistic approaches adhered directly to the Probability Ranking Principle (Robertson, 1977). Documents are
ranked by the probability that they will be found to be relevant, conditioned
on the (fixed) query. From a practical, empirical standpoint, an undercurrent
in this paper is the belief that the scoring of documents by $p(q|d)$ instead of
$p(rel\,|d,q)$ does not account for the success of these models. Success, we
assert, is primarily due to variance reduction. For now, we leave as an open
question exactly how this position may be formally expressed as a falsifiable
hypothesis which can be experimentally tested.

2.2.3   Fertile metaphors.   In his seminal work, Ponte discusses the
influence that language modeling in other fields had had on the approach he
developed for IR (Ponte, 1998). The application of hidden Markov models to
information retrieval is clearly motivated by extensive use of this framework in
speech recognition and other areas of textual language processing. The value
of adapting techniques developed, and leveraging the experience garnered, in
these related areas of research should not be understated. Without minimizing
the potential value of such cross-fertilization, we do not believe that, to date,
this is what has been the primary contributor to the success of LM. That said,
we focus our attention on the fourth, and final, point above.

2.2.4   Estimation and variance reduction.   This paper makes the
claim that it is the recognition of parameter estimation as a fundamental issue
in IR modeling that should be seen as the significant contribution of LMIR.
Further, we believe it is the reduced variance of estimators used in LM approaches that accounts for the positive results that have been obtained. It is
known that simply "shrinking" an estimate toward an arbitrary value can reduce mean squared error (MSE) by trading bias for variance (Carlin and Louis,
1996). A more informed choice for the shrinkage target can produce further
improvement. Of course, reduced MSE does not translate automatically to

improved retrieval performance. This relation must be studied. In Section 3 we will describe how we have used simulation to examine this relation and how variance reduction can in fact have a significant impact on retrieval performance. We believe that an appreciation for and understanding of the role of variance reduction will serve to place IR research on a sounder theoretical foundation, and that a sound theoretical underpinning will be essential if IR is to meet the expanding challenges that face it, as demands on information access technology increase.

2.3   Recent Language Modeling Research

With the objective of connecting the view of language modeling established in the previous section with the research that has been undertaken in the last few years, we present in this section a brief review of recent LMIR research with emphasis on the aspects of this work that relate to the above discussion.

The idea of using language modeling for information retrieval was introduced in 1998 by Ponte & Croft (Ponte and Croft, 1998). In this work they are careful to distinguish between the use of the term "model" in the context of probabilistic modeling, and another sense in which the term is used in IR, where "model" refers to "an abstraction of the retrieval task itself"; this second sense being a more appropriate interpretation of the word when speaking of the vector space *model*. They go on to identify a third sense of the term as used in the phrase "language modeling", where emphasis here is on the generative nature of the statistical models. In this paper, the notion of inferring a language model for a document is imported into the IR community and ranking by the probability of a query is introduced. Perhaps most important, Ponte & Croft consciously focus on the issue of estimation. This leads them to question the automatic use of maximum likelihood estimates and results in their incorporating the use of a potentially more robust shrinkage estimator in their retrieval algorithm.

Where Ponte & Croft import language modeling from other human language technologies, in particular speech recognition, Miller et al. (Miller et al., 1999) go a step further and import hidden Markov models (Rabiner et al., 1983) and the Expectation-Maximization (EM) algorithm (Dempster et al., 1977). Although they justify their modeling framework in terms of a "noisy channel in the mind of the user," the essence of their approach is very similar to that of Ponte & Croft in that an unbiased maximum likelihood estimate is smoothed using information from a background model.

Berger & Lafferty also conceptualize the retrieval problem in terms of communication over a noisy channel. In contrast, however, they bring their experience with language modeling applied to the problem of statistical machine translation to bear. They also make use of the EM algorithm and they also "interpolate parameters away from their maximum likelihood estimates" by way of a linear mixture with a background unigram model

Ng proposes document ranking based on how much more probable a document is in the context of a query than it is in general (i.e. according to a background model). Bayesian inversion, which also comes in to play in the work of Miller et al. and Berger & Lafferty, converts the problem into one of determining how much more likely the query would be in the context of the document than it would be in general. Although the work is similar to the others, the theoretical framework differs; Ng makes different modeling assumptions; and he applies alternate smoothing algorithms.

Hiemstra presents a linguistically motivated probabilistic model of IR and uses estimation by linear interpolation (Hiemstra, 1998), and Hiemstra & deVries compare language modeling to more traditional approaches in IR (Hiemstra and de Vries, 2000). Song & Croft (Song and Croft, 1999) experiment with a number of smoothing techniques including curve fitting functions, model combinations, and Good-Turing estimation.

Lavrenko and Croft return to the notion of relevance in what they have called *relevance-based language models* (Lavrenko and Croft, 2001). After using the query terms to estimate a model of relevant documents, documents are ranked according to how much more likely they are to have been produced from the relevance model than from a background model estimated from the entire collection.

What we see in all this work is a recognition of the importance of the parameter estimation problem for probabilistic approaches to information retrieval. In particular, although it is not always stated in these terms, there is a concern for the variance of an estimate. Statisticians refer to an estimate that is correct on average as unbiased. However an unbiased estimator need not be the best estimator. It is understood that for a number of applications it can be highly advantageous to accept a certain degree of estimation bias if in return there is a reduction in estimation variance. Ponte & Croft explicitly introduce the use of shrinkage estimators to trade off bias for variance. The backoff models and smoothing techniques discussed in the other papers mentioned above are also variance reduction techniques.

Traditionally, probabilistic approaches to information retrieval rank documents according to the probability that a document is relevant. In language modeling documents are ranked according to the probability that the query would be generated from the distributions which have generated the documents. We join Sparck Jones and Robertson in asking "Where's the relevance?" (Sparck Jones and Robertson, 2001). From a theoretical standpoint making the connection should not be seen as inconsequential. Retrieval systems are evaluated on their ability to return relevant documents, and there is no formal reason why, of two documents, the one that was generated from a distribution more likely to produce the query need be more likely to be relevant to that same query. Miller et al., Berger & Lafferty, and Ng all present formal justifications for basing retrieval ranking on the probability of query generation rather than the probability of relevance. However, the authors tend not to make explicit the precise nature of the event space they have in mind or the operational semantics to be associated with the random variables. In their article Sparck-Jones & Robertson also argue for the need to justify ranking by the probability of the query, although they argue from a somewhat different perspective.

3. Simulation Studies of Variance Reduction

As we have stated above, the main position in this paper is that variance reduction plays a key role in the effectiveness of ranking formulae used for information retrieval. At The MITRE Corporation we have embarked on a program to study the effects of variance reduction techniques via simulation. In these studies, simulation is used to create an idealized environment in which questions concerning estimation can be analyzed. Simulation allows for experimentation for which:

true probability distributions are known: In both practical and theoretical research in IR, assumptions are often made about the stochastic nature of the phenomenon; terms are assumed to follow a Poisson distribution, the log-odds of relevance is assumed to be a linear function of document features, etc. These assumptions may or may not hold. When running a simulation, we control how the data is generated. This allows us to study ranking strategies knowing the true nature of the stochastic processes producing the retrieval situation. So, as we will see in Section 3, we can fix the probabilistic assumptions concerning the generation of documents, including hidden characteristics of those documents, and demonstrate the value of adopting variance reduction strategies as part of the retrieval process.

both environment and retrieval engine parameters can be controlled: We can, in a simulation, control various parameters in order to study the relation between input and output variables. For example, in the case of the variance reduction experiments to be discussed below, we have studied the relation between the standard deviation of the noise added to the observation of a latent variable, and the optimal level of shrinkage to be applied as part of the estimation procedure.

confounding issues can be abstracted away: Like all real world problems, IR is messy. Many factors interact in complex and unpredictable ways. For example, IR systems often use stemming. Unfortunately, stemming algorithms are imperfect. For the terms of one query a given algorithm may work well, conflating term variants appropriately. For another, terms with very different semantics may be coalesced, or the relation between two important variations of the same term may be missed. The results of a study of term-weighting formulae will be affected by the stemming algorithm used. In a simulated environment, issues such as these can be left out of the simulation models, allowing the researcher to focus on one aspect of the problem without the interference of confounding factors.

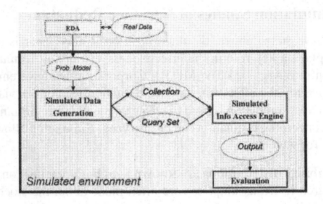

Figure 4.1.   Simulation environment.

Figure 4.1 presents our overall approach to simulation as a tool for the study of theoretical questions in information retrieval. The main block of this diagram shows the simulation environment we have developed. Starting with a well-defined, formal, probabilistic model, we are able to simulate document collections and query sets. Only those characteristics of the documents which are necessary for a particular study are generated.

Typically, document characteristics will include both observable and latent, that is hidden, document features. An example of observable features might be the number of times each of the query terms appears in the document. An example of latent features might be some measure of the extent to which the document treats the concepts corresponding to the query terms. In general, observable features will be related to latent variables, although the dependence of observables on hidden document properties will tend to be stochastic rather than functional.

While it will not be discussed further in this paper, the simulation environment also provides for the stochastic generation of query sets. Once they have been generated, the document collection together with the query set are fed into the simulated retrieval engine. For each query, the engine will apply the specified retrieval algorithm, score each document in the collection, and produce a document ranking. Finally there is an evaluation module which can analyze the effectiveness of the retrieval strategy according to metrics typically used to evaluate the ad-hoc retrieval task.

One question which arises in the context of the previous discussion is, where does the probabilistic model come from. In our initial studies, we will make strong assumptions about the nature of the model, guided entirely by our intuition and experience. This will allow us to study theoretical issues, such as those that are the subject of this paper. If the information retrieval issues we wish to study were not so complicated, and reasonable metrics of retrieval performance were not so algebraically complex, an analytical approach would be a possibility. Imagine the difficulty, however, of applying formal mathematical reasoning to the problem of characterizing the effect estimation variance has on (expected) average precision. Note that the mathematical formulation of average precision, based as it is on document ranking, and not directly on document scores, is in and of itself a daunting proposition. In the age of high-speed computing machines, however, simulation offers a viable alternative in the face of intractable mathematics.

In later stages of our research, a greater effort will be made to have the setting of these simulation variables be informed by distributions extracted from existing test data, such as that provided by the TREC competitions (Voorhees and Harman, 2000). This is shown pictorially in the upper left corner of Figure 4.1.

In the remainder of this section we give a brief, high level view of some of the experimentation we have conducted, and will discuss how these experiments validate the arguments concerning variance reduction made in the previous section. We begin with a description of the specific retrieval model we will be discussing, and then present some of the results of our analysis.

3.1 Retrieval Model

In our simulations we assume that the probability, p_d, that a document will be judged relevant to a query is a function of a set of latent variables associated with the terms of that query. For the experiments reported here we assume that this probability of relevance conforms to a conditional log-linear model. That is, that the log-odds of relevance, which we denote by $\lambda_d = logit(p_d)$, is a linear function of the latent variables:[2]

$$\lambda_d = logit(p_d) = \alpha_0 + \alpha_1 \cdot \xi_1 + \cdots + \alpha_s \cdot \xi_s.$$

---

[2]The *logit* function is given by $logit(p) = \log(p/(1-p))$. When p is interpreted as a probability of relevance, $p/(1-p)$ corresponds to the odds in favor of relevance (typically much less than one), and $logit(p)$ corresponds to the log-odds of relevance (typically negative).

Intuitively, we assume that for each query term, the log-odds of relevance increases linearly with degree to which the document is related to the concept associated with that term. In order to create a pseudo-document collection, we must determine how the latent variables are generated. We have chosen independent normal distributions, $N(\mu_i, \sigma_i)$, each variable with its own mean, μ_i, and standard deviation, σ_i. This modeling family provides sufficient flexibility to model intuitively reasonable distributions of the probability of relevance, such as that exemplified by the histogram displayed in Figure 4.2.

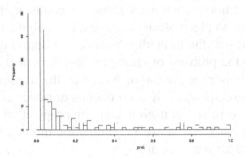

Figure 4.2. Histogram of p_d for 100,000 documents drawn from the distribution used in experiments. (Leftmost bar contains roughly 99, 800 documents.)

Although not typically discussed in these terms, all of the IR language modeling work assumes latent variables. Documents are understood to have been produced from an underlying generative model. The process is stochastic. Hence the latent variables are not directly observed. What are observed are document features randomly generated from the underlying model. The values of the latent variables must then be inferred from the values of the observed features.

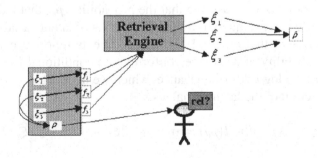

Figure 4.3. Schematic view of probabilistic document model and retrieval strategy.

This scenario is shown pictorially in Figure 4.3. The document (in the context of the supposed query) comprises three latent variables, ξ_i, and an intrinsic probability of relevance, p_d, which is a function of the ξ_i. These are not visible. The observable features are assumed to have been generated independently from three (possibly different) distributions, with one free parameter whose value is given by the value of the corresponding hidden variable ξ_i. In our experiments these are normal distributions, $N(\mu_i, \sigma_i^\epsilon)$, centered about the respective ξ_i with standard deviations, σ_i^ϵ, that can be different for each feature. Effectively the true value of the latent variables are observed in the presence of Gaussian noise.

$$f_2 = \xi_2 + \epsilon_2 \qquad \text{where:} \quad \epsilon_2 \backsim N(0, \sigma_2^\epsilon)$$

Figure 4.3 also shows the retrieval engine, which takes as input the observable document features. From these it estimates the values of the latent variables. With these estimates (and the values of the coefficients, α_i, assumed known), it is able to calculate an estimate of the log-odds of relevance. After all documents are processed, they can be ranked in accordance with these probability estimates. Since *logit* is a monotonically increasing function, the engine can rank by its estimate of the log-odds:

$$\hat{\lambda}_d = \hat{\alpha}_1 \cdot \hat{\xi}_1 + \cdots + \hat{\alpha}_s \cdot \hat{\xi}_s$$

We assume in this study that the engine knows the true value of the coefficients, such that $\hat{\alpha}_1 = \alpha_1, \ldots, \alpha_s = \hat{\alpha}_s$.[3] However, it does not have access to the true values of the latent variables, and must base its ranking on the values of the observable features, f_i, using these to produce estimates, $\hat{\xi}_i$, of the underlying latent variables, ξ_i. A natural and unbiased estimate for ξ_i is $\hat{\xi}_i = f_i$.

With f_i used as a plug-in estimator for $\hat{\xi}_i$ we have been able in others of our experiments to introduce bias and variance and study the effects on performance, in a controlled manner. In the study discussed below, we work only with zero mean noise. Estimation bias is introduced in the inference procedure used by the retrieval engine with the goal of reducing estimation variance. For simplicity of exposition we work with two variables, set the two coefficients of the log-linear model to be equal, and assume the first is observed with negligible noise. More extensive descriptions of the experimentation we have conducted and the results obtained have been prepared in (Greiff et al., 2002).

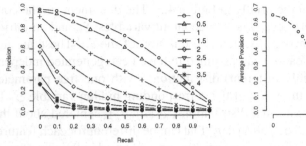
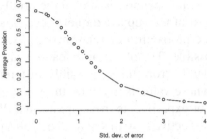

(a) Recall-precision curves for varying levels of noise, σ_2^ϵ, on the observation, f_2.

(b) Corresponding average precision for each level of σ_2^ϵ.

Figure 4.4. Degradation of performance as noise is introduced to the observation of the variables.

3.2   Simulation results

Figure 4.4(a) presents an example of how performance degrades when one of two latent variables is observed with noise. The top curve on the graph is a recall-precision curve corresponding to the (unrealistic) situation in which both latent variables are observed directly. Although the true values of the latent variable are observed without error, performance is not perfect because the simulated retrieval engine does not get to observe whether or not a document is relevant, but only the probability that it will be deemed relevant when judged.[4] Although the retrieval engine does a perfect job of ranking by the true value of λ_d, it is possible for a document with a low probability of relevance (e.g. $p_d = 0.1$) to be judged relevant while a document with higher probability of relevance (e.g. $p_d = 0.4$) to be judged not-relevant. Note that if the most highly ranked document is judged not-relevant, (interpolated) precision will be less than 1.0 at all levels of recall.

The remaining curves on Figure 4.4(a) correspond to situations where noise has been added to the observation of the second latent variable, ξ_2. Now the estimate, $\hat{\xi}_2$, used for the second feature is not the true value ξ_2 but rather $\hat{\xi}_2 = f_2$. In each case the observed feature is the true value of the latent variable plus noise, $f_2 = \xi_2 + \epsilon_2$, which we have assumed is generated according to a

---

[3]We exclude α_0 as it has no effect on ranking.

[4]An alternate, but equivalent, interpretation allows for a document to be either relevant or not relevant to a given query, independent of being *judged*. In this view the engine is still unable to produce a perfect ranking of documents, because it is unable to completely analyze the document in the context of the query. Probabilities again enter the picture because the retrieval engine is limited to consideration of surface features of the document, and relevance is not functionally dependent on these features. Some readers may find this view more natural. Either view can be adopted as an intuitive justification for studying the model family used here. In this sense they are equivalent.

zero mean Gaussian distribution, $\epsilon_2 \backsim N(0, \sigma_2^\epsilon)$. Each curve corresponds to a different value for the standard deviation of the noise, σ_2^ϵ. The top curve can be interpreted as having a standard deviation of $\sigma_2^\epsilon = 0$. As the standard deviation is increased ($\sigma_2^\epsilon = 0.5$, $\sigma_2^\epsilon = 1.0$, ..., $\sigma_2^\epsilon = 4.0$), performance degrades.

Figure 4.4(b) shows the same phenomenon in terms of average precision. Average precision (y-axis) decreases for 19 successively increasing value of σ_2^ϵ (x-axis), between $\sigma_2^\epsilon = 0.0$ and $\sigma_2^\epsilon = 4.0$.

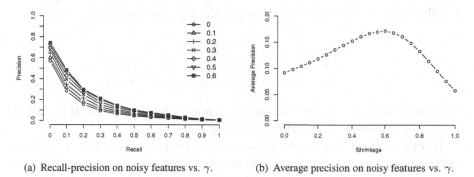

(a) Recall-precision on noisy features vs. γ.   (b) Average precision on noisy features vs. γ.

Figure 4.5.   Effect of shrinkage on retrieval performance.

We are interested in demonstrating that when the true value of the latent variable can only be observed with noise there is an opportunity to improve performance by reducing estimation variance. Figure 4.5(a) shows how performance improves as estimation variance is reduced. The estimator $\hat{\xi}_2 = f_2$ used above is a natural choice. It is the Maximum Likelihood Estimator (MLE). No other value of ξ_2 is as likely to have produced the observed feature. Formally,
[5]

$$\hat{\xi}_2 = \arg\max{}_{\xi_2'} p\text{observing } f_2; \xi_2 = \xi_2',$$

so we choose $\hat{\xi}_2 = f_2$ because

$$\forall \xi_2' : p\text{observing } f_2; \xi_2 = \xi_2' \leq p\text{observing } f_2; \xi_2 = f_2.$$

More pertinent to this discussion is that $\hat{\xi}_2 = f_2$ is an unbiased estimator. If we were given a large sample of observations, f_2, for a fixed value of ξ_2, our estimates would be correct *on average*. That is, the average value of $\hat{\xi}_2$ would be very close to ξ_2:

$$\frac{1}{N} \sum \hat{\xi}_2 = \frac{1}{N} \sum f_2 \approx \xi_2.$$

---

[5]The notation $p...$; ... should be understood as denoting the probability of the specified event (e.g. observing f_2) under the specified modeling situation (e.g. $\xi_2 = f_2$). It is worth cautioning that this is not the same as a conditional probability.

The recall-precision curves of Figure 4.5(a) correspond to biased estimators. Estimates are moved away from f_2 and are *shrunk* toward some other point μ.

$$\xi_2 = f_2 - \gamma(f_2 - \mu) = \gamma\mu + (1 - \gamma)f_2$$

Since document ranking is invariant under linear transformations (i.e. ranking by $a + b \cdot \text{score}$ is identical to ranking by score) the shrinkage target will not have any effect for the particular modeling families used in this experiment. For the purposes of ranking according to the log-odds estimate:

$$\begin{aligned} \hat{\lambda}_d &= \alpha_0 + \alpha_1 f_1 + \alpha_2 f_2 \\ &= \alpha_0 + \alpha_1 f_1 + \alpha_2(\gamma\mu + (1 - \gamma)f_2) \\ &= \alpha_0 + \alpha_1 f_1 + \gamma\alpha_2\mu + (1 - \gamma)\alpha_2 f_2. \end{aligned}$$

The $\gamma\alpha_2\mu$ term is constant and can be ignored along with α_0. It is only the degree of shrinking, γ, that affects ranking.

In Figure 4.5(a), we see how increasing shrinkage can result in improved performance. Recall-precision curves are shown for 7 values of shrinkage ($\gamma = 0.0, 0.1, \ldots, 0.7$). For $\gamma \neq 0.0$, bias is introduced. If we were given a large sample of f_2 values for a fixed value ξ_2, the average estimate would not be ξ_2, but a value, $\xi_2 - \gamma(\xi_2 - \mu)$, closer to μ. In return for bias, we get reduced variance. Estimates will hover about the average value $\hat{\xi}_2(avg) = \gamma\mu - \gamma(\xi_2 - \mu)$ more tightly than they would hover about the value $\hat{\xi}_2(avg) = \xi_2$ for the unbiased estimator. Figure 4.5(a) shows how this reduced variance can result in improved performance. Larger values of the shrinkage coefficient, γ, produce successively better curves. Figure 4.5(b) shows the same effect in terms of average precision, and goes on to show how shrinkage is only helpful up to a point. Excessive shrinkage will hurt performance. For this particular experiment optimal performance is achieved with shrinkage γ of approximately 0.6. For values below 0.6, average precision increases with more and more shrinkage. Beyond $\gamma = 0.6$, average precision drops as γ increases, reaching the original level at approximately $\gamma \approx 0.6$ and dropping even further for levels of shrinkage beyond that.

The ability to effect improved retrieval performance by variance reduction is only possible because the true value of the latent variable is observed with noise. Shrinkage ameliorates the deleterious effects of the noise. If there is no noise, any shrinkage will hurt performance. In the presence of more noise, greater levels of shrinkage are needed to achieve optimal performance, as shown in Figure 4.6. Figure 4.6(a) gives the optimal values of γ for various levels of noise. As the standard deviation of the noise, σ_2^ξ, increases, the optimal amount of shrinkage increases. Figure 4.6(b) shows the corresponding improvement as the percentage increase in average precision over that realized with no shrinkage. For higher levels of noise, greater shrinkage can be

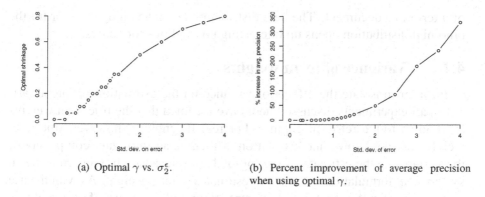

(a) Optimal γ vs. σ_2^ϵ.   (b) Percent improvement of average precision when using optimal γ.

Figure 4.6. Optimal shrinkage, γ, and its effect on performance as a function of noise.

sustained and greater improvement (as measured by percentage increase in average precision) can be realized.

4.   Continued Exploration

In this paper we have used simulation experiments to show that estimation variance is an important factor in term weighting. Unbiased estimates are not necessarily optimal. In the presence of noisy features, shrinkage can be advantageously employed. This research opens numerous directions for continued investigation. In the remainder of this section, we outline four research directions we plan to pursue.

4.1   Alternate generation models

Normal distributions have been used for the generation of both the latent variables and observable features. If estimation variance contributes to reduced retrieval performance, then any retrieval formula based on term frequencies should benefit from estimation procedures that reduce this variance. Other model families can be considered. In particular it would be interesting to consider distributions that would limit the features to values between zero and one, motivated by the *tf* features used in, for example, the Okapi ranking formula (Robertson and Walker, 1994). The Okapi formula is based on the two-Poisson model, but does not consider the introduction of bias in order to reduce variance as part of the estimation procedure. We will experiment with shrinkage estimators such as that used by Ponte & Croft, and study the effect on performance. Another possibility would be to use the beta distribution for the generation of the latent variables. The latent variables could then be interpreted as probabilities and used as parameters to a binomial distribution for the generation of discrete values which would mirror the number of occurrences of a term in a document. The beta distribution being a conjugate prior for the binomial distribution opens up interesting possibilities for analysis.

4.2   Variance of term weights

In order to isolate the effects of variance on the estimation of latent variables, all experiments discussed here have assumed that the true term weights are known to the retrieval engine. For real IR engines, however, true term weights are not known and estimation of them is an important component of the variance in the estimate of the log-odds of relevance. In modern retrieval systems, *idf* formulations are used as estimates of term weight. As with the use of *tf* as an estimator, traditional attempts to provide a theory of *idf* weighting have worked with unbiased estimates. We plan to extend the work presented here to include the effect of the term weight estimation in the simulation and analysis of retrieval performance.

4.3   Model fitting with real data

Via simulation we have been able to show the importance of variance reduction for improving information retrieval. In addition to knowledge gleaned from theoretical analysis, a major contribution of these kinds of studies is that they provide a framework for the design of empirical studies. A difficulty of testing theories of the nature of those presented here, is that the inclusion of latent variables in the theory make it impossible, by definition, to directly observe the assumptions made about them. Nonetheless indirect inferences can be made. Alternate models can be compared with regard to how well they can be made to fit real-world data, even in the presence of hidden variables. We intend to compare the ability of alternate modeling candidates to fit data collections such as those provided by TREC. These studies are a natural follow-on to the work presented here.

4.4   Alternate variance reducing estimators

Ponte & Croft use a shrinkage estimator based on the geometric distribution. This is motivated by an interest in reducing the Bayesian Risk. In his dissertation work, Ponte did initiate an empirical study of alternatives to this smoothing mechanism. We plan to further pursue this line of research with the investigation of alternate estimators and their impact on retrieval performance, in the context of the Ponte/Croft language modeling approach. In particular, we plan to use Empirical Bayes methods (Carlin and Louis, 1996) to exploit information given by the background distribution of term frequencies, in conjunction with information extracted from the document, in a principled way.

References

Abney, S. and Light, M. (1999). Hiding a semantic hierarchy in a Markov model. In *Proceedings of the Workshop on Unsupervised Learning in Natural Language Processing, ACL.*

Bookstein, A. and Swanson, D. R. (1975). Probabilistic models for automatic indexing. *Journal of the American Society for Information Science*, 26(1):45–50.

Brown, P., Cocke, J., Pietra, S. D., Pietra, V. D., Jelinek, F., Lafferty, J., Mercer, R., and Roosin, P. (1990). A statistical approach to machine translation. *Computational Linguistics*, 16:79–85.

Burger, J. D., Palmer, D., and Hirschman, L. (1998). Named entity scoring for speech input. In Boitet, C. and Whitelock, P., editors, *Proceedings of the Thirty-Sixth Annual Meeting of the Association for Computational Linguistics and Seventeenth International Conference on Computational Linguistics*, pages 201–205, San Francisco, California. Morgan Kaufmann Publishers.

Carlin, B. P. and Louis, T. A. (1996). *Bayes and Empirical Bayes Methods for Data Analysis*. Chapman and Hall, London.

Cooper, W. S., Dabney, D., and Gey, F. (1992). Probabilistic retrieval based on staged logistic regression. In Belkin, N., Ingwersen, P., and Mejtersen, A. M., editors, *Proceedings of the 15th Annual International ACM-SIGIR Conference on Research and Development in Information Retrieval*, pages 198–210, Copenhagen, Denmark.

Cutting, D., Kupiec, J., Pedersen, J., and Sibun, P. (1992). A Practical Part-of-Speech Tagger. In *Proceedings of the Third Conference on Applied Natural Language Processing.*

Dempster, A., Laird, N., and Rubin, D. (1977). Maximum likelihood from incomplete data via the em algorithm. *Journal of the Royal Statistical Society – Series B.*, 39:1–38.

Greiff, W., Morgan, A., Fish, R., Richards, M., and Kundu, A. (2001). Fine-grained Hidden Markov Modeling for broadcast-news story segmentation. In *Proceedings of the Human Language Technology Conference*, San Diego, Ca.

Greiff, W. R., Morgan, W. T., and Ponte, J. M. (2002). The role of variance in term weighting for probabilistic information retrieval. In *Proceedings of the Eleventh International Conference on Information and Knowledge Management.*

Harter, S. P. (1975a). A probabilistic approach to automatic keyword indexing, Part I: On the distribution of specialty words in a technical literature. *Journal of the American Society for Information Science*, 26:197–206.

Harter, S. P. (1975b). A probabilistic approach to automatic keyword indexing, Part II: An algorithm for probabilistic indexing. *Journal of the American Society for Information Science*, 26:280–289.

Hiemstra, D. (1998). A linguistically motivated probabilistic model of information retrieval. In *Proceedings of the Second European Conference on Research and Advanced Technology for Digital Libraries (ECDL 98)*, volume 513 of *Lecture Notes in Computer Science*, pages 569–584, New York. Springer Verlag.

Hiemstra, D. and de Vries, A. P. (2000). Relating the new language models of information retrieval to the traditional retrieval models. Technical Report TR-CTIT-00-09, Centre for Telematics and Information Technology, University of Twente.

Jelinek, F. (1998). *Statistical Methods for Speech Recognition*. MIT Press, Cambridge, MA.

Lavrenko, V. and Croft, W. B. (2001). Relevance-based language models. In Croft, W. B., Harper, D. J., Kraft, D. H., and Zobel, J., editors, *Proceedings of the 24th Annual International ACM-SIGIR Conference on Research and Development in Information Retrieval*, New Orleans, Louisiana. ACM Press.

Miller, D. R. H., Leek, T., and Schwartz, R. M. (1999). A hidden markov model information retrieval system. In *SIGIR '99: Proceedings of the 22nd Annual International ACM SIGIR Conference on Research and Development in Information Retrieval, August 15-19, 1999, Berkeley, CA, USA*, pages 214–221. ACM.

Ponte, J. M. (1998). *Probabilistic Language Models for Topic Segmentation and Information Retrieval*. PhD thesis, University of Massachusetts, Amherst, Massachusetts.

Ponte, J. M. and Croft, W. B. (1998). A language modeling approach to information retrieval. In Croft, W. B., Moffat, A., van Rijsbergen, C. J., Wilkinson, R., and Zobel, J., editors, *Proceedings of the 21st Annual International ACM-SIGIR Conference on Research and Development in Information Retrieval*, pages 275–281, Melbourne, Australia. ACM Press.

Rabiner, L. R., Levinson, S. E., and Sondhi, M. M. (1983). On the application of vector quantization quantization and hidden markov models to speaker-independent, isolated word recognition. *The Bell System Technical Journal*, 62(4):1075–1106.

Robertson, S. E. (1977). The probability ranking principle in IR. *Journal of Documentation*, 33:294–304.

Robertson, S. E. and Walker, S. (1994). Some simple effective approximations to the 2-Poisson model for probabilistic weighted retrieval. In Croft, W. B. and van Rijsbergen, C. J., editors, *Proceedings of the 17th Annual Interna-*

tional ACM-SIGIR Conference on Research and Development in Information Retrieval, pages 232–241, Dublin, Ireland.

Song, F. and Croft, W. B. (1999). A general language model for information retrieval. In *Proceedings of the Eighth International Conference on Information and Knowledge Management*.

Sparck Jones, K. and Robertson, S. (2001). LM vs. PM: Where's the relevance? In Callan, J., Croft, B., and Lafferty, J., editors, *Proceedings of the Workshop on Language Modeling and Information Retrieval*, pages 12–15.

Turtle, H. and Croft, W. B. (1990). Inference networks for document retrieval. In Vidick, J.-L., editor, *Proceedings of the 13th Annual International ACM-SIGIR Conference on Research and Development in Information Retrieval*, pages 1–24, Brussels, Belgium.

Voorhees, E. M. and Harman, D. K. (2000). Overview of the eighth Text REtrieval Conference (TREC-8). In Voorhees, E. M. and Harman, D. K., editors, *The Eighth Text REtreival Conference (TREC-8)*, pages 1–24, Gaithersburg, Md. NIST Special Publication 500-246.

Wong, S. K. M. and Yao, Y. Y. (1992). An information-theoretic measure of term specificity. *Journal of the American Society for Information Science*, 43(1):54–61.

Yamron, J. P., Carp, I., Gillick, L., Lowe, S., and van Mulbregt, P. (1998). A Hidden Markov Model approach to text segmentation and event tracking. In *Proceedings ICASSP-98*, Seattle, WA.

Chapter 5

LANGUAGE MODELS FOR
TOPIC TRACKING

The importance of score normalization

Wessel Kraaij
TNO TPD
P.O. Box 155, 2600 AD Delft, The Netherlands
kraaij@tpd.tno.nl

Martijn Spitters
TNO TPD
P.O. Box 155, 2600 AD Delft, The Netherlands
spitters@tpd.tno.nl

Abstract   Generative unigram language models have proven to be a simple though effective model for information retrieval tasks. In contrast to ad-hoc retrieval, topic tracking requires that matching scores are comparable across topics. Several ranking functions based on generative language models: straight likelihood, likelihood ratio, normalized likelihood ratio, and the related Kullback-Leibler divergence are evaluated in two orientations. Best performance is achieved by the models based on a normalized log-likelihood ratio. Key component of these models is the a-priori probability of a story with respect to a common reference distribution.

Keywords: Language Models, Information Retrieval, Score Normalization

1.   Introduction

Topic tracking is one of the tasks of the annual Topic Detection and Tracking (TDT) evaluation workshop, which was first organized in 1996. Main purpose of the TDT project is to advance the state-of-the-art in determining the topical structure of multilingual news streams from various sources, including

W.B. Croft and J. Lafferty (eds.), Language Modeling for Information Retrieval, 95–124.
© 2003 *Kluwer Academic Publishers.*

newswires, radio and television broadcasts, and Internet sites. See (Wayne, 2000) for a detailed overview of the TDT project. The tracking task models the information-need of a user who hears about a certain event on the radio or television and wants to be notified by all follow-up stories in a number of pre-specified information sources in different languages. TDT is challenging because it combines several problems: automatic speech recognition and segmentation of continuous media like radio and television, cross-lingual access to data and a topic tracking task without supervised relevance feedback. A topic tracking system is initialized with one or a few stories describing a certain news event, and must track this topic in a stream of new incoming stories. The most basic form of a tracker makes just binary decisions: a story is on-topic or off-topic. In practice such a decision is based on thresholding a score which is designed to be some monotonic function of the probability that the story is on-topic.

The goal of this study is to investigate whether generative probabilistic models that have been successfully applied to ad-hoc IR tasks (Hiemstra, 1998; Hiemstra and Kraaij, 1999; Kraaij et al., 2000) can be applied to the tracking task as well. The tracking task contains an additional difficulty in comparison with the ad-hoc task because it is required that scores are comparable across topics since the decision threshold is equal across topics. In this paper, we will review several ways to use generative models for tracking and methods to obtain comparable scores across topics. We hope to find a single model which is effective for both the ad-hoc and tracking task.

The remainder of this paper is organized into three main sections. Section 2 discusses different lay-outs for the use of language models for ad-hoc IR and topic tracking. In particular, we will look at model-internal and external normalization methods. In Section 3 we describe experiments with a selection of models that we carried out on the TDT development data and on TREC-8 Ad-hoc data. We conclude the paper with a discussion and conclusions.

2.   Language models for IR tasks

The basic problem underlying most information retrieval problems is that of ranking documents based on relevance with respect to a certain information need. This need could be an ad-hoc query, a long-standing topic of interest or - in a more dynamic fashion - an event of interest. For this class of problems, models have to impose an ordering on documents based on their supposed relevance: the probability ranking principle(Robertson, 1977). An implicit constraint is that these models need to be able to cope with documents of different lengths. In some of the TREC collections for example, document sizes can differ with several orders of magnitude. If a score would be correlated with document length this would cause highly inflated scores for long documents. For another class of IR problems, which is more related to classification, simple ordering is not enough. Here we need to be able to interpret scores in an absolute way, since the score is used to classify a document as relevant or not relevant. This is for example the case in filtering applications. In the TREC adaptive filtering task, the decision threshold can be adjusted for each topic on the basis of relevance feedback. However, in the TDT tracking task the decision threshold is taken to be uniform across all topics. This makes sense, since the task does not allow any supervised relevance feedback. As a consequence scores must be comparable across stories (documents) and topics (queries). For certain applications (e.g. document clustering) it is even desirable that matching scores fulfill another constraint, namely symmetry (Spitters and Kraaij, 2002).

2.1 Score properties of probabilistic models

It is instructive to review the relationship of probabilistic models for IR with regard to the aspect of score normalization. For reasons of legibility, we will present the models from the point of view of an ad-hoc IR problem, i.e. we talk about documents and queries. In most cases (unless stated otherwise) these models also apply to the tracking task, after replacing the query by a topic and documents by stories.

Following (Sparck Jones et al., 2000) we define:

- Q is the event that the user has a certain information need and describes it with description Q (In a tracking setting: The user is interested to track stories related to the topic described by T)

- D is the event that we consider a document with description D (Tracking setting: we are considering a story S)

- L is the event that D is liked (or relevant). (L is the event that S is liked)

- $\bar{L}$ is the event that D is not liked (or relevant). ($\bar{L}$ is the event that S is not liked). to T)

Now, for a certain query, we want to rank documents on the probability that they are liked. This can be done by estimating $P(L|D,Q)$: the probability that a document is liked given its description and the description of the query. In order to simplify further computation[1], documents are ordered on log-odds of being liked, which is an order preserving operation.

---

[1] The logarithm converts products to summations, working with the odds results in a simple likelihood ratio after applying Bayes' rule.

2.1.1   Document likelihood.   The classical next step is to apply Bayes' rule in order to express the matching score based on log-odds in terms of $P(D|L, Q)$ i.e. the probability that a document is described by D_i when we know it is relevant for a certain query Q. This model describes the situation where we have one query and several documents.

$$\log \frac{P(L|D_i, Q)}{P(\bar{L}|D_i, Q)} = \log \frac{P(D_i|L, Q)}{P(D_i|\bar{L}, Q)} + \log \frac{P(L|Q)}{P(\bar{L}|Q)} \qquad (5.1)$$

Since we do not have any information about the prior probability of relevance given a certain query, we assume a uniform prior so the second term in (5.1) can be dropped for ranking purposes. Ranking is then solely based on the log-likelihood ratio $P(D_i|L, Q)/P(D_i|\bar{L}, Q)$. One could interpret this log-likelihood ratio as follows: "How likely is the description of document D_i if we assume the document is relevant to Q?". This likelihood is normalized w.r.t. a model based on descriptions of non relevant documents[2]. Because the model is about one query and several documents, scores are inherently comparable across documents, due to the normalizing denominator likelihood.

Now $P(D_i|L, Q)$ (and $P(D_i|\bar{L}, Q)$) can be estimated in various ways. In the Binary Independence Model (Robertson and Sparck Jones, 1976) also known as the Binary Independence Retrieval (BIR) model(Fuhr, 1992), D is described as a vector of binary features x_k, one for each word in the vocabulary. Further development of the log-odds assuming term independence leads to the classical Robertson-Sparck-Jones formula for term weighting. Estimation of $P(D_i|L, Q)$ is usually based on the assumption that there is prior knowledge about some relevant documents. Such a situation is essentially equivalent to supervised text classification based on the Naive Bayes assumption, where the classes are $L, \bar{L}$ (Lewis, 1998). In the absence of relevance information, the BIR model reduces to *idf* term weighting, which is quite weak. The matching score based on the log-likelihood is basically a sum of term weights over all terms in the vocabulary, but usually it is assumed that $P(x_k|L, Q) = P(x_k|\bar{L}, Q)$ for all terms that do not occur in the query. This means that scores of the 'typical' BIR model are comparable for documents but not comparable for queries, since scores depend on the query length and not on document length. The BIR model can thus be used unchanged for the ad-hoc IR task, but scores have to be normalized for topic length, if we would want to use the BIR model for tracking.

One can also estimate $\frac{P(D_i|L,Q)}{P(D_i|\bar{L},Q)}$ in a generative framework where D_i is defined as a sequence of terms. In such a generative framework we can think of $P(D_i|L, Q)$ as the probability that D_i is generated as a sequence of terms

---

[2]This normalization is in fact the probabilistic justification of *idf* weighting

from a unigram language model M_R which is constrained by Q and L i.e. which describes the probability of observing words in documents relevant to Q. As usual, term independence is assumed. This particular model is also referred to as 'document-likelihood' (Croft et al., 2001a). In a similar way we can think of $P(D_i|\bar{L}, Q)$ as the probability that D_i is generated from a model estimated on non relevant documents, which we can approximate by a model of the collection: $P(w|M_{\bar{R}}) \approx P(w|M_C)$. Since the vast majority of documents are not relevant, this seems a reasonable assumption. Substituting the generative estimates in the log-likelihood ratio results in:

$$\log \frac{P(D_i|L, Q)}{P(D_i|\bar{L}, Q)} \approx \sum_{w \in D_i} d_w \log \frac{P(w|M_R)}{P(w|M_C)} \tag{5.2}$$

where d_w is the term frequency of the word w in the document. Just like the BIR Model, it is difficult to estimate $P(w|M_R)$ for ad-hoc queries in the absence of relevance information. Applying maximum likelihood estimation on a short query would yield a very sparse language model. However, recently a new estimation technique has been developed to estimate $P(w|M_R)$ in a formal and effective way(Lavrenko and Croft, 2001). The so-called Relevance Model is based on estimating the joint distribution P(w,Q) by making use of term cooccurrence in the document collection. For tracking, estimation is easier, since there is at least one example story. Stories are usually considerably longer than the typical ad-hoc query.

Regarding score comparability, the situation is reversed with respect to the BIR model. Scores are independent of query length (a relevance model is a probability distribution function over the complete vocabulary) but are dependent on the length of the generated text, as can be seen in formula (5.2). We can illustrate this by comparing the scores of a document A and a document B, which consists of two copies of document A. Intuitively, both documents are equally relevant, but this is not reflected in the score. A simple correction is to normalize by document (story) length, making the score usable for ad-hoc and tracking tasks. Interestingly, a ratio of length normalized generative probabilities can also be interpreted as a difference between cross entropies:

$$\sum_w \frac{d_w}{\sum_w d_w} \log \frac{P(w|M_R)}{P(w|M_C)} = \sum_w \log P(w|M_{D_i}) \log P(w|M_R)$$
$$- \sum_w \log P(w|M_{D_i}) \log P(w|M_C) \tag{5.3}$$

Here M_{D_i} is a unigram model of document D_i, which is constructed on the basis of maximum likelihood estimation. The basic ranking component in (5.3) is the (negated) cross-entropy $H(M_{D_i}; M_R)$, which is normalized by the cross-entropy $H(M_{D_i}; M_C)$. We will refer to this length normalized likelihood ratio with the shorthand $NLLR(D; Q, C)$.

2.1.2   Query Likelihood.   Coming back to the original log-odds model, Bayes' rule can also be applied to derive a model where the log-odds of being relevant is described in terms of $P(Q_j|L, D)$, i.e. the probability that a query is described by Q_j when we know that a document described by D is relevant (Fuhr, 1992; Lafferty and Zhai, 2001).

$$\log \frac{P(L|D, Q_j)}{P(\bar{L}|D, Q_j)} = \log \frac{P(Q_j|L, D)}{P(Q_j|\bar{L}, D)} + \log \frac{P(L|D)}{P(\bar{L}|D)} \qquad (5.4)$$

Strictly spoken, this model describes the situation where there is one document and a number of queries submitted to the system.Still, the model can be used for document ranking provided that the document models are constructed in a similar manner and do not depend on document length. This time, the likelihood ratio computes how typical the query description Q_j is for document D in comparison to other query descriptions. Key element for the comparability of scores of different queries is the normalizing denominator $P(Q_j|\bar{L}, D)$. Again, there are multiple ways to estimate $P(Q_j|L, D)$. A query representation by a binary feature vector leads to the Binary Independence Indexing (BII) model (Fuhr, 1992), which is closely related to the first formulated probabilistic IR model of Maron and Kuhns (Maron and Kuhns, 1960). Because of estimation problems, these models have to our knowledge not been used for practical IR-tasks like ad-hoc queries or tracking. With regard to score comparability, these models should be normalized for query length in order to be used for tracking, the models can be used unchanged for ad-hoc tasks.

The query-likelihoods in (5.4) can also be estimated in a generative framework. We could think of $P(Q_j|L, D)$ as the probability that Q is generated as a sequence of terms from a model which is constrained by D and L. This means, we have a document with description D, which we know is relevant, so we can use this document as the basis for a generative language model and calculate the query likelihood. Analogously to the document-likelihood model (5.2), we assume term independence and approximate $P(Q_j|\bar{L}, D)$ by the marginal $P(Q)$:

$$\log \frac{P(L|D, Q_j)}{P(\bar{L}|D, Q_j)} = q_w \sum_{w \in Q_j} \log \frac{P(w|M_D)}{P(w|M_C)} + \frac{P(L|D)}{P(\bar{L}|D)} \qquad (5.5)$$

where q_w is the number of times word w appears in query Q. The prior probability of relevance should not be dropped this time, since it can be used to incorporate valuable prior knowledge, e.g. that a web-page with many inlinks has a high prior probability of relevance (Kraaij et al., 2002). This model is directly usable for the ad-hoc task, since scores are comparable across documents of different lengths, due to the maximum likelihood procedure, which is used to estimate $P(w|M_D)$. Usually, the denominator term $P(Q_j|\bar{L}, D)$ is dropped from the ranking formula, since it does not depend on a document property.

$$\log P(L|D, Q_j) = P(L|D) \sum_{w \in Q_j} q_w \log \frac{P(w|M_D)}{P(w|M_C)} \qquad (5.6)$$

This results in the basic language modeling approach (5.6) as formulated in (Hiemstra, 1998) and (Miller et al., 1999).

If we want to use model (5.5) for tracking, scores should be comparable across queries, therefore the denominator, which depends on the query, should not be dropped. In addition, scores have to be normalized for topic (=query) length[3], which leads again to a ranking formula consisting of the difference between two cross entropies (for simplicity, we assume a uniform prior and drop the prior odds of relevance term in (5.5)):

$$\frac{q_w}{\sum_w q_w} \sum_w \log \frac{P(w|D)}{P(w|M_C)} =$$
$$\sum_w \log P(w|M_{Q_j}) \log P(w|M_D) - \sum_w \log P(w|M_{Q_j}) \log P(w|M_C)$$
$$(5.7)$$

Here, the basic ranking component is the (negated) cross-entropy $H(M_Q; M_D)$, which is normalized by the cross-entropy $H(M_Q; M_C)$.

Concluding, the probabilistic formulation of the prototypical IR task, $P(L|D, Q)$, can be developed in two different ways; one starting from documents, the other one starting from queries. After applying Bayes' rule and transforming to log-odds, both variants can be rewritten to a sum of a likelihood ratio and the odds of the prior probability. The denominator in the likelihood ratio is a key element to ensure comparable scores of the events which are compared (document descriptions in the case of the document likelihood variant and query descriptions in the case of the query likelihood variant). Apart from the fact that the likelihoods of documents and queries have to be normalized in order to model $P(L|D, Q)$ (Bayes' rule), we have seen that we have to apply some corrections to account for differences in length, since the basic model is based on descriptions of similar length.

---

[3]Matching scores are already length normalized in the language model of Ponte and Croft, since queries are represented as a binary vector defined on the complete collection vocabulary (Ponte and Croft, 1998).

We summarize the length normalization aspects of the various models in table 5.1, the table lists 'yes' if the particular model inherently accounts for length differences and 'no' if an external length normalization is required.

Model name	query length normalization	document length normalization	reference
BIR	no	yes	Robertson & Sparck Jones
document likelihood ratio	yes	no	Lavrenko & Croft
BII	yes	no	Maron&Kuhns, Fuhr
query likelihood (ratio)	no	yes	Hiemstra, Miller et al.

Table 5.1.   Length normalization of probabilistic IR models

2.2   A single model for ad-hoc and tracking?

From an abstract matching point of view, there are no major differences between the tracking and ad-hoc task. There is some text, which describes the domain of interest of the user, and subsequently a list of documents has to be ranked according to relevance to that description. So, it is a valid question to ask, whether we could define a model, which works well for both tasks. As we have argued, such a model has to be insensitive to length differences both for queries and for documents. Indeed, it seems valid to say that a good tracking system would work well for ad-hoc tasks as well, since the additional constraint concerning score normalization across topics does not affect the rank order of the documents.

However, when we compare the tasks in more detail, there are certainly many differences between the ad-hoc and the tracking task. First of all, the "matching" situation is extremely asymmetric for the ad-hoc task: a query is usually very short in comparison with a document. Moreover, not all words in the query are about the domain of interest, some serve to formulate the query. There are no phrases like "Relevant documents discuss X" in TDT topics. The tracking task does not provide any query at all, just one or more example stories. In that respect, "matching" is much more symmetric for tracking. The asymmetry of the ad-hoc task is probably the reason why the query likelihood approach is so successful: a document contains a much larger foothold of data to estimate a language model than a query (Lafferty and Zhai, 2001). This preference is probably not so clear-cut for tracking. Indeed, BBN has experimented with both directions and found that they complement each other (Jin et al., 1999). Also, relevance in TDT is different from relevance in the traditional ad-hoc task, since TDT is concerned with events. Although the tracking task lacks supervised relevance feedback, unsupervised feedback (topic model adaptation) is allowed. In a way, this procedure is related to pseudo-feedback techniques in IR. However, the tracking task lacks the notion of the "top-N" documents, i.e. unsupervised feedback has to be based on absolute instead of relative scores, which is certainly more complicated.

In our experiments, we do not want to rule out specific models a-priori on the basis of the differences between ad-hoc and tracking, but instead will investigate whether probabilistic language models which are successful for the ad-hoc task can be adapted for tracking. We will study the necessity and relative effectiveness of normalization procedures. Therefore we will test both directions of the generative model for the tracking task.

2.3   Ranking with a risk metric: KL divergence

Recently, Lafferty and Zhai proposed a document ranking method based on a risk minimization framework(Lafferty and Zhai, 2001). As a possible instantiation of this framework, they suggest to use the relative entropy of Kullback-Leibler divergence between a distribution representing the query and a distribution the document $\Delta(M_Q||M_D)$ as a loss function. The KL divergence is a measure for the difference between two probability distributions over the same event space.

$$\Delta(P||Q) = \sum_{x \in X} P(x) \log \frac{P(x)}{Q(x)} \tag{5.8}$$

KL divergence has an intuitive interpretation, since the KL divergence is either zero when the probability distributions are identical or has a positive value, quantifying the difference between the distributions by the number of bits which are wasted by encoding events from the distribution P with a "code" based on distribution Q. However, KL also has some less attractive characteristics: it is not symmetric and does not satisfy the triangle inequality and thus is not a metric(Manning and Schütze, 1999).

The relationship between the KL divergence and language models for IR was initially discussed by Ng (Ng, 2000). The relationship of (5.7) with $\Delta(M_Q||M_D)$ is as follows:

$$\Delta(M_Q||M_D) = \sum_w P(w|M_Q) \log \frac{P(w|M_Q)}{P(w|M_D)} + \sum_w P(w|M_Q) \log \frac{P(w|M_C)}{P(w|M_C)} \tag{5.9}$$

after reformulation:

$$NLLR(Q; D, C) = \Delta(M_Q||M_C) - \Delta(M_Q||M_D) \tag{5.10}$$

It is tempting to interpret this equation as a subtraction of two values of a similar metric. However, this is invalid. Informally, we might interpret the generalized (or story length normalized) log likelihood ratio by taking a closer look at the two components: a score based on NLLR is high when $\Delta(M_Q||M_C)$ is high and $\Delta(M_Q||M_D)$ is low. This means that a story has a higher score when it contains specific terminology, i.e. is dissimilar from the background collection model and when its distribution is close to the topic distribution. For ad-hoc search, $\Delta(M_Q||M_D)$ is essentially equivalent to the length normalized query likelihood (5.6) since the query entropy

$$H(M_Q) = \sum_w P(w|M_Q) \log P(w|M_Q)$$

is a constant which does not influence document ranking. Several authors have presented KL divergence as a valid and effective ranking model for ad-hoc IR tasks (Ogilvie and Callan, 2001; Lavrenko et al., 2002b). They consider query likelihoods as a derived form of the more general KL divergence. Since we are looking for a general model, which is useful for both the ad-hoc and the tracking task, we will evaluate the KL-divergence measure for tracking in addition to the models presented in Section 2.

2.4   Parameter estimation

In the previous sections, we have only marginally talked about how unigram language models can be estimated. A straightforward method is to use maximum likelihood estimates, but just like language models for speech recognition, these estimates have to be smoothed. One obvious reason is to avoid to assign zero probabilities for terms that do not occur in a document because the term probabilities are estimated using maximum likelihood estimation. If a single query term does not occur in a document, this would amount to a zero probability of generating the query. There are two ways to cope with this. One could either model the query formulation process with a mixture model based on a document model and a background model or assume that all document models can in principle generate all terms in the vocabulary, but that irrelevant terms are generated with a very small probability.

A simple yet effective smoothing procedure, which has been successfully applied for ad-hoc tasks in linear interpolation (Miller et al., 1999; Hiemstra, 1998). Recently other smoothing techniques (Dirichlet, absolute discounting) have been evaluated (Zhai and Lafferty, 2001). These authors argued that smoothing actually has two roles: i) improving the probability estimates of a document model, which is especially important for short documents, and ii) "facilitating" the generation of common terms (a *tfidf* like function). Dirichlet smoothing appears to be good for the former role and linear interpolation (which is also called Jelinek-Mercer smoothing) is a good strategy for the latter function. In the experiments reported here, we have smoothed all generating models by linear interpolation. We did some preliminary experiments with Dirichlet smoothing, but did not find significant improvements.

Linear interpolation based smoothing of e.g. a topic model is defined as follows:

$$P(w|M_T) = \lambda P(w|M_T) + (1 - \lambda)P(w|M_C)) \qquad (5.11)$$

The probability of sampling a term w from topic model M_T is estimated on the set of training stories for M_T using a maximum likelihood estimator. This estimate is interpolated with the marginal $P(w|M_C)$ which is computed on a large background corpus (the entire TDT2 corpus).

2.5 Parametric score normalization

We have seen in Section 2.1 that it is easy to normalize generative probabilities for differences in length. Length normalized generative probabilities have a sound Information Theoretic interpretation. Length might not be the only topic dependent score dependency we we have to correct for. For example in a model which is based on the query likelihood: $NLLR(Q; D, C)$ with smoothing based on linear interpolation, the median of the score distribution for each topic will differ, since it is directly correlated with the average specificity of topic terms. Let's look at a couple of extreme cases of title queries from the TREC ad-hoc collection:

Query 403: osteoporosis A query of a single very specific word will yield document scores with high scores for those documents containing "osteoporosis". Since $P(w|M_D)$ is much higher than $P(w|M_C)$, the term weight is essentially determined by the ratio $\log(P(w|M_D)/P(w|M_C))$. Documents that do not contain the term "osteoporosis" do all have the constant score $\log((1 - \lambda))$ due to smoothing.

Query 410: Schengen agreement This query consists of a quite specific proper name and the fairly general term "agreement". The contribution of "Schengen" to the total score of a document is much higher than "agreement". If a document does not contain "Schengen" it will not be relevant, therefore the score distributions between relevant documents are well separated[4].

Query 422: heroic acts This query does not contain any rare terms, consequently document scores of relevant documents are lower.

Even though maximum likelihood procedures normalize for most of the length variations in topics for $NLLR(S; T, C)$ models, we still expect length

---

[4]This can clearly be seen in Figure 5.10, which we will discuss later.

dependencies in the scores because the generating models are smoothed. A longer topic will have a higher probability to have overlapping terms with stories than a shorter topic, which we expect to see in the scores.

The examples make clear that the score distribution of relevant documents (say the documents that contain most of the important terms) is dependent on the query. Queries formulated with mostly specific terms, will produce higher scores. The score distribution of non-relevant documents containing any of the query terms does also depend on the query. A perfect tracking system would produce separated distributions of relevant and non-relevant stories with equal medians and variances across topics, because of the single threshold. In reality, distributions are never perfectly separated (i.e. the situation of $Precision = Recall = 1$). But we might be able to normalize score distributions.

Score distributions have been studied by different researchers in the context of collection fusion (Baumgarten, 1997; Baumgarten, 1999; Manmatha et al., 2001) or adaptive filtering (Arampatzis and Hameren, 2001). These researchers tried to model score distributions of relevant and non relevant documents by fitting the observed data with parametric mixture models (e.g. Gaussian for relevant documents and exponential or Gamma for non relevant documents). If the parametric models are a good fit of the data, it just suffices to estimate the model parameters to calculate the probability of relevance at each point in the mixture distribution. Unfortunately, we have very little training data for the distribution of the relevant documents in the case of tracking, so an approach like (Manmatha et al., 2001) is not feasible here. Instead, we could try to just estimate the parameters of the model for the non-relevant stories and assume that the concentration of relevant documents in the right tail of this distribution is high and hope that there is a more or less similar inverse relationship between the density of non-relevant and relevant stories in this area of the curve. This normalization strategy was proposed and evaluated for TDT tasks by researchers at BBN (Jin et al., 1999). They modeled the distribution of non relevant documents by a Gaussian distribution, which can be justified by the central limit theorem for some of the models we have discussed. Indeed, the topic likelihood model score can be seen as a sum of independent random discrete variables. When a topic is long enough, the distribution can be approximated by the Gaussian distribution. It is unclear, whether this also holds for the story likelihood model, since the score is composed of a different number of variables for each story.

We implemented the Gaussian score normalization as follows: For each topic we calculated the scores of 5000 stories taken from the TDT Pilot corpus, we assumed these were non-relevant, since they predate the test topics[5]. We

---

[5]However, some of these stories could be considered relevant under a more liberal definition. Removal of these outliers has been reported to improve parameter estimation(Jin et al., 1999)

subsequently computed the mean and standard deviation of this set of scores. These distribution parameters were used to normalize the raw score τ in the following way:

$$\tau' = (\tau - \mu)/\sigma \tag{5.12}$$

3. Experiments

The generative models presented in the previous section will now be compared on two different test collections. Before presenting the actual data, the models will be briefly re-presented in Section 3.1 followed by background information about the test collections and test metrics that we used in Sections 3.2 and 3.3.

3.1 Experimental conditions

For our tracking experiments we plan to compare the following models:

Normalized Story likelihood ratio: $NLLR(S; T, C)$ This is the model described in (5.3), which can also be seen as a normalized cross-entropy.

Normalized Topic likelihood ratio: $NLLR(T; S, C)$ This is the model described in (5.7), also a normalized cross-entropy.

KL divergence: $\Delta(S\|T)$ **and** $\Delta(T\|S)$ Recently, several researchers have argued that the Kullback-Leibler divergence can be viewed as a general model underlying generative probabilistic models for IR.

The first two models are motivated by the probability ranking principle. Query likelihood ratio is based on a model for ranking queries, but can be used to rank documents. The KL divergence model is motivated as a loss function in a risk minimization framework, which does not explicitly model relevance.

Apart from comparing the effectiveness of the models as such, we will investigate the relative importance of several normalization components that are inherent to the models, for example the length normalization and the fact that the first two models compare entropy with respect to a common ground. We also evaluate the effectiveness of the Gaussian normalization and its interaction with different smoothing techniques.

3.2 The TDT evaluation method: DET curves

The TDT community has developed its own evaluation methodology. Because some of the plots further on in this article show results that were produced by this method, it is necessary to familiarize the reader with some of its details. All of the TDT tasks are cast as detection tasks. In contrast to TREC experiments, the complete test set for each topic of interest is annotated for relevance. Tracking performance is characterized in terms of the probability of miss and false alarm errors ($P_{Miss} = P(\neg ret|target)$ and $P_{FA} = P(ret|\neg target)$). To speak in terms of the more established and well-known precision and recall measures: a low P_{Miss} corresponds to high recall, while a low P_{FA} corresponds to high precision. These error probabilities are combined into a single cost measure C_{Det}, by assigning costs to miss and false alarm errors (Doddington and Fiscus, 2002):

$$C_{Det} = C_{Miss} \cdot P_{Miss} \cdot P_{target} + C_{FA} \cdot P_{FA} \cdot P_{\neg target} \qquad (5.13)$$

where C_{Miss} and C_{FA} are the costs of a miss and a false alarm respectively; P_{Miss} and P_{FA} are the conditional probabilities of a miss and a false alarm respectively; P_{target} and $P_{\neg target}$ are the a priori target probabilities ($P_{\neg target} = 1 - P_{target}$).

Then C_{Det} is normalized so that $(C_{Det})_{Norm}$ can be no less than one without extracting information from the source data:

$$(C_{Det})_{Norm} = \frac{C_{Det}}{min(C_{Miss} \cdot P_{target}, C_{FA} \cdot P_{\neg target})} \qquad (5.14)$$

Thus the absolute value of $(C_{Det})_{Norm}$ is a direct measure of the relative cost of the TDT system (Doddington and Fiscus, 2002).

The error probability is estimated by accumulating errors separately for each topic and by taking the average of the error probabilities over topics, with equal weight assigned to each topic. The following parameters were determined a-priori: $C_{Miss} = 1$, $C_{FA} = 0.1$, and $P_{target} = 0.02$. The Detection Error Tradeoff (DET) curve is the equivalent of a precision-recall plot for ad-hoc experiments. The DET plot shows what happens when the decision threshold of the tracking system performs a sweep from an (infinitely) high value to an (infinitely) low value. Obviously, at the beginning of the parameter sweep, the system will have zero false alarms but will not detect any relevant stories either and moves to the opposite end of the trade-off spectrum when the threshold is decreased. An example DET plot is Figure 5.1. A good curve in a DET plot is a relatively straight curve with a negative slope. The steeper the curve, the better.

We can prove that there is a simple relationship between the derivative of the DET curve (the slope of a tangent line at each point in the curve) and the probability of relevance. First we define P_{Miss} and P_{FA} as a function of the probability of relevance at rank n[6]:

$$P_{Miss}(n) = \frac{\int_1^N P_r(n) - \int_1^n P_r(n)}{\int_1^N P_r(n)} \tag{5.15}$$

$$P_{FA}(n) = \frac{\int_1^n (1 - P_r(n))}{\int_1^N (1 - P_r(n))} \tag{5.16}$$

In these equations, $P_r(n)$ is the probability of relevance at rank n, N is the total number of stories and R is the total number of relevant stories. Now the slope of the DET curve as a function of n can be defined as:

$$\frac{\partial P_{Miss}}{\partial n} \bigg/ \frac{\partial P_{FA}}{\partial n} = \frac{-P_r(n)}{1 - P_r(n)} \cdot \frac{\int_1^N (1 - P_r(n))}{\int_1^N P_r(n)} = \frac{-P_r(n)}{1 - P_r(n)} \cdot \frac{N - R}{R} \tag{5.17}$$

Formula (5.17) makes it easier to interpret the shape of a DET curve. A straight line means that the probability of relevance is constant for all ranks. An example of such a curve is the system that assigns scores to stories in a random fashion. If the curve is convex at some point, this means that the probability of relevance is decreasing with rank n. If the DET curve is concave at a certain point, the probability of relevance is increasing with n. A good normalized system would have a high relatively constant probability of relevance at the top ranks , followed by a short section where the probability of relevance gradually drops to a lower level and then a low relatively constant probability of relevance for the lower ranks. This would yield an extremely convex DET curve, consisting of two almost straight lines, not far from the axes of the plot and connected by a round convex segment where the probability of relevance drops from a high to a low value.

Note that the DET curves produced by the TDT evaluation software have custom scales - partly linear and partly logarithmic - in order to magnify certain areas of the curve. This has the effect that straight descending curves become concave in the logarithmic parts of the graph. This effect is doubled in the double-logarithmic part of the graph (the lower left corner). Straight curves are not transformed in the linear part of the graph (upper right part). The probability of relevance based definition of slope (5.17) is thus only valid for the linear - linear part of the graph. Still, convexness (or the absence of concave segments) indicates that the system produces well normalized score distributions.

---

[6]The DET curve as a function of the rank is identical to the DET curve as a function of the score. The story with the highest score gets rank 1.

3.3   Description of the test collections

Currently, the Linguistic Data Consortium (LDC) has three corpora available to support TDT research[7] (Cieri et al., 2000). The TDT-Pilot corpus contains newswire and transcripts of news broadcasts, all in English, and is annotated for 25 news events. The TDT2 and TDT3 corpora are multilingual (TDT2: Chinese and English, TDT3: Chinese, English, and Arabic) and contain both audio and text. ASR transcriptions and close captions of the audio data as well as automatic translations of the non-English data are also provided. TDT2 and TDT3 are annotated for 100 and 120 news events respectively.

We conducted several experiments on a subset of the TDT2 corpus to investigate the effect of stemming, the value of the smoothing parameter λ and a comparison of the two different orientations of generative model for tracking: generating the topic or the story. These experiments are reported in (Spitters and Kraaij, 2001). In this paper we describe experiments focused on score normalization. These experiments were conducted using the Jan-Apr part of the TDT2 corpus as training and development data, and the May-June part as the evaluation data (17 topics). Our study is limited to a simplified dataset, we work with the output of automatic speech recognizers, which is pre-segmented. The foreign language material has been processed by a Machine Translation system. We will not study source specific dependencies, i.e. we regard the dataset as a uniform and monolingual collection of news stories. All experiments were done with just one training story per topic.

Because experimentation with tracking is a time consuming process, we also simulated a tracking task by using TREC ad-hoc runs. We replicated an experiment presented by Ng (Ng, 2000) who simulated a binary classification task on TREC ad-hoc data with a fixed threshold. We will discuss further details in Section 3.5.

3.4   Experiments on TDT test collection

We will first present a comparison of the basic models which have $P(S|T)$ as their core element: topic likelihood models. All experiments are based on smoothing by linear interpolation with a fixed $\lambda = 0.85$.

Figure 5.1 shows the results of several variant models in a DET curve. The basic story likelihood model $P(S|T)$ is hardly better than a random system (with a constant $P_r(n)$). This is not surprising, since the likelihood is not normalized. The relative effect of the two normalization components i.e. normalizing by the a-priori story likelihood $NLLR(S; T, C)$ and story length normalization is quite different. Taking the likelihood ratio is the fundamental step,

---

[7]http://www.ldc.upenn.edu/Projects/TDT

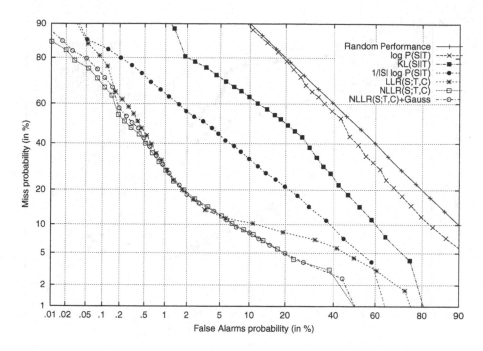

Figure 5.1. Comparison of different tracking models based on $P(S|T)$.

which realizes the *idf*-like term weighting and converts likelihood ranking to log-odds ranking (cf. formula (5.2)). Story length normalization removes some variance in the scores due to length differences and improves upon the LLR model for most threshold levels. Our basic tracking model (NLLR) combines both normalization steps.

Surprisingly, the performance of $\Delta(S||T)$ is even worse than the length normalized likelihood $H(S;T)$. The Kullback-Leibler divergence can be seen as an entropy normalized version of the latter: $\Delta(S||T) = -H(S;T) + H(S)$, whereas the (length) normalized log likelihood ratio normalizes by the cross-entropy with the background collection:

$NLLR(S;T,C) = -H(S;T) + H(S;C)$. Our experimental results make clear that normalizing with entropy deteriorates results, whereas normalizing with $P(S|C)$ (or its length normalized version $H(S;C)$) is an essential step in achieving good results.

We repeated the same experiments for the reversed orientation: generating the topics from the stories. Results are plotted in Figure 5.2. The relative performance of the $P(T|S)$ based variant models is roughly equivalent to the variants of the $P(S|T)$ models with the exception of the models, which are not based on a likelihood ratio. Again, the main performance improvement is achieved by normalizing $P(T|S)$ with the prior likelihood $P(T|C)$, which is

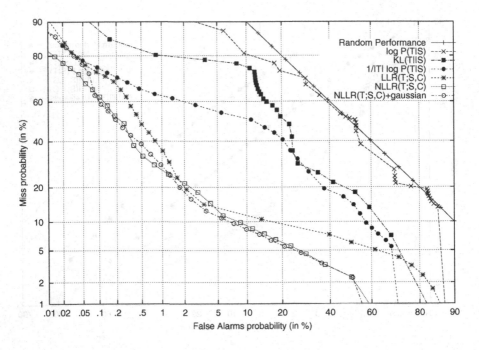

Figure 5.2.   Comparison of different tracking models based on $P(T|S)$.

equivalent to ranking by log-odds of being liked. Length normalization improves performance at both ends of the DET-plot and results in a straighter curve. The length normalized likelihood model $1/|T|\log P(T|S)$ performs worse than its reverse counterpart. This is due to the fact that scores are not normalized for average term specificity across topics. An even more striking phenomenon is the step-like behaviour of the unnormalized $P(T|S)$. This is due to the fact that the score distributions of plain $P(T|S)$ are linearly dependent on topic lengths and consequently their medians are located quite far apart. We will illustrate this effect by some boxplots.

A boxplot is a graphical summary of a distribution, showing its median, dispersion and skewness. Therefore boxplots are extremely helpful to compare many different distributions. A boxplot is defined by five datapoints: the smallest value, the first quartile, the median, the third quartile and the largest value. The area between the first and third quartile (interquartile range) is depicted by a box, with a line marking the median. (Figure 5.5 is a good example.) The boxplots in this paper also have whiskers that mark either the smallest or largest value or the area that extends 1.5 times the interquartile range from the first or third quartile.

Figures 5.3 and 5.4 show boxplots of the distributions of $NLLR(T; S, C)$ and $P(T|S)$ respectively. The first plot shows that the bodies of the distribu-

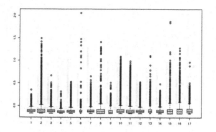

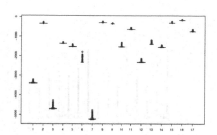

Figure 5.3. Score distributions of $NLLR(T; S, C)$

Figure 5.4. Score distributions of $P(T|S)$

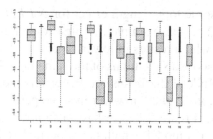

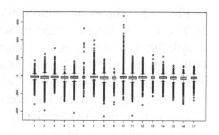

Figure 5.5. $KL(T\|S)$

Figure 5.6. $NLLR(S|T)$

tions for all topics are quite well aligned. The distributions are skewed and have a long right tail, because they are in fact mixtures of a large distribution of relevant stories and a small distribution of non-relevant stories with a higher median. Figure 5.4 gives an explanation why the DET plot curve of this model is so wobbly: the distributions of the individual topics do not even overlap in a few cases: lowering the threshold will bring in the stories of each topic as separate blocks. This means that the probability of relevance will increase and decrease locally as we decrease the threshold, causing convex and concave segments (cf. Section 3.2). Because the boxes are hardly visible in both cases, we show an example of a more dispersed distribution: $KL(T\|S)$ in Figure 5.5. The fact that the distributions lack a long right tail is a sign that relevant and non-relevant documents are probably not well separated. Finally, an example of well-aligned symmetrical distributions is $LLR(S; T, C)$ in Figure 5.6. The symmetry is due to the fact that scores are not length normalized, long stories that do not have word overlap with the topic will have high negative scores, long stories with good word overlap with the topic will have high positive scores.

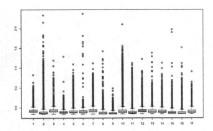

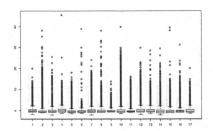

Figure 5.7. $NLLR(S; T, C)$ *Figure 5.8.* $NLLR(S; T, C)$ + Gaussian normalization

Figure 5.7 shows that indeed there is some topic length effect for $NLLR($ $S; T, C)$ as we hypothesized in Section 2.5. For example, the first topic has length 395 and the second has length 43, which results in lower scores for the bulk of the distribution. Figure 5.8 shows score distributions of the same model after applying Gaussian normalization. Indeed the boxes are better aligned, but differences are small. The normalization resulted however in some performance loss in the high precision area, cf. Figure 5.1. We have also applied Gaussian normalization to the $LLR(S; T, C)$ model, which is not normalized for story length. In this case, the Gaussian normalization deteriorated results, even though medians were well aligned. We think that this is due to the fact that the variance in the score distribution is due to differences in length, which can be normalized in a more effective way. Gaussian normalization of the model in the reverse orientation: $NLLR(T; S, C)$ had similar effects: a small performance loss in the high precision area and for the rest roughly equivalent to the not Gaussian normalized version (cf. Figure 5.2). Further investigation is needed in order to understand why the Gaussian normalization is not effective. There are several possibilities: i) scores are already quite well normalized, ii) the score distribution differs too much from the normal distribution, or iii) outliers hurt the estimation of the distribution parameters.

Since both orientations of the NLLR model work well, there might be some potential to improve results by a combination of the scores of both models. We did some initial experiments which were based on a simple score averaging procedure. A side effect of this method is that scores become symmetric. It is exactly this symmetrical NLLR model that had proven to be effective for the TDT detection task (Spitters and Kraaij, 2002). The resulting system performed worse than each of the components, but after applying Gaussian normalization the system was a little bit more effective than a model based on just a single orientation. Further research is needed to find an optimal combination/normalization procedure.

3.5   Simulating tracking on TREC Ad-Hoc data

We complemented the runs on the TDT2 corpus with experiments on TREC ad-hoc data. The main reason is that most data was available already, and provided a rich resource for research on score normalization. Since ad-hoc runs output a list of scored documents, we could simulate a $NLLR(Q; D; C)$ tracking system, by placing a threshold. We applied two methods to implement this idea. The first method is based on trec_eval, the second on the TDT evaluation software.

The basic idea is to evaluate all 50 topics of an ad-hoc run by a single threshold. Standard trec_eval does not support this kind of evaluation. However, it can be simulated by replacing all topic-id's in both the runs and the qrel file by a single topic-id. Of course, this evaluation is different from TDT eval, since this method does not involve topic averaging, so topics with many relevant documents will dominate the results. Still, this evaluation is a quick and easy method to assess score stability across topics when TDT evaluation software is not available. We tested this method on the TREC-8 ad-hoc test collection, for both title and full queries.

run name	title (tracking)	title (ad-hoc)	full (tracking)	full (ad-hoc)
$P(Q\|D)$	0.0874	0.2322	0.1358	0.2724
$LLR(Q; D, C)$	0.1334	0.2321	0.1581	0.2723
$NLLR(Q; D, C)$	0.1294	0.2324	0.1577	0.2723
$\Delta(Q\|\|D)$	0.0845	0.2322	0.1356	0.2723

Table 5.2. Tracking simulation on TREC-8 Ad-Hoc collection (mean average precision)

Table 5.2 shows the results of our experiments, using four weighting schemes: straight (log) query likelihood, log-likelihood ratio, normalized log-likelihood ratio and Kullback-Leibler . We see that the influence of the particular normalization strategy is quite strong on the tracking task, while - as was expected - there is no influence on the ad-hoc task. Indeed the normalization strategies just add topic specific constants, which do not influence the ad-hoc results. There seems to be no big difference between LLR and NLLR, but that might be due to the averaging strategy, which is not weighted across topics. NLLR is a bit less effective than LLR for title queries, but that can be explained by the difference in query term specificity for short (1-3 word) queries. A single word TREC title query must be very specific (e.g. topic 403: "osteoporosis") in order to be effective. Two and three word queries often use less specific words and thus their scores will be lower in the NLLR case, which is normalized for query length. Still two or three word queries can be just as effective as one word queries, so there is no reason to down-normalize their scores. This effect

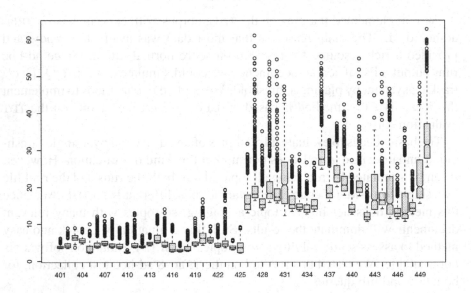

Figure 5.9.   Tracking simulation: LLR

was confirmed by the boxplots for these runs, shown in Figures 5.9 and 5.10. The title queries with the highest NLLR scores (403 and 424) are single word queries. The boxplots show a mix of topics to visualize the topic normalization, the score distributions of the first 25 topics (topic 401-425) are based on title queries, the rightmost 25 distributions are based on the full queries (topic 426-450).

The Kullback Leibler divergence based run really performs disappointingly. We can conclude that KL as such is not a suitable model for tracking, at least not for models estimated with maximum likelihood estimation.

We also ran the TDT evaluation scripts on the TREC data after applying a conversion step. The difference with the previous method, is that the TDT evaluation procedure averages P_{FA} and P_{Miss} across topics. The results of the run based on the full topics are shown in plot 5.11. The best performance is reached by NLLR, which is just a bit better than LLR. Again KL yields a very disappointing result.

4.   Discussion

One of the main challenges of designing a tracking system is to normalize scores across topics. Since topics are of a very different nature, and there is no direct relationship between the score distribution of the models and prob-

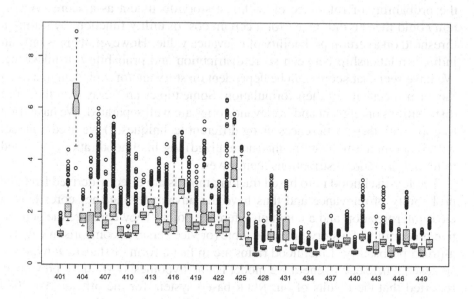

Figure 5.10. Tracking simulation: NLLR

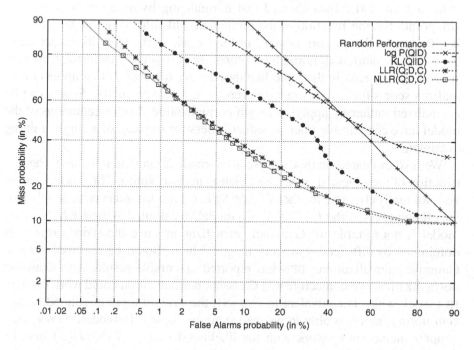

Figure 5.11. DET plot of tracking simulation on the TREC 8 ad-hoc full topics

ability of relevance, this is quite a hard task. An ideal system would produce the probability of relevance of each test story/document as a score. A system could then be optimized for a certain cost or utility function, by setting a threshold on a certain probability of relevance value. However, there is only an indirect relationship between score distribution and probability of relevance. We have seen that scores can be dependent on story and/or topic length and on the term specificity of their formulation. Some topics are "easy" i.e. the score distributions of relevant and irrelevant stories are well separated. We have tried to cope with these differences using different techniques, i) we used a model with inherent normalization: the (normalized) log likelihood ratio ii) we tried to model the score distributions themselves.

The log-likelihood ratio based tracking models are directly derived from the probability of relevance and thus have the advantage that the scores have a clear interpretation and a common reference point. They compare the generative probability of a story given the topic (or vice versa) in comparison with the a-priori probability. Likelihood ratios are in fact a form of statistical hypothesis tests, where each generative model is one hypothesis. We have previously reported that the results of our NLLR based system for the official TDT 2000 tracking task were competitive (Spitters and Kraaij, 2001). We therefore conclude that language models can form the basis for an effective tracking system indeed, provided that the models are properly normalized. Our experiments with TDT and TREC data showed that normalizing by an a-priori model is a key point. But the function of the normalizing likelihood in the denominator is different for the two orientations of the model. In the story likelihood case, the $P(S|C)$ component normalizes scores for across story differences in term specificity, whereas in the topic likelihood case, the $P(T|C)$ component normalizes scores for across topic differences in term specificity. Scores can be normalized further by applying length normalization. Both orientations of the model have comparable tracking effectiveness for the case of a single training document.

We also evaluated methods for score normalization which try to fit the distribution of non-relevant stories by a Gaussian distribution. This normalization was not really effective for the $NLLR(S; T, C)$ model and even seriously hurt the effectiveness of the $LLR(S; T, C)$ model. We think that the $LLR(S; T, C)$ model is not suitable for Gaussian normalization since the score variance is dominated by differences in story length, which should be removed prior to Gaussian normalization. BBN has reported favourable results with Gaussian normalization. We conjecture that Gaussian normalization could work for their IR model, which is equivalent to $P(T|S)$; the straight topic likelihood. Gaussian normalization is able to normalize across topic differences. However, a simpler method is to work with the likelihood ratio $P(T|S)/P(S)$ instead. After all, unlike ad-hoc the denominator $P(S)$ is not a constant.

Despite the intuitive appeal of KL - measuring the dissimilarity between distributions - our experiments with KL for tracking yielded disappointing results for both orientations $\Delta(S||T)$ and $\Delta(T||S)$. The Kullback-Leibler divergence has usually been proposed in an ad-hoc query-likelihood context. In that case KL reduces to pure query-likelihood, since the normalizing entropy $H(Q)$ in the KL divergence can be discarded because it is a constant. This cannot be done in a tracking context and we have seen that normalizing a cross entropy by its entropy is not effective in a tracking context. We have also shown that normalizing by the prior probability of a topic as measured by its cross entropy with the collection model is effective. Informally we could say that the KL divergence based scores are not properly normalized. The problem of using KL divergence for tracking is that the scores lack a common point of reference. Dissimilarity is measured on the basis of different models and since KL is not a metric, these scores cannot be compared. A more formal criticism on the use of KL divergence for tracking is that KL based models lack the notion of relevance. We have seen that both orientations of the normalized log likelihood ratio, which are direct derivations of probability of relevance based ranking are effective for tracking.

This analysis has been recently confirmed by independent research in the area of story link detection (Lavrenko et al., 2002a). Lavrenko found that pure KL is not effective for story link detection and proposed the so-called "Clarity-adjusted KL" topic similarity measure to correct for the fact that KL does not concentrate on informative (in the *idf* sense) terms when computing the (dis)similarity score. This adjusted KL measure is defined as $-\Delta(T||S) + Clarity(T)$, where clarity is defined as $\Delta(T||C)$ (Cronen-Townsend et al., 2002). Indeed, when comparing this definition to formula (5.10), the Clarity-adjusted KL divergence seems to be equivalent[8] to the normalized log-likelihood ratio. The NLLR similarity measure can thus be motivated by two frameworks: i) direct derivation from the log-odds of relevance ii) clarity adjusted version of KL divergence.

We also evaluated the query-likelihood models by a simulation of the tracking task on the TREC-8 ad-hoc collection. We know that there is a real difference between ad-hoc topics and TDT topics, this difference is one of the reasons that score normalization effectiveness differs across these tasks. TDT topics are just stories describing a particular event. Ad-hoc topics are structured queries which are stated in a particular jargon. The bag-of-words approach we took for ad-hoc query construction showed a clearly visible difference between title queries and full queries. Even our best normalization strategy (NLLR) could not "smooth out" the differences in score distributions between these two types of

---

[8]Note however that in Lavrenko's framework, topic models are estimated using the relevance model technique.

queries. We plan to develop topic-type (e.g. title versus full) specific query distribution estimation methods, which we hope will enable us to further normalize scores.

5.   Conclusions

Our aim was to find generative probabilistic models that work well both for the ad-hoc task and the tracking task, because we realized that a tracking system puts just one additional constraint on matching function: across topic comparability of scores. With the probability ranking principle as a starting point, we reviewed two lines of probabilistic modeling, either based on the document likelihood ratio or the query likelihood ratio. We evaluated variants of both models, based on length normalization and Gaussian normalization. We found that both orientations of the log-likelihood ratio work well. The essential normalization component in the NLLR model is the a-priori likelihood (or cross entropy) of the generated text in the denominator. Effectiveness can be further enhanced by length normalization.

We have not been able to show performance increase by Gaussian normalization. The NLLR model is related to the negated KL divergence since both measures are based on the cross entropy. We found that KL divergence is not an effective scoring function for tracking, because the scores are not comparable across topics (for $\Delta(T||S)$) or across stories (for $\Delta(S||T)$). The principal reason seems to be the fact that the application of KL divergence as a similarity measure for the tracking task lacks normalization with respect to a common reference distribution.

Acknowledgements

We would like to thank Kenney Ng for providing details about his normalization experiments with ad-hoc data and Jon Fiscus for implementing the TREC2TDT conversion script.

References

Arampatzis, A. and Hameren, A. (2001). The score-distributional threshold optimization for adaptive binary classification tasks. In (Croft et al., 2001b), pages 285–293.

Baumgarten, C. (1997). A probabilistic model for distributed information retrieval. In Belkin, N. J., Narasimhalu, A. D., and Willet, P., editors, *Proceedings of the 20th Annual International ACM SIGIR Conference on Research and Development in Information Retrieval (SIGIR '97)*, pages 258–266. ACM Press.

Baumgarten, C. (1999). A probabilistic solution to the selection and fusion problem in distributed information retrieval. In (Hearst et al., 1999), pages 246–253.

Beaulieu, M., Baeza-Yates, R., Myaeng, S. H., and Jarvelin, K., editors (2002). *Proceedings of the 25th Annual International ACM SIGIR Conference on Research and Development in Information Retrieval (SIGIR 2002)*. ACM Press.

Cieri, C., Graff, D., Liberman, M., Martey, N., and Strassel, S. (2000). Large multilingual broadcast news corpora for cooperative research in topic detection and tracking: The TDT2 and TDT3 corpus efforts. *Proceedings of the Language Resources and Evaluation Conference (LREC2000)*.

Croft, B., Callan, J., and Lafferty, J. (2001a). Workshop on language modeling and information retrieval. *SIGIR FORUM*, 35(1).

Croft, W., Harper, D., D.H.Kraft, and Zobel, J., editors (2001b). *Proceedings of the 24th Annual International ACM SIGIR Conference on Research and Development in Information Retrieval (SIGIR 2001)*. ACM Press.

Cronen-Townsend, S., Zhou, Y., and Croft, W. (2002). Predicting query performance. In (Beaulieu et al., 2002).

Doddington, G. and Fiscus, J. (2002). The 2002 topic detection and tracking (TDT2002) task definition and evaluation plan. Technical Report v. 1.1, National Institute of Standards and Technology.

Fuhr, N. (1992). Probabilistic models in information retrieval. *The Computer Journal*, 35(3):233–245.

Hearst, M., Gey, F., and Tong, R., editors (1999). *Proceedings of the 22th Annual International ACM SIGIR Conference on Research and Development in Information Retrieval (SIGIR '99)*. ACM Press.

Hiemstra, D. (1998). A linguistically motivated probabilistic model of information retrieval. In Nicolaou, C. and Stephanides, C., editors, *Research and Advanced Technology for Digital Libraries - Second European Conference, ECDL'98, Proceedings*, number 1513 in Lecture Notes in Computer Science. Springer Verlag.

Hiemstra, D. and Kraaij, W. (1999). Twenty-one at TREC-7: Ad hoc and cross language track. In Voorhees, E. M. and Harman, D. K., editors, *The Seventh Text REtrieval Conference (TREC-7)*, volume 7. National Institute of Standards and Technology, NIST. NIST Special Publication 500-242.

Jin, H., Schwartz, R., Sista, S., and Walls, F. (1999). Topic tracking for radio, tv broadcast and newswire. In *Proceedings of the DARPA Broadcast News Workshop*.

Kraaij, W., Pohlmann, R., and Hiemstra, D. (2000). Twenty-one at TREC-8: using language technology for information retrieval. In (Voorhees and Harman, 2000). NIST Special Publication 500-246.

Kraaij, W., Westerveld, T., and Hiemstra, D. (2002). The importance of prior probabilities for entry page search. In (Beaulieu et al., 2002).

Lafferty, J. and Zhai, C. (2001). Probabilistic IR models based on document and query generation. In Callan, J., Croft, B., and Lafferty, J., editors, *Proceedings of the workshop on Language Modeling and Information Retrieval*.

Lavrenko, V., adn Edward DeGuzman, J. A., LaFlamme, D., Pollard, V., and Thomas, S. (2002a). Relevance models for topic detection and tracking. In *Proceedings of HLT 2002*.

Lavrenko, V., Choquette, M., and Croft, W. (2002b). Cross-lingual relevance models. In (Beaulieu et al., 2002).

Lavrenko, V. and Croft, W. (2001). Relevance-based language models. In (Croft et al., 2001b).

Lewis, D. D. (1998). Naive (Bayes) at forty: The independence assumption in informatiion retrieval. In C.Nedellec and Rouveirol, C., editors, *Proceedings of ECML-98, 10th European Conference on Machine Learning*, pages 4–15.

Manmatha, R., Rath, T., and Feng, F. (2001). Modelling score distributions for combining the outputs of search engines. In (Croft et al., 2001b), pages 267–275.

Manning, C. and Schutze, H. (1999). *Foundations of Statistical Natural Language Processing*. MIT press.

Maron, M. and Kuhns, J. (1960). On relevance, probabilistic indexing and information retrieval. *Journal of the Association for Computing Machinery*, 7:216–244.

Miller, D. R. H., Leek, T., and Schwartz, R. M. (1999). A hidden markov model information retrieval system. In (Hearst et al., 1999), pages 214–221.

Ng, K. (2000). A maximum likelihood ratio information retrieval model. In (Voorhees and Harman, 2000). NIST Special Publication 500-246.

Ogilvie, P. and Callan, J. (2001). Experiments using the lemur toolkit. In (Voorhees and Harman, 2001).

Ponte, J. M. and Croft, W. B. (1998). A language modeling approach to information retrieval. In Croft, W., Moffat, A., van Rijsbergen, C., Wilkinson, R., and Zobel, J., editors, *Proceedings of the 21th Annual International ACM SIGIR Conference on Research and Development in Information Retrieval (SIGIR '98)*, pages 275–281. ACM Press.

Robertson, S. (1977). The probability ranking principle in IR. *Journal of Documentation*, 33:294–304.

Robertson, S. and Sparck Jones, K. (1976). Relevance weighting of search terms. *Journal of the American Society for Information Science*, 27(3):129–146.

Sparck Jones, K., Walker, S., and Robertson, S. (2000). A probabilistic model of information retrieval: development and comparative experiments. *ipm*, 36(6).

Spitters, M. and Kraaij, W. (2001). Using language models for tracking events of interest over time. In *Proceedings of the Workshop on Language Models for Information Retrieval (LMIR2001)*.

Spitters, M. and Kraaij, W. (2002). Unsupervised event clustering in multilingual news streams. *Proceedings of the LREC2002 Workshop on Event Modeling for Multilingual Document Linking*, pages 42–46.

Voorhees, E. M. and Harman, D. K., editors (2000). *The Eigth Text REtrieval Conference (TREC-8)*, volume 8. National Institute of Standards and Technology, NIST. NIST Special Publication 500-246.

Voorhees, E. M. and Harman, D. K., editors (2001). *The Tenth Text REtrieval Conference (TREC-2001), notebook*, volume 10. National Institute of Standards and Technology, NIST.

Wayne, C. (2000). Multilingual topic detection and tracking: Successful research enabled by corpora and evaluation. *Proceedings of the Language Resources and Evaluation Conference (LREC2000)*, pages 1487–1494.

Zhai, C. and Lafferty, J. (2001). A study of smoothing methods for language models applied to ad hoc information retrieval. In (Croft et al., 2001b).

Chapter 6

A PROBABILISTIC APPROACH TO TERM TRANSLATION FOR CROSS-LINGUAL RETRIEVAL

Jinxi Xu

BBN Technologies, 10 Moulton St
Cambridge, MA 02138
jxu@bbn.com

Ralph Weischedel

BBN Technologies, 10 Moulton St
Cambridge, MA 02138
weisched@bbn.com

Abstract

This work has three aspects. One is to describe a probabilistic approach to term translations for cross-lingual IR. We will show that such an approach, when used with a probabilistic retrieval model, can produce better retrieval than non-probabilistic techniques such as structural query translation (Pirkola, 1998) and Machine Translation. We will also show that parallel corpora and manual lexicons are complementary and their combination is essential to high performance CLIR. The second aspect of this work is to empirically measure CLIR performance as a function of the sizes of the bilingual resources available for estimating translation probabilities. A measurement like this is useful for two reasons. First, it can help to predict CLIR performance for a new language pair. Second, it can be used as a guidance on how much more data to acquire if existing resources cannot meet a target performance level. The third aspect is to describe a technique that can potentially reduce the cost of manually creating a parallel corpus. Such a technique will be useful for language pairs with no or little parallel text.

1.   Introduction

Statistical language modeling has become an important technique in information retrieval (IR). In Cross-lingual IR (CLIR), queries and documents are

W.B. Croft and J. Lafferty (eds.), Language Modeling for Information Retrieval, 125–140.
© 2003 *Kluwer Academic Publishers.*

in different languages. An important problem in applying statistical language modeling to CLIR is how to translate terms in different languages. This work describes a probabilistic approach to term translation, which derives probabilistic term translations from widely available resources such as manual bilingual lexicons and parallel corpora.

This work has three aspects. One is to empirically compare the proposed approach with two popular non-probabilistic techniques, structural query translation and machine translation (MT). The major difference between our approach and structural query translation is that ours uses translation probabilities while the other treats all translations as equals. A comparison between the two approaches will show the advantages and disadvantages of using probabilistic term translation for CLIR. The major difference between the MT-based technique and our approach is that the former does not use multiple translations for a term while the latter does. A comparison between them will show the advantages and disadvantages of using multiple translations in CLIR. The basic idea of structural query translation was used by a number of studies (Pirkola, 1998; Ballesteros and Croft, 1998; Sperer and Oard, 2000; Hull, 1997). Past studies that used MT systems for CLIR include Oard, 1998; Ballesteros and Croft, 1998.

A common problem with past research on MT-based CLIR is that a direct comparison of retrieval results with other approaches is difficult because the lexical resources inside most commercial MT systems cannot be directly accessed. To overcome the problem we will use a technique to hypothesize the term translations inside a MT system based on the text it translated. By treating the translated text as a pseudo-parallel corpus, we can automatically induce a statistical bilingual lexicon and use it with our system for cross-lingual retrieval. That will establish a lower bound on the performance of our approach if it had direct access to the translation resources in the MT system.

The second aspect of this work is to empirically measure the CLIR performance of the probabilistic translation approach as a function of the sizes of the bilingual lexicon and parallel corpus available for probability estimation. Such a measurement will be useful for predicting CLIR performance for new language pairs and for guiding the acquisition of more resources if existing resources cannot meet a desired performance goal.

The third aspect is to describe and evaluate a technique to reduce the amount of text humans have to translate in manual creation of a parallel corpus. As shown by empirical results, parallel text is critical to high performance CLIR. Such a technique will be useful for language pairs that have no or little existing bilingual text.

In section 2 we describe the CLIR retrieval model used in this work. Section 4 discusses related work. Section 3 describes our procedure of estimating translation probabilities and the lexical resources we used in our experiments.

Section 5 describes the test collections used in our experiments and how they were processed. The test collections are the TREC5&6 Chinese tracks, the TREC9 cross-lingual track and the TREC5 Spanish track (Voorhees and Harman, 1997; Voorhees and Harman, 1998; Voorhees and Harman, 2001). Section 6 compares CLIR performance with a monolingual baseline. Sections 7 and 8 compare our approach with structural query translation and MT-based CLIR. In section 9 we empirically study the relationship between CLIR performance and the sizes of translation resources. Section 10 describes a technique to reduce the amount of the text humans need to translate in manual creation of a parallel corpus. Section 11 summarizes this work.

2.   A Probabilistic Model for CLIR

The basic function of an IR system is to rank documents against a query according to relevance. By Bayes' rule,

$$P(Doc\ is\ rel|\,Q) = \frac{P(Doc\ is\ rel)P(Q|Doc\ is\ rel)}{P(Q)}$$

where *Doc* is a document and *Q* is a query. *P(Doc is rel)* is the prior probability of relevance for *Doc*, which we assume to be a constant.[1] $P(Q)$ is the prior probability that Q is generated; since Q is a constant, $P(Q)$ has no effect on document ranking. We can therefore rank documents by $P(Q \mid Doc\ is\ rel)$, the probability that query Q is generated given document *Doc*.

We use Hidden Markov Models to simulate the process of query generation. Rabiner, 1989, provided an excellent introduction to HMM theory. For convenience, we will assume that queries are in English and documents are in Chinese. We assume two states, the *General English state* and the *document state*. In the General English state, an English word for the query is generated; it may or may not describe the content of the document. In the document state, a word from the Chinese document is chosen and translated to an English word for the query. The following pseudo-code describes the query generation process.

```
Until all query words are generated
{
  Toss a biased coin with probabilities α for heads and
  1 − α for tails. Enter the General English state if it is
  heads and the document state otherwise.

  General English state: Pick an English word from the English
```

---

[1]Previous studies show that all documents are not equal. Longer documents in the TREC corpora, for example, are more likely to be relevant than short ones Singhal et al., 1996. We ignore this issue because it is not a concern in this study.

```
vocabulary according to a probability distribution.

Document state: Pick a Chinese word from the document
according to a probability distribution and translate it
to an English word according to another probability
distribution.
}
```

To minimize the need for training data, we estimate the parameters as follows:

- The parameter α is a constant. We fix it at 0.3 in this study, based on prior experience.

- In the General English (*GE*) state, we estimate the probability distribution as follows:

$$P(e|GE) = freq(e, GE)/|GE|$$

where *freq(e, GE)* is the frequency of English word e in an English corpus and $|GE|$ is the size of the English corpus. Any large English corpus can be used for this purpose. In this study, we used TREC volumes 1-5 of English data.

- In the document state (*Doc*), we estimate the probability distribution as follows:

$$P(c|Doc) = freq(c, Doc)/|Doc|$$

where *freq(c, Doc)* is the frequency of Chinese word c in *Doc* and $|Doc|$ is the length of the document.

- The probability of translation to an English word e given a Chinese word c, $P(e|c)$, depends on c and e only. In section 3, we will discuss how to estimate the translation probabilities from parallel texts and from bilingual lexicons.

With these assumptions, it is easy to verify that:

$$P(Q|Doc) = \prod_{e \, in \, Q} (aP(e|GE) + (1-a) \sum_{chinese \, words \, c} P(c|Doc)P(e|c))$$

This cross-lingual retrieval model is an extension of the monolingual retrieval model proposed by Miller et al., 1999. The model assumes that the translation of a term is independent of the document and query contexts in order to deal with data sparseness.

3. Estimating Term Translation Probabilities

We used two types of resources in estimating term translation probabilities, manual bilingual lexicons and parallel corpora. For manual lexicons, we assume uniform translation probabilities. That is, if a Chinese word c has n translations e_1 to e_n in a lexicon, we assume $P(e_i|c) = 1/n$.

For parallel corpora, we use the statistical machine translation models described by Brown et al., 1993, to automatically derive probabilistic term translations. We used the WEAVER system developed by Lafferty, 1999, for this purpose. The WEAVER system implemented three of the five models proposed by Brown. Model 1 was used in this work for its efficiency. In order to keep the size of the induced lexicon manageable, a threshold (0.01) was used to discard low probability translations.

Given multiple translation sources, separate probability estimates for individual sources are combined using a mixture model to produce a single probability estimate for a pair of terms:

$$P(e|c) = \sum_{s_i} \beta(s_i) P_{s_i}(e|c)$$

where s_i's are lexical sources (manual lexicons or parallel corpora), $\beta(s_i)$'s are mixture weights ($\sum \beta(s_i) = 1$) and $P_{s_i}(e|c)$'s are probability estimates from individual sources.

In this work, we used three lexical sources for estimating translation probabilities for Chinese CLIR using English queries:

- The LDC lexicon. It contains 86,000 English entries, 137,000 Chinese entries and 240,000 translation pairs. It is available from the Linguistic Data Consortium (LDC).

- The CETA lexicon. it contains 35,000 English entries, 202,000 Chinese entries and 517,000 translation pairs. It can be obtained through the MRM Corporation, Kensingston, MD.

- The HKNews (Hong Kong SAR News) parallel corpus. It consists of 18,000 pairs of documents in English and Chinese, with about 6 million English words. The corpus is available from LDC. An algorithm developed in-house was used to align the corpus, resulting in 230,000 pairs of sentences.

In our experiments, we gave each source a weight 1/3. In principle, the mixture weights could be adjusted using training queries to optimize CLIR performance. This was not done because it is not a focus of this work. Table 6.1 shows the statistics of the lexical sources.

Lexical Source	English Terms	Chinese Terms	Translation Pairs
LDC	86,000	137,000	240,000
CETA	35,000	202,000	517,000
HKNews	21,000	75,000	860,000
Combined	104,997	305,103	1,490,000

Table 6.1.   Table 1: Statistics about lexical sources. HKNews is a statistically derived lexicon. The combined lexicon is a combination of LDC, CETA and HKNews. English words are stemmed.

4.   Related Work

Structural query translation was proposed by Pirkola, 1998, whose basic idea can be traced to an earlier study (Hull, 1997). It has been used in a number of studies, including Sperer and Oard, 2000; Ballesteros and Croft, 1998. This technique treats translations of a query term as synonyms of the term: occurrences of the Chinese translations of an English term in the Chinese documents are treated as instances of the English term. The technique is typically applied with a TF.IDF retrieval model.

Studies that used MT systems for CLIR include Oard, 1998; Ballesteros and Croft, 1998. As discussed earlier, direct comparisons with other techniques have been a problem because lexicons in most MT systems are inaccessible. McCarley, 1999, studied both query and document translations and concluded the combination of the two translations can improve retrieval performance.

The use of statistical language modeling techniques for IR has appeared in a number of studies (Ponte, 1998; Berger and Lafferty, 1999; Miller et al., 1999). Our CLIR model is similar to a few other models in that all treat query generation as statistical language generation. One such model was proposed by Hiemstra and de Jong, 1999. A difference is that our model makes use of corpus statistics of the query language while Hiemstra's uses the corpus statistics of the document terms. Similar to this work, Hiemstra and de Jong, 1999 also compared a number of approaches to query translation, but that work was conducted with different objectives.

Brown et al., 1993 described five statistical models for machine translation whose parameters can be derived through automatic alignment of the words in a parallel corpus. Among the parameters in the models are translation probabilities between terms in two different languages, which were used in this work for statistical term translation for CLIR. The models, numbered 1, 2, 3, 4 and 5, differ in the complexity of the alignment scheme used. The more complex models in general produce better word alignments and as a result more accurate translation probabilities than the simpler models, but they incur a much higher computational cost. Our prior, unpublished experimental results using models 1, 2 and 3 showed that for the purpose of CLIR, the simplest model (i.e. model 1) usually suffices. All experiments in this work used model 1.

5.   Test Collections

Several test corpora were used in our experiments: TREC5 Chinese track (TREC5C), TREC6 Chinese track (TREC6C), TREC9 cross-lingual track (TREC9X) and TREC5 Spanish track (TREC5S). TREC5C, TREC6C and TREC9X consist of Chinese documents with queries in English and Chinese. Having two versions of the same queries allows both monolingual and cross-lingual experiments. TREC5S consists of Spanish documents with queries in English and Spanish. English stemming used the Porter stemmer (Porter, 1980) and Spanish stemming used the stemmer described by Xu and Croft, 1998. Unless specified otherwise, all three fields (title, description and narrative) of the TREC topics were used in query formulation. Table 6.2 shows statistics about the test corpora.

Corpus	Query language	Doc language	Query count	Doc count
TREC5C	English	Chinese	28	164,789
TREC6C	English	Chinese	26	164,789
TREC9X	English	Chinese	25	127,938
TREC5S	English	Spanish	25	172,952

Table 6.2. Statistics about test collections.   TREC5C=TREC5 Chinese track. TREC6C=TREC6 Chinese track. TREC9X=TREC9 Crosslingual track; TREC5S=TREC5 Spanish track.

For Chinese text segmentation, we used a simple dictionary-based algorithm. A list of valid Chinese words was obtained by combining the Chinese entries in the LDC and CETA lexicons. To segment Chinese text, the algorithm examines every substring of 2 or more characters and treats it as a word if it appears in the Chinese word list. In addition, a single Chinese character is also treated as a word if it is not part of any of the words recognized in the first step. The goal of the algorithm is to optimize cross-lingual performance, since it allows as many matches between English terms and Chinese terms as possible. For monolingual retrieval in Chinese, however, it has been shown that the best search strategy is to use a combination of bigrams and unigrams of Chinese characters (Kwok, 1997). That strategy was used in our monolingual experiments in order to produce the strongest monolingual baseline.

Throughout this paper, we will use the TREC average non-interpolated precision to measure retrieval performance (Voorhees and Harman, 1997).

6.   Comparing CLIR with Monolingual Baseline

Table 6.3 shows the retrieval results of our CLIR system on TREC5C and TREC9X. Our monolingual results were obtained using Miller et al's HMM monolingual retrieval system (Miller et al., 1999). The monolingual results form a strong baseline; they are better than the best official monolingual results in the TREC Proceedings (Voorhees and Harman, 1997; Voorhees and Harman, 2001). Given the strong baseline, the cross-lingual results are very impressive because they are around 90% of monolingual results (87% on TREC5C and 92% on TREC9X).

	monolingual	LDC	CETA	HKNews	Combined
TREC5C	0.3910	0.2886	0.3067	0.2530	0.3391
TREC9X	0.3362	0.1725	0.2126	0.2418	0.3100

Table 6.3.   Comparing monolingual and CLIR results on TREC5C and TREC9X

Retrieval results using the combined lexicon are significantly better than those using individual lexical sources. Both parallel corpora and manual lexicons have pros and cons. Parallel corpora can produce reliable probability estimates for frequent terms but not for infrequent ones due to data sparseness. In contrast, the flat probability distribution from manual lexicons is unreliable for frequent terms, which tend to have many translations, but is better for infrequent terms, which tend to have few translations. The complementary properties make the combination of the two types of resources essential to good CLIR.

The results show that dialect similarity can also affect retrieval performance. Both the TREC9X corpus and the HKNews parallel corpus are in Cantonese (a Chinese dialect). Therefore, HKNews is more effective on TREC9X than LDC and CETA, which have a strong bias toward Mandarin (standard Chinese). On the other hand, since TREC5C is a Mandarin corpus, LDC and CETA are better than HKNews on TREC5C.

7.   Comparing Probabilistic and Structural Translations

In this section we compare the retrieval results of our system with those of the structural query translation technique. Our experiments followed the query translation procedure described in Pirkola, 1998. A term in a Chinese document is treated as an instance of an English term if it is a translation of the English term according to a bilingual lexicon. Given a Chinese corpus, the term frequency and the document frequency of an English term are computed as:

$$tf(e, Doc) = \sum tf(c_i, Doc)$$
$$df(e) = |\bigcup doc\_set(c_i)|$$

where c_i's are Chinese translations of e and $doc\_set(c_i)$ is the set of Chinese documents containing c_i. The *tf* and *df* values of English terms were used with the INQUERY *tf.idf* function (Allan et al., 2000) to compute the retrieval score of a Chinese document for an English query.

Table 6.4 shows that probabilistic is better than structural in all cases but one, when the LDC lexicon was used on TREC5C. Overall, when manual lexicons (LDC and CETA) were used, probabilistic is better than structural, but the performance gap is small. When the parallel corpus (i.e. HKNews) and the combined lexicon were used, probabilistic is much better than structural.

	LDC	CETA	HKNews	Combined
TREC5C, structural	0.3009	0.2924	0.1886	0.2764
TREC5C, probabilistic	0.2886	0.3067	0.2530	0.3391
TREC9X, structural	0.1696	0.1750	0.2022	0.2285
TREC9X, probabilistic	0.1725	0.2126	0.2418	0.3100

Table 6.4.   Retrieval results of structural and probabilistic translations

Since the procedure we used to obtain translation pairs from parallel texts is statistically based, it is error prone for infrequent terms. Most of the incorrect translations have a small probability estimate. These bad translations are automatically discounted by our approach because they have small probabilities. However, since the structural query translation technique treats all translations equally, the bad translations become a serious problem. Experiments show that removing the low probability translations significantly improves the performance of structural query translation. Figure 6.1 shows the performance curves when we vary the probability cut off values on TREC9X. The results confirm that noisy translations from the parallel corpus are a serious problem for structural query translation. However, these noisy translations are useful information to probabilistic translation as removing them hurts retrieval performance. The advantage of probabilistic translation seems to be its capability of utilizing noisy translations to improve retrieval performance.

The disadvantage of probabilistic translation is that it is less efficient than structural query translation due to the extra computation incurred by the using of probabilities. The efficiency issue can be addressed by pre-computing $P(e|Doc) = \sum_{Chinese\ words\ c} P(c|Doc)P(e|c)$ of the retrieval function. Such optimization techniques have been used in Hiemstra and de Jong, 1999. They were not used in this work because they would prevent us from experimenting with different bilingual lexicons without re-indexing.

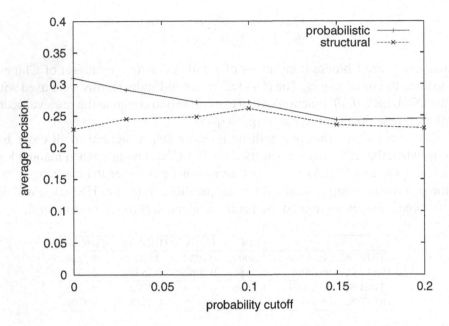

Figure 6.1. The impact of dropping low probability translations on the performance of structural and probabilistic translations. TREC9X was used.

8. Comparing Probabilistic Translation and MT

The major difference between MT-based CLIR and our approach is that the former uses one translation per term and the latter uses multiple translations. It has been suggested that CLIR can potentially utilize the multiple useful translations in a bilingual lexicon to improve retrieval performance (Klavans and Hovy, 1999). In our experiments, we used SYSTRAN version 3.0 (http://www.systransoft.com) for query and document translation. SYSTRAN is generally accepted as one of the best commercial MT systems for English-Spanish translation.

We performed four retrieval runs on the TREC5S corpus:

1 Query translation. English queries are translated to Spanish via SYSTRAN. Retrieval was performed using the translated queries on the Spanish corpus.

2 Document translation. The Spanish corpus is translated to English via SYSTRAN. Retrieval was performed using English queries on the translated corpus.

3 Combined run. The two retrieval scores for each document obtained in 1 and 2 were multiplied to produce a combined score for that document.

Documents were then ranked based on the combined scores. Previous studies (McCarley, 1999) suggested that such a combination can improve CLIR performance.

4 Probabilistic translation. We used WEAVER to induce a probabilistic bilingual lexicon from the translated corpus by treating the translated corpus as a pseudo-parallel corpus.

Table 6.5 shows that probabilistic translation outperforms the three runs using SYSTRAN, but the improvement over the combined MT run is very small. Its performance is around 85% of monolingual retrieval. Please note that the induced lexicon is probably a trimmed version of the true lexicon in SYSTRAN. Had we had direct access to the relevant linguistic knowledge (including lexicon and disambiguation knowledge) in the MT system, we could probably make a better probabilistic bilingual lexicon than the one induced from a pseudo-parallel corpus. As a result, we could produce better retrieval performance.

Monolingual	Query translation	Doc translation	Doc and query translation	Probabilistic translation
0.4275	0.2943	0.3197	0.3466	0.3615

Table 6.5.   Comparing MT and probabilistic translation

The goal of our experiments is not to dismiss the MT-based approach; it is viable for at least two reasons. First, it is much faster than our approach. It is about 10 times as fast as our CLIR system in the above experiments. Even though pre-computation can improve the efficiency of our system (as we discussed earlier), we expect MT-based CLIR would still be faster due to a sparser term-document matrix. Second, the retrieved documents are readable by end users. These properties make it the ideal search strategy in an interactive CLIR environment. The advantage of the probabilistic translation approach is also twofold. It is relatively inexpensive to build and it can potentially produce better retrieval results by using more than one translation per term.

9.   Measuring CLIR Performance as a Function of Resource Sizes

Availability of bilingual resources varies from one pair of languages to another. While such resources abound for high density language pairs (e.g. English and Chinese), they are scarce for many so-called low density language pairs. Considering this variability, it would be very useful if we can determine what level of CLIR performance is achievable given the existing bilingual resources. Furthermore, if existing data cannot meet our goal for CLIR, we would like to know how much more data has to be created. In this section we will empirically measure CLIR performance as a function of two variables, the size of the manual lexicon and the size of the parallel corpus.

Our experiments were carried out on TREC5C and TREC6C. The experiment set up is slightly different in that only the title and description fields of the TREC topics were used in query formulation. In Figure 6.2, each curve corresponds to a parallel corpus of a certain size. A n words parallel corpus was created by using the first m sentences pairs in the HKNews corpus that contain n English words. The X axis corresponds to the size of the manual lexicon. A n words lexicon contains the most frequent n English words with their Chinese translations in combined LDC-CETA lexicon. The frequency of the English words were compiled from TREC English volumes 1-5. The Y axis shows the retrieval performance.

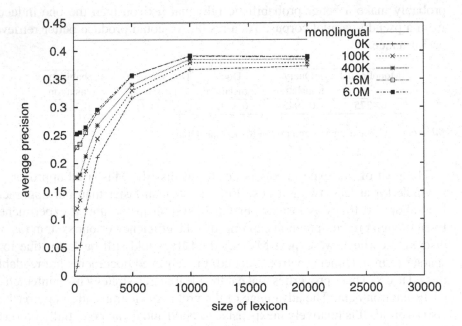

Figure 6.2. CLIR performance as a function of sizes of manual lexicon and parallel corpus. Each curve shows average precision as a function of manual lexicon size, holding the size of the parallel corpus fixed. The curve labeled 0K reflects the manual lexicon alone while the leftmost point in each curve reflects the parallel corpus alone.

Several observations can be made. First, as expected, the combination of a parallel corpus and a manual lexicon is always better than either resource alone, regardless of their sizes. Second, without any parallel text, there is a limit on the CLIR performance when we increase the size of the manual lexicon. To do better than that, parallel text has to be used. Although Figure 6.2 shows that the value of parallel text is modest when we have a large manual lexicon, this is largely due to the dialect mismatch between the HKNews parallel corpus (Cantonese) and the TREC5&6C collections (Mandarin). As shown in Table 6.3, the combined translations produced much better performance than using either type of resources alone on the TREC9X collection for which dialect mismatch is not a problem. The results suggest that manual lexicons alone are not sufficient for high performance CLIR; parallel text has to be used together with manual translations. Third, different combinations of lexicon and parallel corpus sizes can produce the same performance. This gives us some freedom in choosing what types of resources to acquire if our goal is to achieve decent but not the best possible CLIR. For example, to achieve 85% of monolingual IR, Figure 6.2 shows that we could either have a 10,000 words lexicon with no parallel text or have a 5,000 words lexicon and a medium size parallel corpus of a few million words.

We should point out that our results are based on a few dozen queries and are by no means conclusive. Nonetheless, we hope that the results can at least give us some insight into realistic cross-lingual search situations.

10. Reducing the Translation Cost of Creating a Parallel Corpus

We have shown that parallel text is necessary for high performance CLIR. Unfortunately, for many language pairs, there is little or no parallel text available. In such cases, we will need to create a parallel corpus by translating a body of monolingual text.[2] We will demonstrate that by carefully selecting the candidate sentences to be translated we can significantly reduce the translation cost.

In our experiments we used the following algorithm to select candidate sentences from a larger monolingual corpus. The algorithm iteratively removes the most redundant sentence from the remaining corpus until the size of the corpus is no greater than a pre-determined number n.

```
corpus = initial corpus;
while(size of corpus > n)
{
  For each sentence s in corpus, calculate novelty(s, corpus);

  Remove the sentence with smallest novelty from corpus;
}
  output the corpus;
```

---

[2]There are tools that mine the World Wide Web for bilingual text Resnik, 1998, but such tools are not useful if there is no parallel text online for a language pair.

Note that the novelty score for each sentence needs to be computed at each iteration because it changes with the corpus. We define the novelty of a sentence s as the average reciprocal frequency of the words in the sentence:

$$novelty(s, corpus) = \sum_{w \in s} 1/freq(w, corpus)$$

where $freq(w, corpus)$ is the frequency of w in $corpus$. The metric penalizes sentences containing frequent words.

Figure 6.3 shows retrieval performance as a function of parallel corpus size n on TREC9X under two conditions. Under one condition, the English sentences were selected from HKNews using the above algorithm. Under the other, the first m sentence pairs in HKNews with no more than n English words were used. The former is significantly better than the latter with the exception that when n is very small or approaches the size of the full HKNews, the two are close. When n=1.5 million (i.e. 1/4 of the size of full HKNews), the former showed almost no degradation in performance (0.2402 vs 0.2418) while the latter produced miserable result (0.1396). The results suggest that significant reduction in translation cost can be achieved by properly selecting the candidate sentences to be translated.

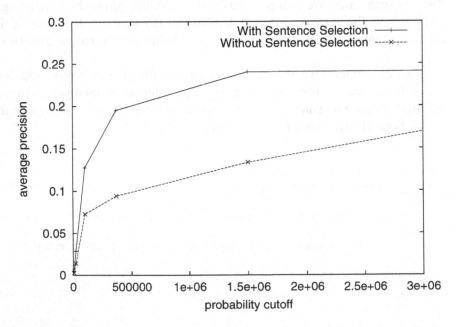

Figure 6.3. The impact of using a reduced parallel corpus on CLIR with and without sentence selection. TREC9X was used.

An assumption we made is that the lack of document contexts does not significantly affect the accuracy and the speed of translating a sentence. Whether the assumption is true needs further investigation.

11. Conclusions

We have shown that for CLIR a probabilistic approach to term translation is more effective that non-probabilistic techniques such as structural query translation and Machine Translation. Retrieval is slower with probabilistic term translation, but the degradation in speed seems to be reasonable given the retrieval benefit. We have empirically measured retrieval performance as a function of the sizes of bilingual resources. Such a measurement is useful for predicting CLIR performance for new language pairs and for guiding the acquisition of more resources. Retrieval results suggest that combining manual lexicons and parallel corpora is essential to high performance CLIR. Finally, we has proposed a technique to reduce the cost of manually creating a parallel corpus. The technique is promising based on preliminary experimental results but needs further investigation.

Acknowledgments

Thanks to Chanh Nguyen who carried out the Spanish experiments.

References

Allan, J., Callan, J., Feng, F., and Malin, D. (2000). INQUERY at TREC8. In *TREC8 Proceedings*. NIST.

Ballesteros, L. and Croft, W. (1998). Resolving Ambiguity for Cross-language Retrieval. In *Proceedings of ACM SIGIR 1998 Conference*, pages 64–71.

Berger, A. and Lafferty, J. (1999). Information Retrieval as Statistical Translation. In *Proceedings of ACM SIGIR 1999 Conference*.

Brown, P., Pietra, S. D., Pietra, V. D., and Mercer, R. (1993). The Mathematics of Statistical Machine Translation: Parameter Estimation. *Computational Linguistics*, pages 263–311.

Hiemstra, D. and de Jong, F. (1999). Disambiguation Strategies for Cross-language Information Retrieval. In *Proceedings of the third European Conference on Research and Advanced Technology for Digital Libraries*, pages 274–293.

Hull, D. (1997). Using Structured Queries for Disambiguation in Cross-language Information Retrieval. In *AAAI Symposium on Cross-Language Text and Speech Retrieval*.

Klavans, J. and Hovy, E. (1999). Multilingual (or Cross-lingual) Information Retrieval. In Hovy, E., editor, *Multilingual Information Management, current levels and future abilities*.

Kwok, K. L. (1997). Comparing Representations in Chinese Information Retrieval. In *Proceedings of ACM SIGIR 1997 Conference.*

Lafferty, J. (1999). Personal Communications.

McCarley, J. (1999). Should We Translate the Documents or the Queries in Cross-language Information Retrieval. In *Proceedings of ACL 1999*, pages 208–214.

Miller, D., Leek, T., and Schwartz, R. (1999). A Hidden Markov Model Information Retrieval System. In *Proceedings of ACM SIGIR 1999 Conference*, pages 214–221.

Oard, D. (1998). A Comparative Study of Query and Document Translation for Cross-language Information Retrieval. In *Third Conference of the Association for Machine Translation in the Americas.*

Pirkola, A. (1998). The Effects of Query Structure and Dictionary Setups in Dictionary-based Cross-language Information Retrieval. In *Proceedings of ACM SIGIR 1998 Conference*, pages 55–63.

Ponte, J. (1998). A Language Modeling Approach to Information Retrieval. In *Proceedings of ACM SIGIR 1998 Conference*, pages 275–281.

Porter, M. (1980). An Algorithm for Suffix Stripping. *Program*, 14(3):130–137.

Rabiner, L. (1989). A Tutorial on Hidden Markov Models and Selected Applications in Speech Recognition. *Proceedings of IEEE 77*, pages 257–286.

Resnik, P. (1998). Parallel Strands: A Preliminary Investigation into Mining the Web for Bilingual Text. In *Third Conference of the Association for Machine Translation in the Americas.*

Singhal, A., Buckley, C., , and Mitra, M. (1996). Pivoted Document Length Normalization. In *Proceedings of ACM SIGIR 1996 Conference.*

Sperer, R. and Oard, D. (2000). Structured Query Translation for Cross-language Information Retrieval. In *Proceedings of ACM SIGIR 2000 Conference.*

Voorhees, E. and Harman, D., editors (1997). *TREC5 Proceedings*. NIST.

Voorhees, E. and Harman, D., editors (1998). *TREC6 Proceedings*. NIST.

Voorhees, E. and Harman, D., editors (2001). *TREC9 Proceedings*. NIST.

Xu, J. and Croft, W. (1998). Corpus-based Stemming Using Co-occurrence of Word Variants. *ACM TOIS*, 18(1):79–112.

Chapter 7

USING COMPRESSION-BASED LANGUAGE MODELS FOR TEXT CATEGORIZATION

William J. Teahan
School of Informatics
University of Wales, Bangor
Bangor, Gwynedd LL57 1UT, Wales, UK
wjt@informatics.bangor.ac.uk

David J. Harper
School of Computing
The Robert Gordon University
Aberdeen AB25 1HG, Scotland, UK
djh@scms.rgu.ac.uk

Abstract   Text compression models are firmly grounded in information theory, and we exploit this theoretical underpinning in applying text compression to text categorization. Category models are constructed using the Prediction by Partial Matching (PPM) text compression scheme, specifically using character-based rather than word-based contexts. Two approaches to compression-based categorization are presented, one based on ranking by document cross entropy (average bits per coded symbol) with respect to a category model, and the other based on document cross entropy difference between category and complement of category models. Formally, we show the equivalence of the latter approach to two-class Bayes classification, and propose a method for performing feature selection within our compression-based categorization framework.

An extensive set of experiments on a range of classification tasks is reported. These tasks in increasing order of difficulty are language and dialect identification, authorship ascription, genre classification and topic classification. The results show that text categorization based on PPM is extremely effective for language and dialect identification, and for authorship ascription. PPM-based categorization is very competitive for genre and topic categorization compared with other reported approaches.

W.B. Croft and J. Lafferty (eds.), Language Modeling for Information Retrieval, 141–165.
© 2003 *Kluwer Academic Publishers.*

Keywords: text categorization, language modeling, text compression

1.   Background

Text categorization is the problem of assigning text to any of a set of pre-specified categories. It is useful in indexing documents for later retrieval, as a stage in natural language processing systems, for content analysis, and in many other roles (Lewis, 1994).

The traditional machine learning approach to text categorization is based on a four step process (Dumais et al., 1998): first, performing word and sentence segmentation on the training files; second, performing feature selection on the word counts; third, applying a machine learning algorithm; and last, applying the learned model to the test data produced after performing the same segmentation and feature feature selection process that was applied in steps one and two. A wide variety of machine learning algorithms have been applied based on this approach, including: probabilistic Bayesian classifiers, decision trees, neural networks, multivariate regression models, symbolic rule learning and support vector machines (Lewis and Ringuette, 1994; Apte et. al., 1994; Schutze et al., 1995; Weiner et al., 1995; Cohen and Singer, 1996; Yang and Pederson, 1997; 1998; Joachims, 1998; Yang, 1999; Dumais et al., 1998).

Traditional approaches to text categorization share several problems: the need to perform feature extraction before processing; the need to define where word boundaries occur; and the need to deal uniformly with morphological variants of words (Frank at al., 2000). The problem of word and sentence segmentation is an especially vexing one, and indeed for some languages, the Western notion of a word may be inappropriate (Teahan et al., 2000).

We wish to use language models developed for text compression as the basis of a text categorization scheme and potentially for other applications in Information Retrieval (although the latter will not be discussed here). The motivation for using these models is that they are well grounded in information theory, and that they also have proven performance at many Information Retrieval related tasks such as word segmentation (Teahan et al., 2000), text mining (Witten et al., 1999), language/dialect identification and authorship attribution (Teahan, 2000).

For text categorization, our compression-based language modeling approach has several advantages. By using models that are character-based, not word-based, we can avoid the segmentation issue altogether. Additionally, we can sidestep to some extent the issue of which features to use by examining potential features within the framework of standard Markov-based approximations commonly used in language modeling.

Anecdotal evidence indicates that the idea of using compression for text categorization has been re-invented many times (Frank at al., 2000). However, compression-based approaches to date have produced inferior results compared to state-of-the-art schemes based on traditional machine learning techniques more reliant on feature extraction (Frank at al., 2000; Teahan, 2000). Indeed, Frank et al. state that it is their belief that compression-based approaches will not be capable of competing with the machine learning approaches. In this paper, we seek to allay this mis-apprehension.

The main contribution of this work is threefold. Firstly, we demonstrate that compression-based language models work well for a number of categorization tasks. Secondly, in contrast to Frank et al., we show how a variation of the compression-based approach can in fact produce competitive results for genre and topic categorization compared with the traditional machine learning methods. And thirdly, we propose a method for performing feature selection within a compression-based framework, and show how it can lead to improved performance in certain circumstances.

This paper is organized as follows. The next two sections provide the theoretical background to our approach showing its basis in information theory and Bayesian classification. Section 4 briefly describes the particular text compression scheme (PPM) that we use in our experiments with the results discussed in Section 5. Further discussion is provided in the final section.

2. Compression models

As stated, we wish to use compression-based language models as the basis of a text categorization scheme. The crux of our reasoning hinges on the notion of *entropy* as a measure of the "information content" of a message (Shannon, 1948), and importantly that text compression can be used directly to estimate an upper bound to it (Brown et. al., 1992). Various treatments of entropy are given in (Shannon, 1948; Brown et. al., 1992; Manning and Schutze, 1999) and these are drawn upon in the following discussion.

Formally, suppose we have a language defined by an alphabet of k symbols s_i, and a probability distribution over these symbols $p(s)$. The fundamental coding theorem (Shannon, 1948) states that the lower bound on the average number of bits per symbol needed to encode messages of the language (i.e. sequences of the symbols) is given by the entropy of the probability distribution (and often referred to as the "entropy of the language"):

$$H(language) = H(p) = -\sum_{i=1}^{k} p(s_i) \log_2 p(s_i). \qquad (7.1)$$

The information content of a particular symbol is given by $-\log_2 p(s_i)$, and is the number of bits required to encode that symbol. Thus, $H(p)$ can be viewed as an expectation over the number of bits per symbol. Hence, we can obtain minimum code lengths, or alternatively maximal compression rates, by encoding symbols in accordance with the actual probability distribution $p(s)$.

Generally, we do not have access to the actual probability distribution underlying a language, but rather some model of that language. Suppose we have a language, L, in which sequences of symbols $x_1, x_2, \ldots, x_n$ (denoted x_{1n} hereafter) are generated according to probability distribution $p(x)$, for which we have constructed a model $p_M(x)$. The *cross-entropy* of the language with respect to the model provides a measure of the extent to which the model departs from the actual distribution, and is given by:

$$H(L, p_M) = - \lim_{n \to \infty} \frac{1}{n} \sum_{x_{1n}} p(x_{1n}) \log_2 p_M(x_{1n}). \qquad (7.2)$$

The cross-entropy is the average number of bits per symbol required to encode language L using the model p_M, and thus $H(L, p_M)$ is an upper bound on the entropy of the language, and $H(L) \leq H(L, p_M)$. $H(L, p_M)$ can be approximated by observing that Equation 7.2 is simply the expected value of $- \log_2 p_M(x_{1n})$ over an infinite sample of language examples, and we approximate it using one very large sample as follows:

$$H(L, p_M) \approx - \frac{1}{n} \log_2 p_M(x_{1n}), \quad n \; very \; large. \qquad (7.3)$$

For a given document, D, we can compute the *document cross-entropy*, the average number of bits per symbol to encode the document using the model as:

$$H(L, p_M, D) = - \frac{1}{n} \log_2 p_M(D), \quad D = x_{1n}. \qquad (7.4)$$

Suppose that p_M is a good model for L, then the lower the document cross-entropy, the more likely it is that the document D is generated by the language. This key observation lies at the heart of using text compression for text categorization. Categories are viewed as languages, and documents are compressed using models constructed over the categories.

3.   Bayes Classifiers

We would like to establish the relationship between Bayes classifiers, and using cross-entropy for categorization, and in that context discuss feature selection for compression models.

Suppose we want to classify documents such that they are assigned independently to one or more categories. Assuming we have a training collection of categorized documents, then for any given category, C, we can construct a model for that category p_C, and model for its complement p_N (hereafter the "negative" model). Bayes formula gives us a mechanism for deciding whether a particular document, D, belongs to category C, and using the more familiar notation $P(D|C) = p_C(D)$ and $P(D|\overline{C}) = p_N(D)$, decide D belongs to C if:

$$P(D|C)P(C) > P(D|\overline{C})P(\overline{C}) \tag{7.5}$$

where $P(C)$ is the prior probability of a document belonging to C. Equivalently, the documents can be ranked with respect to the category using the following expression:

$$\log_2 \frac{P(D|C)}{P(D|\overline{C})} \tag{7.6}$$

and a cutoff is selected, which gives optimal categorization, according to some measure of categorization goodness.

Equation 7.6 has a dual formulation in the cross-entropy and compression world, namely

$$
\begin{aligned}
\log_2(P(D|C)/P(D|\overline{C})) & \\
&\equiv -\log_2 P(D|\overline{C}) - (-\log_2 P(D|C)) \\
&\equiv -\log_2 p_N(D) - (-\log_2 p_C(D)) \\
&\equiv H(\overline{C}, p_N, D) - H(C, p_C, D).
\end{aligned}
\tag{7.7}
$$

The inverse relationship between cross-entropy, and probability of a given document, is well-known. Thus, maximizing the cross entropy difference (i.e. the code length difference) between a document encoded using the negative model and category model respectively, is equivalent to constructing an independent Bayes classifier for each category. Frank et al. provided a similar analysis in (Frank at al., 2000). In applying text compression to categorization, we will determine an optimal cutoff for the cross entropy difference computed in Equation 7.7 on a category-by-category basis, which will be referred to as the *category cutoff*.

More interestingly, this relationship suggests ways in which feature selection might be incorporated within text compression models when applied to categorization. The need for feature selection was highlighted by Frank et al.— they found that in some cases the occurrence of just a few words determines whether an article belongs to a category or not. Although one might expect an information-theoretic measure to recognize and discount features with poor predictive value, Frank et al. did not propose doing feature selection within a compression framework.

Our method for performing feature selection is as follows. Features are selected for Bayes classification on the basis of their discrimination power, which is computed based on the relative density of the feature in the category compared with its density in the complement (or similar). Likewise, we propose selecting features that exceed some cross entropy difference threshold. Hence, features will be ranked based on their potential contribution to the overall cross entropy difference (as given by Equation 7.7). Again, we will apply feature selection on an individual category basis, and the resultant cutoff will be referred to as the *feature cutoff*.

A benefit of performing thresholding (i.e. category and feature cutoff in our case) noted in (Frank at al., 2000) is that it automatically adjusts for the fact that the models p_C and p_N are formed using different amounts of training data. This is a potential problem since in general, one expects to achieve better compression with more training data.

4.   PPM-based language models

The Prediction by Partial Matching (PPM) text compression scheme has consistently set the standard in lossless compression of text since it was originally published in 1984 by (Cleary and Witten, 1984). Other methods such as those based on Ziv-Lempel coding are more commonly used in practice but their attractiveness lies in their relative speed rather than any superiority in compression (Bell, Cleary and Witten, 1990). Although adequate categorization performance can be achieved by Ziv-Lempel methods in restricted circumstances (Benedetto et al., 2002), experiments show that they are significantly outperformed by other compression methods (Khmelev, 2000; Kukushkina et al., 2001).

Compression models encode a document according to a given model, and the resultant cross-entropy is given by Equation 7.4. In the case of the PPM family of models, the individual symbols are encoded within the context provided by the preceding symbols appearing in a document. Taking Equation 7.4 as a starting point, we can achieve optimal compression for the model p_M, by observing that:

$$H(L, p_M, D)$$
$$= -\frac{1}{n} \log_2 p_M(D), \quad D = x_{1n}$$
$$= -\frac{1}{n} \log_2 \prod_{i=1}^{n} p_M(x_i | context_i) \quad [by \ Chain \ Rule]$$
$$= \frac{1}{n} \sum_{i=1}^{n} - \log_2 p_M(x_i | context_i)$$

where $context_i = x_1, x_2, \ldots x_{i-1}$. Thus each symbol is encoded according to its *information content* within the context provided by all the preceding symbols. In practice, PPM uses a Markov approximation and assumes a fixed order context. A fixed order context of five is found to perform well, and increasing it further does not generally improve compression (Cleary and Witten, 1984, Teahan, 1998).

PPM uses an approximate blending technique called *exclusion* based on the *escape* mechanism to exclude lower order predictions from the final probability estimate. This includes an order 0 model which predicts symbols based on their unconditioned probabilities, and a default model which ensures that a finite probability (however small) is assigned to all possible symbols. Prediction probabilities for each context in the model are calculated from frequency counts, and the symbol that actually occurs is encoded relative to its predicted distribution.

The PPM method is character-based, although the blending mechanism can equally be applied to other classes of symbols such as words and parts of speech. Compression experiments with a wide range of English text (Teahan, 1998) show that word-based models consistently outperform the character-based methods, although the difference in performance is only a few percent. A fuller description of the PPM algorithm can be found in (Bell, Cleary and Witten, 1990); two variants of the algorithm that perform well in compression experiments are PPMC (Moffat, 1990) and PPMD (Howard, 1993). These methods differ in the way they estimate the "escape" probability when a model uses a lower order context to make a prediction. PPMC uses the number of times a novel symbol has occurred before as the basis for this probability. PPMD is a slight variation of PPMC that usually provides a small but noticeable improvement in prediction in many cases.

Feature selection   In contrast to previous compression-based approaches to text categorization, we seek to investigate the possibility of incorporating feature selection in some manner. In our approach, when we apply feature selection using PPM models, we determine on a category-by-category basis an optimal cutoff by only selecting features that exceed some code length difference threshold $h_N - h_C$ where the feature code lengths are $h_N = -log_2 p_N(x_i|context_i)$ and $h_C = -log_2 p_C(x_i|context_i)$.

5.   Experimental results

Experimental results are given for different categorization tasks in the next sections.[1] The tasks (language identification, authorship attribution, genre categorization and topic categorization) are arranged in order of increasing difficulty. The first three tasks use cross-entropy to rank the documents, whereas the last task uses the cross-entropy difference measure defined in Equation 7.7.

---

[1] Part of the work described here has already been published as an extended abstract in (Teahan, 2000).

The results show that the PPM-based categorizer is extremely effective both for language identification and for authorship attribution. Experiments with the latter show that, perhaps surprisingly, results are excellent even when testing for authorship of similar styles. Very competitive results are also obtained for the more difficult tasks of genre and topic categorization.

We wish to stress that for all of these experiments *no* lexical preprocessing was done to the texts beforehand (this includes no case conversion or whitespace substitution). An exception was that, in some cases, certain header information was removed from the documents (such as headers in Usenet news articles) when it was deemed that the information might unfairly affect categorization performance. The technique we adopt is purely character-based and does not require any a-priori knowledge about the representation of the documents—the methods would work just as well, for example, with UTF-encoded Unicode symbols.

5.1 Language identification

Language identification concerns the problem of identifying from examples of written or spoken language which language is being used. Dunning (1994) describes several statistical methods for identifying the language of small pieces of text (such as *e pruebas bioquimica* and *faits se sont produits*). Ganeson and Sherman (1993) adopt various statistical modelling methods to perform various language recognition problems such as: recognizing a known language; distinguishing a known language from uniform noise; and detecting a non-uniform unknown language. Cross-entropy calculated using PPM-based models may equally be applied to each of these problems as it provides the means to rank the performance of statistical models. The text being analysed is compressed using PPM character based language models trained on representative texts written in various languages. The most likely language is the one used to train the model that has the best compression performance.

In an experiment, a selection of Web documents were collected for sixteen different languages using the search engine www.google.com. A diversified pool of text of at least 100,000 bytes was obtained for each language by a three step process: firstly, restricting the search to the specified language; secondly, entering a general query (for example, containing frequently-used terms such as "one" for English or "oui" for French); and thirdly, concatenating a representative selection of the highest ranked documents returned by the search engine after first eliminating those (relatively few) documents whose language was designated incorrectly (for example, when the document contained a mixture of languages). These texts were then split into two 50,000 byte texts, one used for training and the other for testing. The testing text was further split into different sized segments, each from 50 bytes up to 500 bytes. The training text

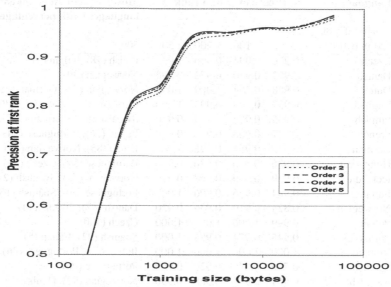

Figure 7.1. Precision at first rank at identifying the language of Web documents for different order PPM models trained on various sized training texts.

was used to train PPM models for each of the different languages, and each segment of testing test was then ranked (in ascending order) by cross-entropy with respect to these models.

Results for different order PPM models on the 500 bytes segments are graphed in Figure 7.1. The vertical axis plots the precision of the first-ranked documents at determining the correct language, whereas the horizontal axis plots on a log scale the size of the training text in bytes ranging from just over 100 bytes up to the full 50,000 bytes that was available. The graph shows that surprisingly very little training text is required (around 2,500 bytes) to achieve a high degree of precision (over 0.95) and that different order models do not have a significant affect on the precision.

Table 7.1 provides further details of results for the different languages for varying sized testing segments (50, 100, 200 and 500 bytes). The rightmost column lists the languages that were ranked second for the 500 byte case. For example, Polish was chosen as the 2nd ranking for the Czech 500-byte test segments in 78% of cases. The results provide an indication of which languages are similar to each other. For example, English is most similar to German (57% of English segments have German as their 2nd ranking), but German is most similar to Dutch (85% of German segments have Dutch as their 2nd ranking). The table shows that the best results are obtained on 500-byte segments with 50% of the languages achieving a precision at first rank value of 1.0, but very

Language	Precision at first rank				Most frequent 2nd-ranked languages (with percentages)
Length of testing text in bytes	50	100	200	500	500
Czech	0.976	0.994	0.996	1.000	Polish (78), Italian (9)
Danish	0.905	0.950	0.972	0.990	Norwegian (99)
Dutch	0.988	0.994	1.000	1.000	Norwegian (61), German (28)
English	0.933	0.980	0.992	1.000	German (57), Portuguese (30)
Finnish	0.935	0.952	0.960	0.970	Swedish (82), German (9)
French	0.937	0.966	0.976	0.990	Italian (56), Portuguese (34)
German	0.959	0.984	0.992	1.000	Dutch (85), Norwegian (10)
Hungarian	0.936	0.960	0.976	0.990	Portuguese (59), Czech (29)
Icelandic	0.939	0.960	0.968	0.970	Norwegian (75), Swedish (2)
Italian	0.984	0.996	0.996	1.000	Portuguese (59), Spanish (15)
Norwegian	0.829	0.910	0.936	0.920	Danish (87), Swedish (4)
Polish	0.999	1.000	1.000	1.000	Czech (100)
Portuguese	0.945	0.974	0.984	1.000	Spanish (92), Italian (5)
Rumanian	1.000	1.000	1.000	1.000	Italian (63), Portuguese (36)
Spanish	0.796	0.876	0.920	0.960	Portuguese (96)
Swedish	0.959	0.978	0.988	0.990	Norwegian (93), Danish (5)
Average	0.939	0.967	0.979	0.986	

Table 7.1. Various results for PPM-based language identifier on Web documents.

good results are also possible even with 50-byte segments with only Spanish and Norwegian having a precision less than 0.9.

Dialect identification Another interesting possibility is the problem of identifying the dialect for a sample text. This is useful in many applications; in information retrieval, for example, we could index "English" text using an appropriate stemmer (English or American), which each then produces standardized stems. The Brown (Francis and Kucera, 1982) and LOB (Johansson, 1986) corpora represent diverse samples from two different dialects, American and British English; as such, they provide a means for rigorously testing how well PPM performs at dialect identification. In an experiment, equal-size partitions of 100,000 characters were successively extracted from the two corpora, and then compressed using order 5 PPMD models trained on the remaining text from each (i.e. all the text in the corpora with just the partition deleted).

The Brown-trained model compressed the Brown corpus partitions up to 3.6% better than did the LOB-trained model. Correspondingly, the LOB-trained model compressed the LOB-partitions up to 3.1% better than did the Brown-trained model. There were no cases in which a model performed worse on its respective partitions, and in only three cases was the performance the same for a particular partition. Consequently, these results show it is possible to classify "English" text as American or British English using PPM models with a high degree of accuracy.

5.2   Authorship attribution

A similar PPM-based process to determine the cross-entropy is possible for the task of authorship attribution. It is widely known that style and statistical properties differ markedly for different authors (Boggess, Argawal and David, 1991). This can be exploited by training models using text written by each of the disputed authors, and then compressing each text in question using all these models. The hope is that the style of each author will be sufficiently different to clearly distinguish between them. Experiments with English texts reported here show that this is true in most cases.

The following two problems are investigated in this section—determining known authorship; and determining disputed authorship. The known authorship experiments described in this section use the Reuters-21578 collection. This collection is publicly available[2] and contains Reuters news articles on various topics. It is a standard data set used for text categorization research. Each article has had specific topic labels (such as `earnings` and `trade`) assigned to it manually by Reuters employees. This collection is usually used for research on what we term "topic categorization", and indeed, we use the collection for just such a purpose in section 5.4. In this section, however, we describe a quite different (and novel) use for the collection. Many of the articles in the collection also have author labels assigned to them (such as `Rich Miller` and `Patti Domm`). Various information concerning the most frequently found of these labels are listed in Table 7.2. The table lists information only for articles of single authorship—articles with multiple authorship were not considered for these experiments. The second column in the table lists the number of documents that were found for each author. For example, `Peter Torday` was designated as the author of 24 articles in the collection. The last column in the table provides a list of topics that were assigned to the same articles. As you would expect, authors write articles on similar topics, and this is reflected in the number of multiple occurrences shown in the list. Nine articles authored by `Cal Mankowski`, for example, primarily concern the topic `acq` (acquisitions), and only one concerns `earn` (earnings). (Many of the authored articles have no topic assigned to them which explains why the number of assigned topics is less than the document frequency listed in the second column.)

We use this data to determine how well our PPM-based categorizer does at the problem of determining known authorship. In an experiment, pools of

---

[2]http://kdd.ics.uci.edu/databases/reuters21578/reuters21578.html

Author	Doc. freq.	Text size (bytes)	List of assigned topics (with number of occurrences if > 1 shown in brackets)
Peter Torday	24	98550	dlr (4), gnp, interest (2), money-fx (5), trade (2), yen
Rich Miller	23	71064	gnp (2), interest (2), money-fx (2), trade (7), yen
Patti Domm	23	83060	acq (18), crude
Chaitanya Kalbag	23	74546	coconut, coconut-oil, copra-cake, earn, gnp (2), meal-feed, money-fx, palm-oil, veg-oil, sugar
Cal Mankowski	18	60453	acq (9), earn
Mark O'Neill	15	62073	bop, grain (2), sugar (2), trade
Alan Wheatley	15	60207	money-fx, money-supply (2), interest

Table 7.2. Various information concerning the most frequent authors found in the Reuters-21578 collection.

text were obtained by concatenating articles written by the same author together. The size of these texts is shown in column three of Table 7.2. These were then split into segments of 250 lines (approximately 14000 bytes each) and alternately used for testing and/or training purposes on a rotating basis for cross-validation (ensuring that testing and training data were disjoint in all cases). PPM models were constructed for each author from the training data, and used to categorize each of the testing segments using the cross-entropy ranking method as before. Out of the resulting 42 tests that were made, just two were incorrectly labelled, a precision at first rank of 95%. One segment written by Alan Wheatley was mis-categorized as belonging to Peter Torday, and one by Cal Mankowski was mis-labelled as Patti Domm's—in both these cases, the list of assigned topics between the two authors noticeably overlap (for example, articles by both Patti Domm and Cal Mankowski concentrate on the acquisition topic).

Another interesting possibility concerns the problem of determining unknown or disputed authorship. A famous problem in authorship attribution concerns the Federalist Papers written by Alexander Hamilton, John Jay and James Madison (Mosteller and Wallace, 1984). Between the years 1787–1788, eighty-five short essays addressed to the citizens of New York on the U.S. Constitution were published in newspapers under the pseudonym "Publius". Of these papers, it is generally agreed that Jay wrote 5, Hamilton 43, Madison 14 with the authorship of the remaining 12 being in flat dispute between Hamilton and Madison.

Mosteller and Wallace (1984) determine odds of authorship for the papers by applying Bayes' theorem to evidence based upon 30 common words (such as *as* and *upon*). Their work supports the claim made by historians (and by Madison himself) that Madison wrote the disputed papers.

| | Disputed papers | | | | |
No.	Madison (bpc)	Hamilton (bpc)	No.	Madison (bpc)	Hamilton (bpc)
49	**1.79**	1.93	55	**1.86**	1.97
50	**1.92**	2.07	56	**1.70**	1.85
51	**1.72**	1.88	57	**1.85**	1.98
52	**1.78**	1.94	58	**1.80**	1.93
53	**1.79**	1.93	62	**1.83**	1.84
54	**1.73**	1.89	63	**1.82**	**1.82**

| Papers known to have been written by Madison | | | Papers known to have been written by Hamilton | | |
No.	Madison (bpc)	Hamilton (bpc)	No.	Madison (bpc)	Hamilton (bpc)
44	**1.76**	1.90	59	**1.82**	1.88
45	**1.67**	1.81	60	1.78	**1.71**
46	**1.78**	1.85	61	1.78	**1.73**
47	**1.70**	1.81	65	1.87	**1.82**
48	**1.85**	1.99	66	1.80	**1.75**

Table 7.3. Ascribing authorship to the Federalist Papers.

Experiments with PPM character based computer models also supports this claim.[3] Each of the disputed papers was compressed using computer models trained on text taken from the non-disputed papers. The same models were also used to test papers with known authorship. To minimize the fluctuations due to differing periods, the papers tested are all in consecutive order from paper number 45 through to 66 (excluding paper number 64 written by John Jay). Table 7.3 lists the results obtained. Compression ratios (listed in bits per character or "bpc") for Madison are much lower for the disputed papers (excluding 62 and 63), supporting the claim that Madison was the primary author for those papers. For the non-disputed papers, only one paper (59) has a result which is contradictory. Mosteller and Wallace state that historians feel least settled about papers 62 and 63, which is reflected in the results. They draw attention to the difficulty of the task confronting researchers—both Hamilton and Madison had remarkably similar prose styles, which was no unique phenomenon as for most educated Americans of the late eighteenth century they employed "the same stylistic devices, the same standard phrases, and remarkably similar sentence structure." These results are also surprising in that only a relatively small amount of training text (a few hundred kilobytes) was required to train the models.

---

[3] Similar results using compression models to tackle the Federalist Papers authorship problem have been reported by Juola (1998) who used a different method of calculating the cross-entropy.

5.3   Genre categorization

Genre categorization is the problem of identifying the subject domain of a document. Some sample genres are: politics, religion, history, sport and science. A number of studies (Biber (1988); Kessler et al., 1997; Wolters and Kirsten, 1999; Stamatatos et al., 2001) have investigated this problem usually by adapting methods found suitable for the related problem of topic categorization (see next section). The terms "domain categorization" and "genre categorization" are often used confusedly in the literature—most take the approach we adopt here of defining a "genre" to be a domain subject area such as history and sport, although Lee and Myaeng (2002) investigate the slightly different problem of identifying the style of the text that characterizes the purpose for which the document has been written (such as a research article, novel, poem, news article, editorial, home page, advertisement, manual etc.). Furthermore, many other researchers have not distinguished between genre and topic categorization (see for example, McCallum & Nigam, 1998), although clearly each task may present its own problems that need to be investigated independently. As a case in point, the task of identifying *sentiment*, or the overall opinion that the author of a document has to its subject matter, has highlighted the need for more sophisticated techniques than the traditional machine learning methods adopted for topic categorization which are found to perform poorly (Pang and Lee, 2002).

An investigation into using PPM for genre categorization was performed using the Newsgroups data set (McCallum & Nigam, 1998). This collection contains 20,000 articles evenly divided among 20 Usenet discussion groups. This data set is particularly interesting as many of the newsgroup categories fall into confusable clusters: for example, three discuss religion (alt.atheism, soc.religion.christian, talk.religion.misc), three discuss politics (from the talk.politics.* hierarchy) and five are from the comp.* hierarchy. In an initial experiment, 20 separate order 5 PPMD models were trained on the text contained in the first 80% of the articles, and the remaining 20% of the articles were compressed against each of them to see which model performed best. The Usenet headers (including the subject, followup and newsgroup lines) were removed from each of the articles beforehand. By assigning the newsgroup of the top-ranked model as the newsgroup of the article, the newsgroup category was correctly deduced in 82.1% of the articles, which compares favourably with the results reported by McCallum & Nigam (1998) who achieved a precision at first rank accuracy level of 74% using a multivariate Bernoulli event model, and 85% using a multinomial model using the same training/testing split of the data.

A confusion matrix of the errors made by the PPM-based classifier for ten of the newsgroups is shown in Table 7.4. The columns show results for

	aa	sc	se	sm	ss	src	tpg	tpme	tpmi	trm
aa	**149**				2	4		1	2	40
sc		**177**	3	3	1	1	4		2	
se	2	3	**136**	13	4			1	3	
sm	2	1	4	**165**	3	1	2		6	2
ss		1	3	1	**172**		1	1	8	5
src						**191**	1			3
tpg	1			2	1	2	**171**		11	9
tpme	1					5		**185**	6	1
tpmi	1				2	1	19	12	**139**	26
trm	35	1			2	9	5	1	6	**141**

Table 7.4. Cross-entropy confusion matrix for the **Newsgroups** data set. The columns show results for each model trained on text taken from the respective newsgroup; rows show test results for each newsgroup based on articles not included in the training data. Only 10 (of the 20) newsgroups are shown. These are: alt.atheism (i.e.*aa*), sci.scrypt, sci.electronics, sci.med, sci.space, soc.religion.christian, talk.politics.guns, talk.politics.mideast, talk.politics.misc and talk.religion.misc.

each model trained on text in the respective genres; rows show test results for each genre based on text not included in the training data. As is typical for a PPM-based classifier, the leading diagonal correctly accounts for most of the categorizations. For most of the newsgroups, there are only a few outliers, the major exception between the confusion between the alt.atheism and talk.religion.misc newsgroups, which seems a reasonable confusion to make, and which accounts for 11% of the overall mis-categorizations. For many of the mis-categorizations, the correct newsgroup category has been ranked second or third-best, with only a small difference in cross-entropy from the best. Choosing the best two improves accuracy to 91.5%, and the best three to 94.2%. However, each test article is now multiply classified, a penalty that some retrieval-based applications may be willing to pay for the increased accuracy. This penalty can, however, be significantly reduced by choosing to discard the second or third best categories if the difference in cross-entropy from the best is above some threshold. For example, examining the best three categories and choosing a difference threshold of as little as 0.2 bits per character in cross-entropy will discard nearly 62% of the multiple categorizations while still ensuring a very high accuracy level of 90.9%.

5.4   Topic categorization

The task of topic categorization concerns the problem of assigning one or more categories to a document from a list of pre-defined categories where the categories reflect the "topics" or subjects the document is concerned with. The

Category	Number Training Documents	Number Testing Documents	Training size (bytes)	Avg. size of document (bytes)
earn	2877	1087	1488519	517.4
acq	1650	719	1330793	806.5
money-fx	538	179	623599	1159.1
trade	369	118	579607	1570.8
crude	389	189	532919	1370.0
grain	433	149	490372	1132.5
interest	347	131	335260	966.2
wheat	212	71	239843	1131.3
ship	197	89	218093	1107.1
corn	182	56	217246	1193.7

Table 7.5.   Various statistics for the Reuters-21578 collection.

categories are likely to be more fine-grained than the broad categories used for genre classification.

The topic-based experiments described in this section all use the Reuters-21578 collection that was used in section 5.2. Using the ModApte split (Dumais et al., 1998), the collection is separated into a training set, testing set and an unused set (9603, 3299 and 7634 documents respectively). This collection comes with manually assigned categories for all the documents in the training and testing sets.

For the experiments, we have further split the training set into a training subset and a validation subset (6338 and 3266 documents respectively). We use the validation subset for choosing the category and feature cutoff values that maximizes the average of recall and precision (i.e. "breakeven" point) for each category based on the cross entropy difference ranking formula defined in Equation 7.7. Once the cutoff values have been obtained, the models p_C and p_N are rebuilt to take maximum use of the full training data in the same manner as (Frank at al., 2000).

Although there are 118 categories in the entire Reuters collection, our experiments only concentrate on the ten largest categories (since by common practice results are seldom published in the literature for the smaller categories). The categories are ordered by the size of training data available, in bytes: *earn, acq, money-fx, trade, crude, grain, interest, wheat, ship* and *corn*. This cuts the validation subset and testing set down to 2152 and 3019 documents respectively. Table 7.5 lists the number of training and testing documents available for each category; also listed is the total size of the training data in bytes after concatenating all the training files together once irrelevant text (including tags) has been removed. The average size per document is shown in the last column. The figures show that the distribution of the collection is highly skewed—there

Category	Order 2	Order 3	Order 4	Order 5	Order 6
earn	0.964	0.970	0.967	0.947	*0.953*
acq	0.942	0.954	0.959	*0.954*	0.953
money-fx	0.838	0.835	*0.816*	0.834	0.810
trade	0.776	0.772	0.759	0.778	*0.772*
crude	0.837	*0.888*	0.878	0.867	0.857
grain	0.870	0.905	0.915	*0.899*	0.911
interest	0.749	0.735	0.723	0.728	*0.759*
wheat	0.721	0.717	0.706	*0.735*	0.757
ship	0.757	*0.783*	0.750	0.771	0.765
corn	0.635	0.666	0.668	0.669	*0.646*
Weighted average	0.899	0.910	0.907	0.900	*0.901*

Table 7.6. Average recall/precision breakeven points for PPM-based categorization for the Reuters-21578 collection using PPMD models with feature cutoff.

Category	Naïve Bayes	LSVM	PPMC (Order 2)	PPMD (Order 3) *without feature cutoff*	PPMD (Order 3) *with feature cutoff*
earn	0.959	**0.980**	0.963	0.968	0.970
acq	0.878	0.936	0.910	0.950	**0.954**
money-fx	0.566	0.745	0.763	0.831	**0.835**
trade	0.639	0.759	0.650	0.734	**0.772**
crude	0.795	**0.889**	0.807	0.871	0.888
grain	0.788	**0.946**	0.746	0.883	0.905
interest	0.649	**0.777**	0.604	0.685	0.735
wheat	0.697	**0.918**	0.649	0.744	0.717
ship	0.854	**0.856**	0.819	0.749	0.783
corn	0.653	**0.903**	0.542	0.667	0.666
Weighted average	0.848	**0.919**	0.863	0.902	0.910

Table 7.7. Average recall/precision values for PPM-based categorization compared with various schemes on the Reuters-21578 collection.

is a varying amount of training data available from nearly 1.5 Mb for the most frequent category *earn* down to just over 200 Kb for the smallest category *corn*; the sizes of the documents also vary noticeably, with just over 500 bytes for *earn*, to over three times that for *trade*.

Table 7.6 shows the average precision/recall breakeven points for our PPM categorizer that are achieved on the Reuters-21578 collection at the testing stage when using the category and feature cutoffs obtained from the validation stage. The italic values indicate the orders that performed the best at the validation stage. Shown at the bottom of the table is the average of the top ten categories weighted according to their frequency of occurrence in the testing set. From Table 7.6, we can see that no one context order is particularly predominate at achieving the best average precision/recall, with the best values

scattered across all orders. These results show that each category has features that make a particular context order most effective for it. This is not too
surprising when we consider the language used in some of these categories.
Considering *earn, acq, money-fx* and *trade*, these categories quite often use
acronyms that are only two or three characters long, or contain numerical data,
and therefore are best served with models that have a context order different
from the order 5 models found most effective for general English text. Also,
higher orders (4 to 6) feature strongly, which closely match well-documented
results from standard compression experiments on text-like data (Bell, Cleary
and Witten, 1990; Teahan, 1998). The overall results, however, are sufficiently
similar for orders ≥ 3 that we can regard it as stable, and arbitrarily pick one—
we have chosen order 3 for subsequent experiments.

Table 7.7 compares the order 3 model results from Table 7.6 (reproduced
in the last column) with results published in (Dumais et al., 1998) for Na"ve
Bayes and linear support vector machines (LSVMs), and with previously published results for PPM. Results in the last two columns are new results using
our models. (The best result for each category is shown in bold font). The results show that our approach is uniformly better than Na"ve Bayes (except for
ship), and performs better than LSVMs in three out of the ten categories (*acq,
money-fx* and *trade*) and are competitive in a further four categories (*crude,
earn, grain* and *interest*). Lack of training data clearly affects performance for
the three poorest performing categories, *corn, ship* and *wheat*, which correspond to the three smallest categories from Table 7.5.

Shown in the third column of Table 7.7 are the results reported by Frank
et al. who used order 2 PPMC models (Frank at al., 2000). In their method,
they used a single category cutoff for optimizing precision/recall; this is clearly
improved across nearly all categories using the order 3 PPMD models and the
feature cutoff approach that we adopt. They also found that models higher than
order 2 achieved degraded performance in almost all cases. They attributed
this to the amount of training data being insufficient to justify more complex
models. This is in direct contrast to the results that we have obtained—we have
found that higher order models perform as well (and in some cases better).
Unfortunately, Frank et al. did not include results for higher order models
in their paper, so it is difficult to speculate as to the reasons for the variance
between our results and theirs.

Results for order 3 PPMD models without feature cutoff are shown in the
second to last column of Table 7.7. They show a consistent but slight improvement across all categories when using feature cutoff, except for *corn* (a
very slight decrease) and *wheat*. Results for other orders show that feature
cutoff leads to better performance for two categories in particular, *interest* and
money-fx, but to inconsistent results for other categories (sometimes better and
sometimes worse than when just applying category cutoff without feature cut-

	$h_C \rightarrow$	Relevant Documents (Percentage of occurrences)					Non-relevant documents (Percentage of occurrences)				
		< 1	1–2	2–4	4–8	≥ 8	< 1	1–2	2–4	4–8	≥ 8
	< 1	*43.91*	3.94	2.98	**0.91**	**0.07**	*33.95*	6.33	7.43	**5.01**	**1.25**
	1–2	*3.96*	4.23	3.01	**0.95**	**0.06**	*1.67*	3.11	3.90	**2.30**	**0.45**
interest	2–4	*2.26*	3.13	3.01	4.53	0.29	*0.68*	1.85	3.90	7.16	0.95
	4–8	*0.67*	0.75	3.01	9.03	1.18	*0.10*	0.30	3.90	9.30	2.15
	≥ 8	*0.06*	0.05	3.01	0.73	0.76	*0.00*	0.01	3.90	0.84	1.12
	< 1	*37.56*	4.09	3.07	**1.05**	**0.07**	*32.15*	7.52	8.08	**5.63**	**0.88**
	1–2	*3.50*	3.10	2.84	**0.95**	**0.05**	*1.59*	3.05	4.05	**2.32**	**0.49**
wheat	2–4	*2.28*	3.01	2.84	4.82	0.37	*0.54*	1.69	4.05	7.06	0.84
	4–8	*1.16*	1.24	2.84	11.83	1.79	*0.10*	0.31	4.05	9.15	1.84
	≥ 8	*0.06*	0.10	2.84	1.76	1.71	*0.00*	0.01	4.05	0.90	0.97
	$h_N \uparrow$										

Table 7.8. Percentage of occurrences within various ranges for symbol code lengths obtained when coding documents for the *interest* and *wheat* categories in the Reuters-21578 testing set.

off). However, these results are encouraging, and show that the approach is worthy of further investigation.

To investigate the effect of applying feature cutoff further, we analyzed the percentage of occurrences of the symbol (i.e. character) code length differences that were observed during coding of the relevant (category) and non-relevant (non-category) documents in the testing set. Table 7.8 summarizes the results for the two categories *interest* and *wheat* (these were chosen because they had the biggest positive and negative difference in values between the last two columns shown in Table 7.7). The columns in the table correspond to the category model's code length ranges ($h_C < 1; 1 \leq h_C < 2; \ldots$), and the rows to the negative model's code length ranges ($h_N < 1; 1 \leq h_N < 2; \ldots$) where h_C and h_N are the character code lengths (in bits) obtained when coding using the category and negative models respectively. Similar results were found for all categories, and not just the two shown in the table.

The results highlighted in bold and italics font in the table show a marked difference between the relevant and non-relevant documents in the observed code lengths. The results in italics are when the category models are performing very well (i.e. $h_C < 1$)—as shown, this occurs much more frequently for the relevant documents. The figures in bold font show a similar contrast— these occur when the category models are performing poorly (h_C is high) and the negative models are doing relatively well (h_N is low). This is likely to occur due to lack of training when a feature is unobserved in the relevant training documents but is common in the non-relevant ones (such as a sequence of text that occurs frequently in standard English, say).

These results are likely to have a significant impact on the overall decision, even though the number of occurrences of these cases ranges between 5 and

10% in total. This is because these code length values are high, whereas for a substantial proportion of the values, the difference in code lengths is small (i.e. the table shows that 30 to 40% of the values occur when both h_C and h_N are < 1). Of particular interest is the over one per cent difference in percentage for *interest* observed for the case when $h_C \geq 8$ and $h_N < 1$. In general, we found that the feature cutoff values chosen for each category varied between -4 and -8 (i.e. when the category model was performing very poorly compared to the negative model). The primary effect of this, as evidenced by the results in the table, is to discard features which are "suspiciously" rare in the non-relevant documents.

6.   Discussion

In this paper, we have presented the results of a study in the use of text compression models for text categorization. Compression models are firmly grounded in information theory, and we have exploited this theoretical under-pinning in applying text compression to categorization. We have argued that document cross-entropy (the average number of bits per symbol to encode the document using the model) provides an excellent ranking measure for many categorization tasks. We have demonstrated that another compression-based approach, namely maximization of the recall/precision average based on the cross entropy difference between category and complement of category mod-els, leads to improved performance for the specific task of topic categorization. We have also shown that this second method is equivalent to a two class (cate-gory, complement of category) Bayes classification.

We have argued that the PPM-family of compression models, and in particu-lar the character-based variants, have a number of advantages over word-based approaches. Problems of text segmentation (determining word boundaries), normalization such as stemming, and to a lesser extent word sense disambigua-tion, can be largely avoided. Instead, the PPM model discovers the important character contexts, which capture word boundary, morphology and word sense. Furthermore, we can apply our approach to languages where word segmenta-tion is far more problematic. And, models can be constructed over very diverse texts, which may include coded and numeric data.

We have performed a comprehensive set of experiments on the use of com-pression based language models for the following categorization tasks: lan-guage identification, authorship and genre categorization. The experiments demonstrate high levels of categorization performance that show these tech-niques are useable in operational environments. For the language identifica-tion experiments, suitable Web training and testing data for 16 different lan-guages were obtained using a popular search engine, and our PPM-based cross-entropy measure was able to identify the correct language in most cases, even for small samples of testing text (50 bytes). We were also able to accurately distinguish between dialects (e.g. American and British English) using this method.

Two tasks were investigated for the authorship experiments—that of determining known and disputed authorship. We were able to make novel use of the Reuters-21578 collection to test how well our cross-entropy based method performed at the first task, and we found that the method was able to accurately predict the Reuters authors in all but two cases, the contrary results occuring for authors who had substantial overlap in their topics of interest. For the second task, we applied the cross-entropy method to a famous problem in authorship attribution—that of determining the authorship of the Federalist papers—and we arrived at the same conclusions as other studies on the subject.

Experiments were performed using the `Newsgroups` data set for the more difficult problem of classifying by genre. The performance of the PPM-based categorizor compares favourably with the results reported by McCallum & Nigam (1998) who used a multi-variate Bernoulli event model and a multi-nomial model. Biber (1988) uses factor analysis to identify six dimensions of variation on the basis of linguistic co-occurrence patterns across 23 spoken and written genres. An interesting possibility for future work in this area is to compare the effectiveness of the PPM based classifier at distinguishing these variations.

We have also conducted preliminary experiments in topic categorization. For this task, we applied the cross-entropy difference measure. Our results indicate that PPM character-context compression models perform significantly better than word-based Na"ve Bayes classifiers, and approach the performance of the linear vector support machine text classifiers. Unlike earlier work presented in (Frank at al., 2000), we have shown that the performance of various PPM n-order models are comparable (for $n \geq 2$), although overall order 3 models are best.

Feature selection in the context of compression models has shown small improvements (see the final two columns of Table 7.7). We based our feature selection on selecting features which will maximize recall/precision based on the code length difference. Our analysis of the distribution of feature code lengths over relevant (category) and non-relevant (non-category) documents indicates that our thresholding strategy was effective in removing some evidently poor features, but that many features are retained with poor discrimination values. Currently, features are ranked and selected based on the "local" code length difference for an individual symbol (and context). We conjecture that ranking features by the likely "global" effect they would have on code length difference may result in improved feature selection.

An important issue is the size of the training data. We have found that for certain applications such as language identification and authorship ascription, a relatively small amount of training data yields excellent results (see Sections 5.1 and 5.2). However, our topic-based categorization experiments show that lack of training data can have an affect on performance and possibly this will remain an impediment to compression-based approaches in future. However, it may be possible to use a hierarchy of models, whose purpose is to progressively select features (and hence text), for subsequent compression-based categorization. For example, one could imagine a hierarchy of models for this application comprising: English model, Reuter's model (and we have evidence to suggest such a model exits), and Category models. Alternatively, one could combine genre categorization, which provides a broader classification of the data, with topic categorization in a two-tiered approach.

The idea of using text compression models is not new. Text compression models have been used for various categorization problems: language identification, dialect identification, and authorship attribution, to name but some. Recently, they have been applied to the arguably more demanding problems of subject/genre categorization, as exemplified by the Reuter's categorization task. However, unlike (Frank at al., 2000), we remain optimistic about compression-based text categorization, both because of the ease of applying the approach, and because our results indicate performance is comparable to other well-performed approaches, and capable of being still further improved. For example, some compression-based research we have conducted into combining multiple models through switching methods (Teahan and Harper, 2001) has shown significant improvements in compression over single model approaches, and these gains might transfer across into the text categorization arena. Lastly, it seems highly likely that new applications will emerge in which the combination of text compression and text categorization, when used in tandem, will be a potent mixture, especially given the huge amounts of uncategorized text which is stored on the Internet, and on Intranets.

References

Apte, C., Damerau, F. and Weiss, S. "Text mining with decision rules and decision trees,", *ACM Transactions on Information Ssystems*, 12:3, 23-251.

Bell, T. C., Cleary, J. G. and Witten, I. H. (1990). *Text compression*. New Jersey: Prentice Hall.

Benedetto, D., Caglioti, E. and Loreto, V. (2002) "Language trees and zipping," *Physical Review Letters*, 88:4, 048702-1–4.

Biber, D. (1988). *Variations across speech and writing*. Cambridge: Cambridge University Press.

Boggess, L. Argawal, R. and Davis, R. (1991). "Disambiguation of prepositional phrases in atomatically labelled technical text," *AAAI'91*, 155–159.

Brown, P. F., Della Pietra, S. A., Della Pietra, V. J., Lai, J. C. and Mercer, R. L. (1992). "An estimate of an upper bound for the entropy of English,", *Computational Linguistics*, 18:1, 31–40.

Charniak, E. (1993). *Statistical language learning*. Cambridge, Massachusetts: MIT Press.

Cleary, J. G. and Witten, I. H. (1984). "Data compression using adaptive coding and partial string matching," *IEEE Transactions on Communications*, 32:4, 396–402.

Cohen, W.J. and Singer, Y. (1996). "Context-sensitive learning methods for text categorization," *SIGIR '96: Proceedings 19th Annual International ACM SIGIR Conference on Research and Development in Information Retrieval*, 307–315.

Dumais, S., Platt, J., Heckerman, D. and Sahami, M. (1998). "Inductive learning algorithms and representations for text categorization," *Proceedings International Conference on Information and Knowledge Management*, 148–155.

Dunning, T. (1994). "Statistical identification of language," Computing Research Laboratory, New Mexico State University: Technical Report 94–273.

Francis, W.N. and Kucera, H. (1982). *Frequency analysis of English usage: lexicon and grammar*. Boston: Houghton Mifflin.

Frank, Eibe, Chui, Chang and Witten, Ian H. (2000). "Text categorization using compression models," *Proceedings IEEE Data Compression Conference*, Snowbird, Utah.

Ganeson, R. and Sherman, A.T. (1993). "Statistical techniques for language recognition: an introduction and guide for cryptanalysts," *Cryptologia*, 17:4, 321–366.

Howard, Paul G. (1993). *The design and analysis of efficient lossless data compression systems*. Ph.D. thesis. Providence, Rhode Island: Brown University.

Joachims, T. (1998). "Text categorization with support vector machines: Learning with many relevant features," *Proceedings of the 10th European Conference on Machine Learning*. Springer-Verlag.

Johansson, S. Atwell, E., Garside, R. and Leech, G. (1986). *The tagged LOB Corpus*. Bergen: Norwegian Computing Centre for the Humanities.

Juola, P. (1998). "What Can We Do With Small Corpora? Document Categorization Via Cross-Entropy," *Proceedings of the Workshop on Similarity and Categorization*.

Kessler, B., Nunberg, G. and Schutze, H. (1997) "Automatic detection of text genre," *Proceedings of the 35th Annual Meeting of the Association for Computational Linguistics*.

Khmelev, D. V. (2000). "Disputed authorship resolution through using releative empirical entropy for Markov Chains of letters in human language text," *Journal of Quantitative Linguistics*, 7:3, 201–207.

Kukushkina, O.V., Polikarpov, A.A. and Khmelev, D. V. (2001). "Using literal and grammatical statistics for authorship attribution," letters in human language text," *Problems of Information Transmission*, 37:2, 96–108.

Lee, Y. and Myaeng, S.H. (2002). "Text genre classification with genre-revealing and subject revealing features," *SIGIR '02: Proceedings 25th Annual International ACM SIGIR Conference on Research and Development in Information Retrieval*, 145–150.

Lewis, D. D. (1994). "Guest editorial," *ACM Transactions on Information Systems,* 12:3, 231.

Lewis, D. D. and Ringuette, M. (1994). "A comparison of two learning algorithms for text categorization," *Proceedings Annual Symposium on Document Analysis and Information Retrieval,* 37–50.

Manning, C. D. and Schutze, Hinrich. (1999). *Foundations of statistical natural language processing.* Cambridge, Massachusetts: MIT Press.

McCallum, A. and Nigam, K. (1998). "A comparison of event models for Naive Bayes text classification," *AAAI-98: Workshop on learning for text categorization.*

Moffat, Alistair. (1990). "Implementing the PPM data compression scheme," *IEEE Transactions on Communications,* 38:1, 1917–1921.

Mosteller, F. and Wallace, D.L. (1984). *Applied Bayesian and classical inference: the case of the Federalist papers.* New York: Springer-Verlag.

Pang, B. and Lee, L. (2002). "Thumbs up? Sentiment classification using machine learning techniques," *Proceedings of the 2002 Conference on Empirical Methods in Natural Language Processing.*

Shannon, C. E. (1948). "A mathematical theory of communication," *Bell System Technical Journal,* 27, 379-423,623-656.

Rose, T.G., Stevenson, M. and Whitehead, M. (2002). "The Reuters Corpus Volume 1—from yesterday's news to tomorrow's language resources," *Proceedings of the Third International Conference on Language Resources and Evaluation* Las Palmas de Gran Canaris, 29–31.

Schutze, H., Hull, D. and Pedersen, J.O. (1995). "A comparison of classifiers and document representations for the routing problem," *SIGIR '95: Proceedings 18th Annual International ACM SIGIR Conference on Research and Development in Information Retrieval* 229–237.

Stamatatos, E., Fakotakis, N. and Kokkinakis, G. (2001). "Automatics text categorization in terms of genre and author," *Computational Linguistics*, 26:4, 471–495.

Teahan, W. J. (1998). *Modelling English text.* Ph.D. thesis. Hamilton, New Zealand: Waikato University.

Teahan, W. J. (2000). "Text classification and segmentation using minimum cross-entropy," *Proceedings RIAO'2000.* Paris, France. April, 2, 943–961.

Teahan, W. J. and Harper, D.J. (2001). "Combining PPM models using a text mining approach," *Proceedings DCC'2001*. Snowbird, Utah. 153–162.

Teahan, W. J., Wen, Y. Y., McNabb, R., Witten, I. H. (2000). "Using compression models to segment Chinese text," *Computational Linguistics,* 26:3, 375–393.

Witten, I. H., Bray, Z., Mahoui, M. and Teahan, W. J. (1999). "Using language models for generic entity extraction," *ICML-99 Worskhop: Machine learning in text data analysis.*

Weiner, E., Pedersen, J.O., and Weigend, A.S. (1995) "A neural network approach to topic spotting," *Proceedings of the Fourth Annual Symposium on Document Analysis and Information Retrieval.*

Wolters, M. and Kirsten, M. (1999). "Exploring the use of linguistic features in domain and genre classification," *Proceedings of the Meeting of the European Chapter of the Association for Computational Linguistics*, Bergen, Norway.

Yang, Y. (1999) "An evaluation of statistical approaches to text categorization," *Information Retrieval.* 1:1, 69–90.

Yang, Y. and Pederson, J.O. (1997) "A comparative study on feature selection in text categorization," *Proceedings International Conference on Machine Learning.* 412–420.

Chapter 8

APPLICATIONS OF SCORE DISTRIBUTIONS IN INFORMATION RETRIEVAL

R. Manmatha

Center for Intelligent Information Retrieval
Computer Science Department
University of Massachusetts
Amherst, MA 01003
manmatha@cs.umass.edu

Abstract   Researchers have recently shown that document scores of a number of different text search engines may be fitted on a per query basis using an exponential distribution for the set of non-relevant documents and a normal distribution for the set of relevant documents. This model fits a large number of different search engines including probabilistic search engines like INQUERY, vector space search engines like SMART and also LSI search engines and a language model engine. The model also appears to be true of search engines operating on a number of different languages. This leads to the hypothesis that all 'good' text search engines operating on any language have similar characteristics.

We then show that given a query for which relevance information is not available, a mixture model consisting of an exponential and a normal distribution can be fitted to the score distribution. These distributions can be used to map the scores of a search engine to probabilities.

This model has many possible applications. For example, the outputs of different search engines can be combined by averaging the probabilities (optimal if the search engines are independent) or by using the probabilities to select the best engine for each query. It has also been applied to filtering. We discuss these and other applications of score modeling in information retrieval.

1.   Introduction

In the 1960's and 70's, Swets, 1963 and other researchers attempted to model the score distributions of search engines for relevant and non-relevant documents and then use statistical detection theory to find a threshold to decide what was relevant. This approach seems to not have been successful for several

W.B. Croft and J. Lafferty (eds.), Language Modeling for Information Retrieval, 167–188.
© 2003 *Kluwer Academic Publishers.*

reasons. First, the data from several queries was often combined in attempts to model it. In general, it is difficult to find a model which works when the data from different queries is averaged. Second, the choice of the models often seems to have been incorrect; Swets, for example, assumed that the scores of both the relevant and non-relevant documents could be modeled using Gaussians. Early on, recognizing that this was probably incorrect, van Rijsbergen, 1979 commented that for search engines like SMART there was no evidence that the two distributions were similarly distributed let alone normally. Third, early researchers in the 60's and 70's often did not have sufficient computational power or the data necessary for modeling. Finally and most important, estimating the score distribution required knowledge of the relevance of at least some set of the documents. While this may be reasonable for some tasks like information filtering, in general, relevance information is not available for most information retrieval tasks.

Recently, it has been shown that score distributions for a given query may be modeled using an exponential distribution for the set of non-relevant documents and a normal distribution for the set of relevant documents. This has been demonstrated by Manmatha et al., 2001 for search engines and by Arampatzis et al., 2001; Arampatzis and van Hameren, 2001 for information filtering. Manmatha et al., 2001 also showed that when relevance information is not available, these distributions can be recovered by fitting a mixture model with a Gaussian and an exponential component to the output scores of search engines on a per query basis. To the best of our knowledge, this is the first attempt at recovering the relevant and non-relevant distributions when no relevance information is available.

This model has been tested on a large number of different search engines on TREC data. For every search engine tested, the above model has been shown to approximate the data well. The search engines tested have included probabilistic search engines like INQUERY and OKAPI, vector space search engines like SMART as well as Bellcore's LSI search engine. Even language model based search engines follow the same distributions. The model also works for search engines in other languages.

We hypothesize that all 'good' text search engines operating on any language have similar characteristics. Since other information retrieval tasks like filtering and topic detection and tracking have search at their core, it is likely that the same score distributions underly them and in fact this has been demonstrated for filtering by Arampatzis and van Hameren, 2001; Arampatzis et al., 2001. These score distributions probably reflect some underlying model of language itself and in Manmatha et al., 2001 there is a discussion of how the shape of the score distributions may arise given certain assumptions about word distributions in documents.

There are different ways to use score distributions in information retrieval applications. For example, in the case of filtering Arampatzis and van Hameren, 2001 and Zhang and Callan, 2001 show how to select thresholds assuming that the relevant and non-relevant distributions can be estimated using relevance judgments on a subset. Manmatha and Sever, 2002 show how to use estimates of the non-relevant distribution to combine the outputs of different search engines.

An alternative approach assumes that the relevant and non-relevant score distributions may be used to map scores to probabilities using Bayes' Rule. Note that no training is required for this approach and in addition no assumption is made on the kind of search engine used. The probabilities of relevance obtained from this model have many possible applications. For example thresholds for filtering and topic detection and tracking may be selected using this approach. Alternatively, the probabilities may be used to combine the results of using different engines to search a common database (Manmatha et al., 2001) or to combine the search from many distributed databases or multilingual or multi-modal databases.

In this chapter, we first discuss how scores may be modeled and we then discuss different possible applications of score modeling. More details about score modeling may be found in Manmatha et al., 2001.

The rest of the chapter is divided as follows. The next section discusses related work. This is followed by Section 3 which discusses the modeling of score distributions of relevant and non-relevant documents and how these distributions may be recovered in the absence of relevance information by using a mixture model. Solving for the mixture model using Expectation-Maximization (EM) is also discussed. Finally, Bayes' Rule is used to map the scores to probabilities of relevance. Section 4 discusses the theoretical intuition behind using such models. Section 5 discusses how the model and the probabilities derived from it can be used for evidence combination. Section 6 discusses possibilities of future work in this area. Finally, Section 6 concludes the paper.

2. Related Work

Very early on a number of different researchers realized that fitting score distributions to relevant and non-relevant data would be useful. Swets, 1963 proposed fitting both the relevant and non-relevant scores using normal distributions and then using statistical decision theory to find a threshold for deciding what was relevant. Bookstein, 1977 pointed out that Swets implicitly relied on an equal variance assumption. Bookstein also raised the issue of whether it might be more appropriate to model the score distributions using Poissons. This modeling does not appear to have been done. van Rijsbergen, 1979 commented that for search engines like SMART there was no evidence that the distributions were similarly distributed let alone normally. We observe here that the empirical data for a large number of search engines clearly shows that the two distributions are not similar. Vogt and Cottrell, 1999 showed that in many cases (but not always) the scores for non-relevant documents *averaged over all 50 queries* were exponentially distributed. We note that the work in this paper focuses on score distributions on a per query basis. The results are not likely to be true when averaged over multiple queries.

Baumgarten, 1999 discussed fitting the scores of all (roughly the top 1000) documents (not just relevant or non-relevant) of one particular search engine using a Gamma distribution in the context of distributed retrieval. We note that when the number of relevant documents is small, a good approximation to the combined distribution is an exponential distribution. In such a situation the Gamma distribution, which is a generalization of an exponential distribution, will model the score distribution of all documents. However, there are a number of disadvantages of this model. First, the relevant and non-relevant distributions are not estimated separately hence limiting its usefulness. For example a posterior probability can no longer be computed from the complete distribution. Second, the approximation breaks down when the number of relevant distributions is large. Finally, the Gamma distribution (in this case) tends to give a lot of weight to the scores near zero. However, the estimates of the distribution of the scores near zero are likely to be misleading since the data provided only consists of a small fraction of all documents.

In related and independent work Arampatzis and van Hameren, 2001; Arampatzis et al., 2001 discussed how the relevant scores could be modeled using a Gaussian distribution and the non-relevant scores using an exponential distribution. They applied this to selecting the threshold dynamically for a filtering application where the relevance of a small subset of the data is known ahead of time. This subset can then be used to derive the relevant and non-relevant distributions separately. Zhang and Callan, 2001 argued that the distribution recovered by Arampatzis et al were biased and suggested ways to improve the estimation.

All previous researchers (including Arampatzis and van Hameren, 2001; Arampatzis et al., 2001) assume that relevance information for some or all of the set is available. To our knowledge, there is no literature on recovering the relevant and non-relevant distributions when no relevance information is available and Manmatha et al., 2001; Manmatha et al., is the first attempt to do this.

3. Modeling Score Distributions of Search Engines

Without prior knowledge it is impossible to actually mark individual documents as relevant or non-relevant. However, we will show that one can obtain a statistical distribution of relevant and non-relevant documents which is useful for many information retrieval tasks. Two different questions arise when modeling score distributions. First, can score distributions be modeled. That is, is there a parametric representation of the relevant and non-relevant score distributions. Second, can these distributions be recovered when relevance information is not available.

A number of different approaches suggest themselves. For example, one could in theory train a model over a few queries and then apply it to the remaining queries. This approach does not work as there is considerable variation from query to query. Instead, the model must learn the model parameters from the data for a given query. Thus, the approach we adopt is to try to obtain a parametric representation given relevance data.

In this section we briefly describe how the outputs of different search engines are modeled using data from the text retrieval conferences (TREC). TREC data provides the scores and relevance information for the top 1000 documents for different search engines. Data from the ad hoc track of TREC were used for the experiments here. We will show examples of the modeling on queries from INQUERY. INQUERY is a probabilistic search engine from the University of Massachusetts, Amherst.

There are 50 queries available with document scores and relevance information for each query. We examine the relevant and non-relevant data separately. The data are first normalized so that the minimum and maximum score for a query are 0 and 1 respectively.

Figure 8.1 shows a histogram of scores for query 151 from TREC-3 for a set of non-relevant documents. The histogram clearly shows the rapid fall in the number of non-relevant documents with increasing score. A maximum-likelihood fit of an exponential curve to this data is also shown. For the purposes of fitting the exponential, the origin is shifted to the document with the lowest score. Figure 8.2 shows a histogram of scores for the set of relevant documents for the same query. The histogram approximates a normal distribution. The exponential fit previously obtained for the non-relevant documents is also plotted in the figure.

The same process was repeated for all 50 queries in this track and in most cases it was found possible to approximate the non-relevant data with exponentials and the relevant data using Gaussians. The relevant data can be fitted with a Gaussian reasonably well when there is a sufficient number of relevant documents. Usually more than about 30 relevant documents were needed. When the number of relevant documents was small, the fit was bad. However, we

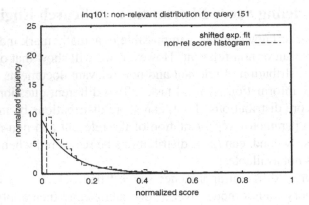

Figure 8.1. Histogram and shifted exponential fit to non-relevant data for query 151 IN-QUERY (inq101)

believe this is not because the Gaussian was a bad fit but because we don't have enough relevant documents to compute the statistics in these cases. The exponential was also a good fit to the non-relevant data.

Our modeling has focused on using the top 1000 documents. This is because TREC only provides the results for the top 1000 documents. There is a second practical reason for focusing on the top 1000 documents. The aim of the experiment is to accurately model the transition between relevant and non-relevant documents and this region is found (in every case we have looked at) in the top 1000 documents. However, we note that our results will not change in any practical way if the top 2000 or the top 5000 documents were used (this has been experimentally verified for some search engines for which we have data). If anything, the Gaussian distributions are estimated better since the number of relevant documents will usually increase.

When relevance information is known, one can fit the scores using either a non-parametric distribution like a histogram or a parametric distribution as done here. When running a new query, however, relevance information is not available. Clearly, it would be useful to fit the score distributions of such data. A natural way to do this is to fit a mixture model of a shifted exponential and a Gaussian to the combined score distribution and this is discussed in the next section. We note that it is not practical to use a non-parametric technique like a histogram when relevance information is not available.

3.1 Estimating Score Distributions in the Absence of Relevance Information

How can one estimate the score distributions in the absence of relevance information? There are a couple of different ways which have been proposed for estimating the non-relevant score distribution but there is only one way to estimate the relevant distribution.

The fraction of relevant documents returned by a search engine is usually quite small for most queries. Thus, in many cases a good estimate of the non-relevant distribution may be obtained by assuming that it can be approximated by the distribution of all documents. Note that the same strategy cannot be used to estimate the relevant distribution. One may wonder whether there is any advantage to recovering an estimate of just the non-relevant distribution. In fact, the non-relevant score distribution alone is useful in some cases. For example, in meta search, the scores of two different search engines may be normalized by equalizing the non-relevant distributions. This has been successfully done in Manmatha et al., and will be briefly mentioned later in this chapter.

The more interesting question is whether the relevant and non-relevant distributions may both be recovered simultaneously without any knowledge of relevance. This can in fact be done using a mixture model and solving for the mixture model using the Expectation-Maximization algorithm (EM). We now discuss how a mixture model may be fitted to the score distributions.

3.1.1 Mixture Model Fit.
Consider the situation where a query is run using a search engine. The search engine returns scores but there is no relevance information available. We show below that in this situation, a mixture model consisting of an exponential and a Gaussian may be fitted to the score distributions. We can then identify the Gaussian with the distribution of the relevant information in the mixture and the exponential with the distribution of the non-relevant information in the mixture. Essentially this allows us to find the parameters of the relevant and non-relevant distributions without knowing relevance information apriori.

The density of a mixture model $p(x)$ can be written in terms of the densities of the individual components $p(x|j)$ as follows (Bishop, 1995):

$$p(x) = \sum_j P(j)p(x|j) \tag{8.1}$$

where j identifies the individual component, the $P(j)$ are known as mixing parameters and satisfy $\sum_{j=1}^{2} P(j) = 1, 0 \leq P(j) \leq 1$. In the present case, there are two components, an exponential density with mean λ

$$p(x|1) = \lambda \exp(-\lambda x) \tag{8.2}$$

and a Gaussian density with mean μ and variance σ^2

$$p(x|2) = \frac{1}{\sqrt{2\pi}\sigma} \exp(-\frac{(x-\mu)^2}{2\sigma^2}) \qquad (8.3)$$

A standard approach to finding the mixing parameters and the parameters of the component densities is to use Expectation Maximization (EM) Bishop, 1995. This is an iterative procedure where the Expectation and Maximization steps are alternated. Space precludes us from discussing the details of the EM algorithm and the update equations used. The reader is referred to Bishop, 1995 for a good introduction to EM.

In the E-step the current value of the parameters is used to compute the expectation of

$$E[E^{comp}] = \sum_{n=1}^{N} \sum_{j=1}^{M} P^{old}(j|x^n) ln\{P^{new}(j)p^{new}(x^n|j)\} \qquad (8.4)$$

where

$$P(j|x) = \frac{p(x|j)P(j)}{p(x)} \qquad (8.5)$$

The M-step involves maximizing the expectation (after using the expressions for the densities of the two components). This maximization leads to a set of update procedures for the parameters of the densities and the mixing parameters. The EM procedure leads to the following update equations for the parameters:

$$\mu^{new} = \frac{\sum_n P^{old}(2|x^n)x^n}{\sum_n P^{old}(2|x^n)} \qquad (8.6)$$

$$(\sigma^{new})^2 = \frac{\sum_n P^{old}(2|x^n)||x^n - \mu^{new}||^2}{\sum_n P^{old}(2|x^n)} \qquad (8.7)$$

$$\lambda^{new} = \frac{\sum_n P^{old}(1|x^n)}{\sum_n P^{old}(1|x^n)x^n} \qquad (8.8)$$

$$P(1)^{new} = \frac{1}{N}\sum_n P^{old}(1|x) \qquad (8.9)$$

More details about the derivation of these update equations are available in Manmatha et al., . The procedure needs an initial estimate of the component densities and mixing parameters. Given that, it rapidly converges to a solution. Using EM to fit the data gives the mixture fit shown in Figure 8.3. The figure plots the mixture density as well as the component densities for the exponential and Gaussian fits. For comparison Figure 8.2 shows the exponential and Gaussian fits to the non-relevant and relevant data. Comparing the two figures, it appears that the strategy of interpreting the Gaussian component of the mixture with the relevant distribution and the exponential component of the mixture with the non-relevant distribution is a reasonable one. We should note that the correspondence between the mixture components and the fits to the relevant/non-relevant data is not always as good as that shown here but in general it is a reasonable fit.

This model has been fitted to a large number of search engines on TREC and TREC data including probabilistic engines like INQUERY and OKAPI, a vector space engine (SMART), Bellcore's LSI engine as well as a language model search engine (that of Lavrenko and Croft, 2001. The fit appears to be better for "good" search engines (engines with a higher average precision in TREC-3) and worse for those with a lower average precision. The model has also been able fitted to document scores for searches on search engines indexing other languages like Chinese. See Manmatha et al., 2001; Manmatha et al., for more details.

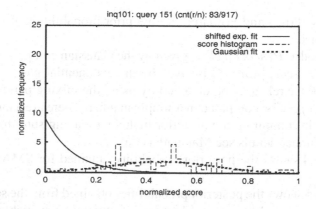

Figure 8.2. Exponential fit to non-relevant data and Gaussian fit to relevant data for query 151 INQUERY (inq101)

3.2 Computing Posterior Probabilities

Using Bayes' Rule one can compute the probability of relevance given the score as

$$P(rel|score) = \frac{P(score|rel)P(rel)}{P(score|rel)P(rel) + P(score|nonrel)P(nonrel)} \quad (8.10)$$

where $P(rel|score)$ is the probability of relevance of the document given its score, $P(score|rel)$ and $P(score|nonrel)$ are the probabilities of score given that the document is relevant and score given that the document is non-relevant

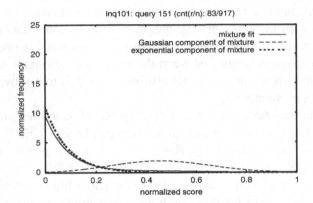

Figure 8.3. Mixture model fit showing exponential component, Gaussian component and the combined mixture for query 151 INQUERY (inq101). Compare with Figure8.2

respectively. P(rel) and P(nonrel) are the prior probabilities of relevance and non-relevance.

In our model, $P(score|rel)$ is given by the Gaussian component of the mixture while $P(score|nonrel)$ is given by the exponential part of the mixture. P(rel) and P(nonrel) may be obtained by using the mixing parameters. Thus, $P(rel|score)$ can be computed in a simple manner. There are a number of considerations in computing the posterior including making sure that it is monotonic. For further details see Manmatha et al., 2001.

Figure 8.4 shows the posterior probability obtained for SMART for query 164.

Figure 8.5 shows the posterior probabilities obtained from the separate Gaussian and exponential fits when relevance information is available and also the posterior probabilities obtained from the Gaussian and exponential part of the mixture. P(rel) and P(nonrel) are taken to be the mixing parameters in this case. Note that the differences in the two curves reflect fitting errors both for the mixture fit as well as the separate Gaussian and exponential fits obtained when relevance information is available.

In general we expect the posterior probabilities to be a monotonic function of the score. In other words as the score increases so should the posterior probability. In some cases we may have the situation depicted in Figure 8.5 where the posterior seems to decrease with increasing scores. The figure depicts the posterior probabilities for INQUERY for query 154 using TREC-3 data. This situation arises because the Gaussian density falls much more rapidly than the exponential and hence the two densities intersect twice. Note that in this case the posterior probabilities obtained both from the mixture fit (no relevance information available) as well as that obtained using relevance data show this

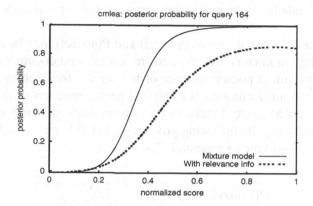

Figure 8.4. Posterior probability for query 164 for the SMART engine for TREC-3 data. The dotted line is obtained from the separate Gaussian and exponential fits computed using relevance information. The solid line is obtained from the mixture fits.

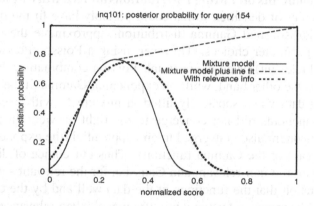

Figure 8.5. Posterior probability for query 154 for the INQUERY engine for TREC-3 data. The bold dotted line is obtained from the separate Gaussian and exponential fits computed using relevance information. The solid line is obtained from the mixture fits. The dotted line joins the maximum point of the mixture to the point(1,1). The final posterior mapping follows the solid line up to the maximum point and then the straight line curve thus preserving monotonicity

problem. One solution would be not to use a Gaussian density but to use another function which has the same form (like a Gamma distribution) but decreases less rapidly. As we discuss below the problem with this approach is that the mixture model does not converge to a reasonable solution. Instead we force the posterior probability to be monotonic by drawing a straight line from the point where the posterior is maximum to the point (1,1). The final posterior probability curve is given by the portion of the posterior probability computed using Bayes' rule up to the maximum portion of the curve and the straight line thereafter.

We have assumed that the priors P(rel) and P(nonrel) may be estimated using the mixing parameters. When there are few relevant documents the mixing parameters provide a poorer estimate of the priors. In a normal retrieval the number of relevant documents is small and hence estimates of the mixing parameters are less accurate. Extensive experiments have shown that P(nonrel) is best estimated using the following procedure. Let P(1) be the mixing parameter corresponding to the exponential. Then

$$P(nonrel) = \{ \begin{array}{ll} P(1) & if\ P(1) \leq 0.8 \\ 0.8 & otherwise \end{array} \tag{8.11}$$

and P(rel) = 1 - P(nonrel). This approach to estimating the priors improves the average precision results slightly when we combine results.

3.2.1   Comments on Fitting Distributions and Mixture Models.   There

is a large family of densities which could possibly have fit the data. For example, the Poisson and Gamma distributions approximate the Gaussian for appropriate parameter choices. However, using a Poisson/Poisson (for non-relevant and relevant) or an exponential/ Poisson combination did not fit the data well. On the other hand, while an exponential/Gamma fit the non-relevant and relevant data when separately fitted, a mixture fit with exponential and Gamma components did not converge to the right answer. In this case the Gamma component also converged to an exponential (the exponential density is a special case of the Gamma function). Thus our choice of distributions - exponential for the non-relevant and Gaussian for the relevant - is dictated by the consideration that the functions fit the data well and by the consideration that they can be recovered using a mixture model when relevance information is not available.

Surprisingly, a mixture of an exponential and 2 Gaussians does not work any better than a mixture of an exponential and 1 Gaussian.

4.   Combining Search Engines Indexing the Same Database

It is often useful to combine the results of search engines indexing the same database. The combination results are often better than those for the best single engine. Early approaches to combining score distributions have focused on normalizing the range of the scores and then combining them by simple techniques like linear combination or by taking the minimum and maximum scores. However, a simple (linear) range normalization does not take into account the actual distribution of the scores. We first discuss related literature in the area of combining search engines before discussing two different score modeling techniques.

4.1 Prior Work

A recent and extensive survey of evidence combination in information retrieval is provided by Croft, 2000. Fox and Shaw, 1994 proposed a number of combination techniques including operators like the MIN and the MAX. Other techniques included one that involved setting the score of each document in the combination to the sum of the scores obtained by the individual search engines (COMBSUM), while in another the score of each document was obtained by multiplying this sum by the number of engines which had non-zero scores (COMBMNZ). Note that summing (COMBSUM) is equivalent to averaging while COMBMNZ is equivalent to weighted averaging. Lee (Lee, 1995; Lee, 1997) studied this further with six different engines. His contribution was to normalize each engine on a per query basis improving results substantially. Lee showed that COMBMNZ worked best, followed by COMB-SUM while operators like MIN and MAX were the worst. Lee also observed that the best combinations were obtained when systems retrieved similar sets of relevant documents and dissimilar sets of non-relevant documents. Vogt and Cottrell, 1998 also verified this observation by looking at pairwise combinations of systems. A probabilistic approach using ranks rather than scores was proposed last year by Aslam and Montague (Aslam et al., 2000; Aslam and Montague, 2001). This involved extensive training across about 25 queries to obtain the probability of a rank given a query. Aslam and Montague were able to demonstrate that rank information alone can be used to produce good combination results. The main difficulty with this technique seems to be the extensive training required of every engine on a substantial number of queries.

Montague and Aslam (Montague and Aslam, 2001) proposed three different normalization schemes for meta-search. The methods involved linearly shifting and scaling scores so that the mappings in Table 8.1 were achieved. They tested these with some well known combination techniques including Comb-Sum and CombMNZ (Fox and Shaw, 1994; Lee, 1995; Lee, 1997).

Name	Method
Standard	Map min to 0 and max to 1.
Sum	Map min to 0 and the sum to 1.
ZMUV	Map mean to 0 and variance to 1.

Table 8.1. Normalization Methods Suggested by Montague and Aslam

For more discussions of related work on previous work on score modeling and on combining different search engines see Manmatha et al., 2001.

4.2   Score Normalization by Equalizing Non-relevant Distributions

Instead, a better approach to normalization involves equalizing the non-relevant distributions (Manmatha and Sever, 2002). The rationale for doing this is that what one wants to do is to normalize the distribution of scores of random documents. In some sense, the non-relevant documents returned are random. Since the non-relevant distributions are exponentials, this may be done by simply dividing by the means of the non-relevant distributions (the resulting mean is 1 for all engines). How does one estimate the non-relevant distribution? There are three ways this can be done.

1 One can assume that most documents are non-relevant. Then, the total distribution is a good approximation to the non-relevant distribution. One can, therefore, fit an exponential to the total distribution and assume that this is a good approximation to the non-relevant distribution. This works reasonably well in many cases. It is also equivalent to the sum normalization suggested by Montague and Aslam Montague and Aslam, 2001

2 One can use the exponential part of the mixture model as an estimate of the non-relevant distribution. This also works fairly well in some cases.

3 The best approximation turns out to be to take an average of the means from the two estimates above and use that as an estimate of the mean of the non-relevant distribution

The different search engines may then be combined by averaging the normalized scores. This approach yields very good results (see Manmatha and Sever, 2002). An advantage of this approach is that the relevant distribution is not required and hence the technique is likely to be successful even when there are few relevant documents.

4.3   Posterior Probability Approach

A second approach involves using the posterior probabilities computed in the previous section.

There are a number of possible ways the probabilities can be used to combine the search engines. A simple approach involves averaging the probabilities. This is optimal in the sense of minimizing the Bayes' error if the search engines are independent. Of course the outputs of search engines are not necessarily independent but this is a reasonable first approximation. In the following discussions, data are taken from TREC-3, INQUERY and SMART are the individual engines to be combined, META200 denotes combination by averaging the posteriors obtained using the mixture model, while META900 denotes the

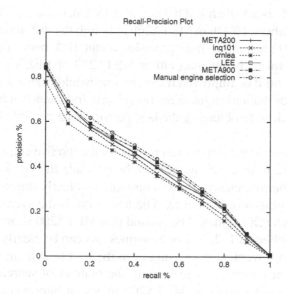

Figure 8.6. Recall precision graphs for combining inq101 and crnlea using different techniques (see text). Data from TREC-3

combination by averaging the posterior probabilities using the Gaussian and exponential fits assuming relevance is given. Thus, any difference between META200 and META900 is caused by the errors in performing a mixture fit to the model. LEE denotes Lee's COMBMNZ Lee, 1997 technique which is one of the best ad hoc (in the sense of being empirically motivated) techniques around. LEE's technique involves normalizing the socre of each engine on a per query basis. The score of each document in the combination is then obtained by multiplying this sum by the number of engines which had non-zero scores (COMBMNZ). COMBMNZ is equivalent to weighted averaging. The manual engine selection technique involves selecting the best engine(s) and discarding the worst engine(s) on a per query basis using the average precision for that query. Manual engine selection provides an indication of the best combination result we can achieve. Note that both META900 and manual engine selection require relevance information and are only plotted to provide a baseline for understanding the limits of combination.

Figure 8.6 shows recall-precision plots for combining INQUERY and SMART on TREC-3 data. Precision is defined as the fraction of retrieved documents which are relevant while recall is the fraction of relevant documents which have been retrieved. The recall-precision graph is usually created by averaging over a certain number of queries - in this case 50. As the figure shows META200 performs considerably better than either INQUERY and SMART -

in fact about 6% better than INQUERY and 13% better than SMART. LEE is slightly better (about 1%) than META200 although the difference is not significant. META900 has an average precision about 10% better than INQUERY and clearly performs better than either META200 or LEE's implying that if the mixture fit could be improved the technique would perform even better. Finally, the plot for manual engine selection clearly indicates that both META200 and LEE's are close to obtaining the best performance possible from combination.

Figure 8.7 describes combination results for the top five engines in TREC-3. The x-axis is the number of engines combined while the y-axis is the average precision. As the plot clearly shows combination clearly improves the results. There are four graphs in the figure. The first curve is the average precision of the individual search engines. The second plot META200 shows the combination method applied to 1, 2, 3, 4 or 5 engines. As can be clearly seen there is a considerable improvement over using even the best search engine and overall the improvement seems to increase with the number of search engines combined. With the top 2 engines, META200 shows an improvement of 6% over the best single engine and using the top 3 engines, META200 shows an improvement of almost 12%. LEE's COMBMNZ technique is also shown in the same graph. It's average precision is seen to be slightly worse than META200 but the difference is not really significant. The performance obtained using META900 (i.e. combination with the posterior probabilities obtained with relevance information) is 15% better than the best single engine. Again this indicates that if the mixture fit were improved we could do even better.

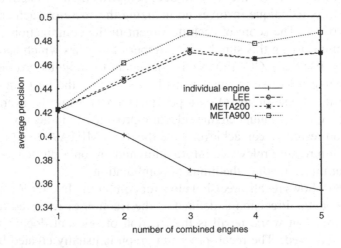

Figure 8.7.   Recall precision graphs for combining the best five techniques from TREC-3.

This approach to combination works for other engines and on documents operating on other languages. The probabilities may also be used to select engines on a per query basis. For more details see Manmatha et al., 2001; Manmatha et al., .

The probabilistic approach is slightly inferior to the approach discussed earlier which involved normalizing the non-relevant distributions. This is probably due to the problems involved in estimating the parameters of the mixture model. Since there are often few relevant documents, the mixture model estimates may sometimes be poor.

5. Applications to Filtering and Topic Detection and Tracking

Arampatzis et al (Arampatzis and van Hameren, 2001; Arampatzis et al., 2001) and Zhang and Callan, 2001 show how to use score modeling to compute the threshold in information filtering. In their approach, they assume that the relevance information for some subset of documents is available. Further, once a given document is retrieved, relevance information is provided for it. This relevance information can be used to refine the model for documents which need to be judged later (it cannot be used to change anything for the past).

We briefly examine the approach used by Arampatzis et al. In filtering, the T9U cost function is defined as the difference between twice the number of detected relevant documents N_{det} minus the number of false alarms N_{fa}.

$$T9U = 2N_{det} - N_{fa} \tag{8.12}$$

Now we can write N_{det} and N_{fa} using the relevant and non-relevant distributions. The system decides that documents with scores above a certain threshold θ are relevant. Then

$$N_{det} = r \int_{\theta}^{\infty} p(x|\text{rel}) \text{ and } N_{fa} = (n - r) \int_{\theta}^{+\infty} p(x|\text{nrel}) \tag{8.13}$$

where n and r are the total number of documents and the number of relevant documents. Substituting the expressions for N_{det} and N_{fa} in the expression for the cost function we have:

$$T9U = 2r \int_{\theta}^{\infty} p(x|\text{rel}) - (n - r) \int_{\theta}^{+\infty} p(x|\text{nrel}) \tag{8.14}$$

The optimal threshold can be determined by minimizing the cost function. that is by setting $\frac{d(T9U)}{d\theta} = 0$. This gives:

$$2rp(\theta|\text{rel}) = (n - r)p(\theta|\text{nrel}) \tag{8.15}$$

This equation may be solved analytically for the threshold θ by substituting for the relevant and non-relevant distributions. Note that this threshold will be in terms of the ratio of the number of relevant to the number of non-relevant documents (that is, $\frac{r}{n-r}$

One can compute the posterior probability of relevance given the scores $P(rel|x)$ from the above densities. Using Bayes rule we have:

$$P(rel|x) \quad = \quad \frac{p(x|\text{rel})P_{rel}}{p(x)} \qquad (8.16)$$

$$= \quad \frac{p(x|\text{rel})P_{rel}}{P_{rel}p(x|\text{rel}) + P(\text{nrel})p(x|\text{nrel})} \qquad (8.17)$$

The threshold in the posterior probability space may be computed by using the relationship between $p(x|\text{rel})$ and $p(x|\text{nrel})$ at the optimal threshold from equation 8.15 and from the fact that $P_{rel} = r/n$ and $P_{nrel} = (n-r)/n$ giving:

$$P(rel|\theta) \quad = \quad \frac{p(\theta|\text{rel})r}{p(\theta|\text{rel})r + 2\frac{r}{n-r}p(\theta|\text{rel})(n-r)}$$

$$= \quad \frac{1}{1+2} = 1/3 \qquad (8.18)$$

That is, one should deliver documents when the posterior probability P(rel|score) > 0.033.

Arampatzis and van Hameren, 2001; Arampatzis et al., 2001 use the total distribution as an approximation to the non-relevant distribution. They also an initial relevant documents to estimate the relevant distribution. This gives an initial threshold. As filtering proceeds, relevance information is provided for all the documents retrieved so far. This enables the relevant distribution to be recomputed as well as the quantity $\frac{r}{n-r}$ and a new threshold may be computed to judge future documents. This updating process is carried out adaptively. The results are quite good.

One problem with this approach is that a bias is introduced since relevance judgements are only provided for retrieved documents. Zhang and Callan, 2001 discuss an approach to handling this problem.

An alternative approach to avoiding the bias problem would be to use the mixture model to compute the relevant and non-relevant distributions and compute a posterior probability.

In Topic Detection and Tracking (TDT), on topic documents are selected using a threshold over a similarity score. A similar approach to that in filtering can, therefore, be applied in TDT. We will indicate the approach to be followed.

The TDT cost function is defined as as a linear combination of P_{miss}, the probability of a miss, and P_{fa}, the probability of a false alarm Fiscus and Doddington, 2002:

$$C_{det} = 0.02P_{miss} + 0.098P_{fa} \qquad (8.19)$$

where

P_{miss} and P_{fa} may be computed using the relevant and non-relevant densities. A similar approach to the filtering case gives:

$$P_{miss} = \int_{-\infty}^{\theta} p(x|\text{rel}) \text{ and } P_{fa} = \int_{\theta}^{+\infty} p(x|\text{nrel}) \qquad (8.20)$$

As in the filtering case, the cost function may be minimized and the posterior probability p(rel|score) at the threshold may be computed. Documents with a higher posterior probability p(rel|score) are considered as on topic. Initial results are positive (Ao Feng and Allan,).

6. Combining Search Engines Indexing Different Databases or Different Languages

How does one combine the output of search engines indexing different databases or different languages? At first glance, this seems to be a simple extension of the case where one wishes to combine multiple search engines indexing a single database. The use of the techniques for combining engines indexing a single database does not always produce good results. There is a very good reason why such techniques are insufficient.

Consider three search engines. Let the first one index a French database, the second an English database and the third an Indonesian database. Consider a query about the election of the mayor of Jakarta. Common sense tells us that the answer is more likely to be found in the Indonesian database. Thus, there needs to be some mechanism to weight the Indonesian database more. A second problem that arises is that the French and English databases may have few or no relevant documents in response to this query and hence the mixture modeling (which assumes a mixture of a relevant and non-relevant components) may break down. Finally, the size of the database may also make a difference. Thus, for example, a database which is ten times as large may have ten times as many relevant documents and should probably be selected over a much smaller database even though the smaller database may have a slightly higher probability of having a relevant document.

These additional considerations complicate the application of score modeling to the multi-database, multilingual problem. Thus, for example, one possible approach would involve the following steps:

1 Normalize the scores by equalizing the non-relevant distributions.

2 Multiply by a function of the prior probability of having relevant documents.

3 Multiply by a function of the number of documents in the database.

Of course the prior probability of having relevant documents must be estimated without knowing relevance. In some situations where some databases contain lots of relevant documents and others contain few relevant documents, it may be desirable to eliminate the databases containing few relevant documents from the fusion step. Since relevance depends on the query, this whole process can become quite complicated.

This is an interesting area of research and existing techniques are mostly ad hoc. Thus, the application of score modeling to this area will be quite beneficial.

7.   Conclusion

We have discussed how the score distributions of a number of text search engines mau be modeled on a per query basis. Specifically, it was shown empirically that the score distributions on a per query basis may be fitted using an exponential distribution for the set of non-relevant documents and a normal distribution for the set of relevant documents.

It was then shown that given a query for which relevance information is not available, a mixture model consisting of an exponential and a normal distribution may be fitted to the score distribution. These distributions were used to map the scores of a search engine to probabilities.

These score distributions have proved useful in different areas of information retrieval including the fusion of search engines searching a common database as well as information filtering. We have also indicated how score distributions could apply to other areas like topic detection and tracking as well as the fusion of engines searching multiple databases or over databases in multiple languages. It would be interesting to see if the application of score distributions in these areas leads to some interesting results.

8.   Acknowledgements

The origins of this work can be traced back to a discussion with Bruce Croft and also for pointing and relevant literature on score modeling in information retrieval. Toni Rath elaborated and implemented the initial score modeling ideas to create a combination technique using it. Fangfang Feng provided much programming support for different aspects of this work. Hayri Sever implemented the ideas for equalizing exponential distributions for combination. With Ao Feng and James Allan I have an ongoing collaboration relating to the application of score modeling to TDT.

This material is based on work supported in part by the CIIR, in part by the National Science Foundation under grant number IIS-9909073, and in part by SPAWARSYSCEN-SD grant number N66001-99-1-8912. Any opinions, findings and conclusions or recommendations expressed in this material are the author(s) and do not necessarily reflect those of the sponsor(s).

References

Ao Feng, R. M. and Allan, J. Unpublished work.

Arampatzis, A., Beney, J., Koster, C. H. A., and van der Weide, T. P. (2001). Incrementality, half-life and threshold optimization for adaptive document filtering. In *Proc. of the 9th Text Retrieval Conference (TREC-9)*, pages 589–600.

Arampatzis, A. and van Hameren, A. (2001). The score-distributional threshold optimization for adaptive binary classification tasks. In *In the Proc. of the 24th ACM SIGIR conf. on Research and Developement in Information Retrieval*, pages 285–293.

Aslam, J. and Montague, M. (2001). Models for metasearch. In *In the Proc. of the 24th ACM SIGIR conf. on Research and Developement in Information Retrieval*, pages 276–284.

Aslam, J. A., , and Montague, M. (2000). Bayes optimal metasearch: A probabilistic model for combining the results of multiple retrieval systems. In *the Proc. of the 23rd ACM SIGIR conf. on Research and Developement in Information Retrieval*, pages 379–381.

Baumgarten, C. (1999). A probabilistic solution to the selection and fusion problem in distributed information retrieval. In *In the Proc. of the 22nd ACM SIGIR conf. on Research and Developement in Information Retrieval*, pages 246–253.

Bishop, C. M. (1995). *Neural Networks for Pattern Recognition*. Oxford University Press.

Bookstein, A. (1977). When the most Pertinent document should not be retrieved - an analysis of the Swets model. *Information Processing and Management*, 13:377–383.

Croft, W. B. (2000). Combining approaches to information retrieval. In Croft, W. B., editor, *Advances in Information Retrieval*, pages 1–36. Kluwer Academic Publishers.

Fiscus, J. and Doddington, G. R. (2002). Topic detection and tracking evaluation overview. In Allan, J., editor, *Topic Detection and Tracking: Event-based Information Organization*, pages 17–31. Kluwer Academic Publishers.

Fox, E. and Shaw, J. (1994). Combination of multiple searches. In *the Proc. of the 2nd Text Retrieval Conference (TREC-2)*, pages 243–252. National Institute of Standards and Technology Special Publications 500-215.

Lavrenko, V. and Croft, W. B. (2001). Relevance based language models. In *In the Proc. of the 24th ACM SIGIR conf. on Research and Developement in Information Retrieval*, pages 120–127.

Lee, J. H. (1995). Combining multiple evidence form different properties of weighting schemes. In *the Proc. of the 18th Intl. Conf. on Research and Development in Information Retrieval (SIGIR'95)*, pages 180–188.

Lee, J. H. (1997). Analyses of multiple evidence combination. In *the Proc. of the 20th Intl. Conf. on Research and Development in Information Retrieval (SIGIR'97)*, pages 267–276.

Manmatha, R., Rath, T., and Feng, F. Modeling score distributions for meta search. *In preparation*.

Manmatha, R., Rath, T., and Feng, F. (2001). Modeling score distributions for combining the outputs of search engines. In *the Proc. of the 24th ACM SIGIR conf. on Research and Developement in Information Retrieval*, pages 267–275.

Manmatha, R. and Sever, H. (2002). A formal approach to score normalization for meta search. In *In the Proceedings of the Human Language Technology Conf.,(HLT2002)*.

Montague, M. and Aslam, J. (2001). Relevance score normalization for meta search. In *In the Proc. of the ACM Tenth International Conference on Information and Knowledge Management (CIKM)*, pages 427–433.

Swets, J. A. (1963). Information retrieval systems. *Science*, 141:245–250.

van Rijsbergen, C. J. (1979). *Information Retrieval*. Butterworths.

Vogt, C. and Cottrell, G. (1998). Predicting the performance of linearly combined IR systems. In *the Proc. of the 21st ACM SIGIR conf. on Research and Developement in Information Retrieval*, pages 190–196.

Vogt, C. and Cottrell, G. (1999). Fusion via a linear combination of scores. In *Information Retrieval*, pages 1–22.

Zhang, Y. and Callan, J. (2001). Maximum likelihood estimation for filtering thresholds. In *In the Proc. of the 24th ACM SIGIR conf. on Research and Developement in Information Retrieval*, pages 294–302.

Chapter 9

AN UNBIASED GENERATIVE MODEL FOR SETTING DISSEMINATION THRESHOLDS

Yi Zhang and Jamie Callan
Language Technologies Institute
School of Computer Science
Carnegie Mellon University
Pittsburgh, PA 15213, USA
{yiz,callan}@cs.cmu.edu

Abstract   Information filtering systems based on statistical retrieval models usually compute a numeric score that indicates how well each document matches each profile. Documents with scores above profile-specific dissemination thresholds are delivered. Optimal dissemination thresholds are usually difficult to determine a priori, so they are often learned during filtering, using relevance feedback about disseminated documents. However, the scores of disseminated documents are a biased sample of the complete distribution of document scores, which causes some algorithms to learn suboptimal thresholds.

This chapter presents a generative method of adjusting dissemination thresholds that explicitly models and compensates for this bias. The new algorithm, which is based on the Maximum Likelihood principle, jointly estimates the parameters of the density distributions for relevant and non-relevant documents and the ratio of relevant to non-relevant documents in the region around the dissemination threshold. Experiments demonstrate its effectiveness when its underlying assumptions about document scores are true, and illustrate its behavior when its assumptions don't match the actual distribution of document scores.

1.   Introduction

Information filtering systems monitor a document stream to find documents that match information needs described by user profiles consisting of queries and related context or history. Filtering systems based on statistical models (e.g., vector space, probabilistic, inference network, and statistical language models) use a numeric score (the *relevancy measure*) to indicate how well a document matches a profile, and only disseminate a document when its score

W.B. Croft and J. Lafferty (eds.), Language Modeling for Information Retrieval, 189–217.
© 2003 *Kluwer Academic Publishers.*

is above some threshold (the *dissemination threshold*). As the information stream is processed, the system may be provided with relevance judgments for some of the documents it delivers. An *adaptive information filtering system* can learn from these user feedback so that it becomes more accurate over time.

A common approach to learning user profiles is an incremental version of the Rocchio algorithm (Rocchio, 1971; Allan, 1996; Callan, 1996):

$$Q' = \alpha Q + \beta \frac{\sum_{d_i \in R} d_i}{\|R\|} - \gamma \frac{\sum_{d_i \in NR} d_i}{\|NR\|}$$

where Q is the initial profile vector, Q' is the new profile vector, R is the set of relevant documents, NR is the set of non-relevant documents, d_i is a document vector, and α, β, γ are constants indicating the relative value of each type of evidence. Machine learning algorithms for text classification have also been used for this task, for example, k-nearest neighbor, naive Bayes, statistical language modeling, and boosting (Schapire et al., 1998; Hull and Robertson, 2000; Robertson and Hull, 2001; Kraaij et al., 2000; Kim et al., 2000; Ault and Yang, 2001).

The problem of how to set filtering thresholds received little attention until the mid 1990s, in part because many operational environments relied upon Boolean queries and exact-match retrieval models. Researchers working with statistical retrieval algorithms typically delayed dissemination decisions while scores were computed for each document in the stream, sorted documents by their scores, and then disseminated the top N documents, as was done in the TREC Routing task (e.g., (Robertson et al., 1996)). This approach is effective when it is not necessary to disseminate information quickly. When dissemination decisions cannot be delayed, it is necessary to find dissemination thresholds for each profile. In the late 1990s dissemination thresholds were recognized as a crucial component of information filtering systems, and a variety of heuristic algorithms were developed (e.g., (Zhai et al., 1999; Zhai et al., 2000; Zhang and Callan, 2001b; Ault and Yang, 2001; Robertson and Walker, 2000; Robertson and Walker, 2001)).

This chapter focuses on using a generative model to dynamically determine dissemination thresholds while filtering. We assume that there is some filtering system, presumably based on a statistical model of information retrieval, that assigns a relevance-based score to each document. Our problem is to learn thresholds that determine whether to disseminate a document given its relevance score. We assume that a user provides relevance feedback about each disseminated document, enabling the system to adjust thresholds dynamically. In this chapter threshold quality is evaluated primarily by how well it optimizes a linear utility measure, as is common in the TREC Filtering Tracks (Hull and Robertson, 2000; Robertson and Hull, 2001; Robertson and Soboroff, 2002), but occasionally it is evaluated using other metrics.

Table 9.1. The values assigned to relevant and non-relevant documents that the filtering system did and did not deliver.

	Relevant	Non-Relevant
Delivered	R^+/A	N^+/B
Not Delivered	R^-/C	N^-/D

The next section of this chapter introduces model based approaches to optimizing utility functions, using a Normal-Exponential model as an example. Section 3 discusses the sampling bias problem that occurs when using a generative model for threshold selection, and provides a solution that explicitly models the bias. Section 4 introduces our experimental methodology, including data sets, system settings, and evaluation metric. Section 5 presents experimental results that compare biased and unbiased versions of the algorithm on several different datasets; these experiments demonstrate the effectiveness of the algorithm when the model's underlying assumption is true, and the effects when the model itself is a poor fit to the actual distribution of document scores. Section 6 concludes.

2. Generative Models of Dissemination Thresholds

The goal of setting a dissemination threshold for a filtering system is to satisfy the user. User satisfaction can be modeled by a utility function, as in recent TREC Filtering Track evaluations (Robertson and Hull, 2001; Hull and Robertson, 2000).

$$Utility = A \cdot R^+ + B \cdot N^+ + C \cdot R^- + D \cdot N^- \qquad (9.1)$$

This model corresponds to assigning a positive or negative value to each element in the categories of Table 9.1, where R^-, R^+, N^-, and N^+ correspond to the number of documents that fall into the corresponding category, and A, B, C, and D correspond to the credit/penalty for each element in the category. For example, the TREC 2001 Filtering Track Utility was $T10U = 2R^+ - N^+$; the TREC 2002 Filtering Track used a normalized version of $T10U$ for evaluation.

Another commonly used evaluation metric is the F measure, which is a combination of Recall and Precision.

$$F = \frac{1}{\frac{a}{Recall} + \frac{b}{Precision}} \qquad (9.2)$$

For example, the TREC 2001 and TREC 2002 Filtering Tracks also used $F = 1/(1/Recall + 4/Precision))$ for evaluation.

The problem of setting dissemination thresholds is to find a threshold that maximizes the utility metric used to evaluate the filtering system. Let $P(R|d)$

represent the probability that document d is relevant to the profile. Maximizing the utility in Equation 9.1 is equivalent to delivering d to the user if and only if $A \cdot P(R|d) + B \cdot (1 - P(R|d)) > C \cdot P(R|d) + D \cdot (1 - P(R|d))$.[1] We express this requirement as shown below.

$$\text{Deliver } d \text{ if } P(R|d) > \frac{D - B}{A - B - C + B} \qquad (9.3)$$

Unfortunately, most retrieval models provide only a score that is correlated (in some unknown way) with relevance, rather than the probability of relevance $P(R|d)$; this is true even for systems using probabilistic models. Our task is to transform the relevance score to $P(R|d)$. This task is similar to some other classification tasks where it is necessary to know the posterior $P(R|score)$. There are two major approaches to solving this problem in recent research.

Discriminant analysis: The posterior distribution $P(R|score)$ is modeled directly. For example, a research group from CLARITECH used a heuristic that allowed the threshold to vary between a lower bound utility value (zero) and an upper bound optimal value (Zhai et al., 2000). A group from Microsoft Cambridge mapped the score to the probability of relevance using a modified form of logistic regression (Robertson and Walker, 2001; Robertson and Walker, 2000).

Generative analysis: The distributions $P(score|R)$, $P(score|NR)$, $P(R)$, and $P(NR)$ are modeled. In this approach, once the model is decided, $P(R|score)$ can be derived using Bayes rule.

$$
\begin{aligned}
P(R|score) &= \frac{P(R, score)}{P(score)} \\
&= \frac{P(score|R) \cdot P(R)}{P(score|R) \cdot P(R) + P(score|NR) \cdot P(NR)}
\end{aligned}
$$

For example, a research group from Katholieke Universiteit Nijmegan (KUN) assumed a Gaussian distribution for the scores of relevant documents and an Exponential distribution for the scores of non-relevant documents, and then found the threshold that maximized a given linear utility measure. This approach was extremely effective in one test, achieving the best result for utility oriented runs in the TREC-9 Filtering Track evaluation (Arampatzis et al., 2001).

Discriminative analysis approaches to modeling $P(R|score)$ tend to have lower bias and higher variance; generative analysis approaches usually have higher

---

[1]This is greedy optimization. In some cases, such as the early stage of filtering, it may be desirable to deliver even when $P(R|d)$ is smaller than required by this formula, e.g., to get more training data. There is little research on this topic and it is not discussed in this chapter.

bias (because of the model assumptions), but lower variance (they use data more efficiently) (Hastie et al., 2001; Rubinstein and Hastie, 1997; Ng and Jordan., 2002).

In an information filtering environment, when the amount of training data is small, variance is a primary cause of error, thus generative approaches are a good choice. In addition to $P(R|score)$, generative analysis also estimates the marginal probability of relevance, which makes it possible to estimate Precision *and* Recall for a given threshold; discriminative models can estimate only Precision, because Recall can not be derived from only the conditional probability $P(R|score)$. The ability to estimate both Precision and Recall from generative models makes it possible to optimize for the F measure, if desired.

The ability of generative models to use training data efficiently, and their ability to optimize for either Utility or F measure, make them an attractive choice for learning dissemination thresholds. We restrict our attention to generative analysis in the remainder of this chapter.

2.1 Normal and Exponential Models Of Document Score Distributions

If the system had an accurate model of the distribution of document scores for the top ranking documents (relevant and non-relevant), the dissemination threshold could be set accurately. Several researchers suggest using a Gaussian distribution for modeling the scores of relevant documents and an Exponential distribution for modeling the scores of the top ranking non-relevant documents (Arampatzis and Hameren, 2001; Manmatha et al., 2001). These distributions are modeled as:

$$P(score|R) = \frac{1}{\sqrt{2\pi}\sigma}e^{-\frac{(score-\mu)^2}{2\sigma^2}} \tag{9.4}$$

$$P(score|NR) = \lambda e^{-\lambda(x-c)} \tag{9.5}$$

$$P(R) = p \tag{9.6}$$

where:
μ is the mean of the Gaussian distribution;
σ is the variance of Gaussian distribution;
λ is the variance of Exponential distribution;
c is the minimum score a non-relevant document can get; and
p is the the ratio of relevant documents to all documents in the region
   being modeled.

The parameter p does not represent the ratio in the corpus as a whole, because the Exponential model fits only the top non-relevant scores. The model

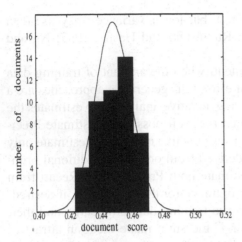

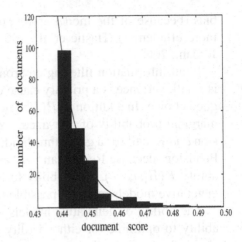

Figure 9.1. Density of relevant document scores for OHSU Topic 5. OHSUMED collection.

Figure 9.2. Density of non-relevant document scores for OHSU Topic 5. OHSUMED collection.

is focused on, and is most accurate modeling, the scores of the top-ranking documents, where thresholds are typically set.

Analysis of experimental results on TREC-9 Filtering Track data support this approach. Figures 9.3 and 9.1 illustrate how the normal distribution fits relevant document scores for two TREC-9 topics. Figures 9.2 and 9.4 illustrate how the Exponential distribution fits the top 100 non-relevant document scores for the same topics.

This model is not perfect, especially for low scoring documents. However, it can provide a relatively accurate estimate of the distribution of scores for higher-scoring documents, and in the information-filtering task the area of interest (i.e., the area in which thresholds are likely to be located) usually is around the higher-scoring documents. A model that fits the higher-scoring documents well can be used for setting thresholds.

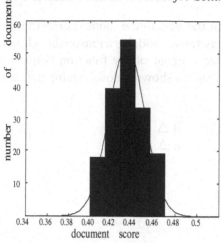

Figure 9.3. Density of relevant document scores for OHSU Topic 3. OHSUMED collection.

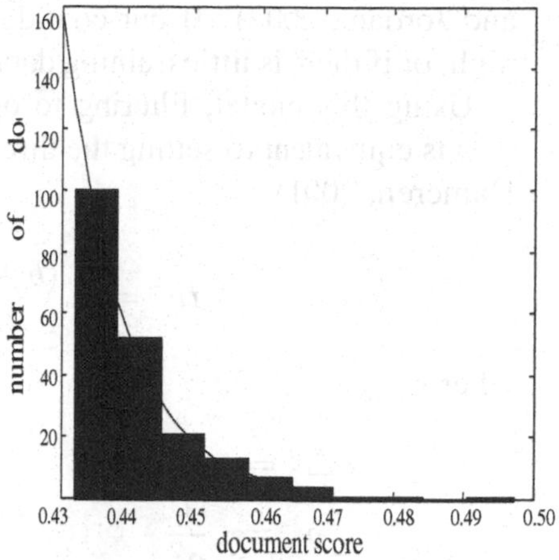

Figure 9.4. Density of non-relevant document scores for OHSU Topic 3. OHSUMED collection.

Based on this generative model for score distributions, we can calculate the probability of a document being relevant given its score.

$$P(R|score) = \frac{P(score|R)P(R)}{P(score)} \tag{9.7}$$

$$= \frac{P(score|R)P(R)}{P(score|R)P(R) + P(score|NR)P(NR)}$$

$$= \frac{p\frac{1}{\sqrt{2\pi}\sigma}e^{-\frac{(score-\mu)^2}{2\sigma^2}}}{p\frac{1}{\sqrt{2\pi}\sigma}e^{-\frac{(score-\mu)^2}{2\sigma^2}} + (1-p)\lambda e^{-\lambda(score-c)}}$$

$$= \frac{1}{1 + \frac{(1-p)\lambda\sqrt{2\pi}\sigma}{p}e^{-\lambda(score-c) + \frac{(score-u)^2}{2\sigma^2}}} \tag{9.8}$$

$$= \frac{1}{1 + e^{c_1 + c_2 \cdot score + c_3 \cdot score^2}} \tag{9.9}$$

Equation 9.9 shows the relationship between generative and discriminative analysis: The discriminative function that corresponds to the Normal-Exponential model is a quadratic logistic regression. There are two options: Train a generative model to find the parameters $(\mu, \sigma, \lambda, p)$, or train a discriminative model to find the parameters (c_1, c_2, c_3). Prior research indicates that a generative model borrows strength from the marginal density and uses training data more efficiently, even when the goal is discriminative (Rubinstein and Hastie, 1997; Ng and Jordan., 2002). If our confidence in the generative model correctness is high, or if there is little training data, a generative model is a reasonable choice.

Using this model, filtering to optimize a linear utility function (Equation 9.3) is equivalent to setting the threshold th^* as shown below (Arampatzis and Hameren, 2001).

$$th^* = \begin{cases} (b - \sqrt{\Delta})/a & \text{if } \Delta \geq 0 \\ +\infty & \text{if } \Delta < 0 \end{cases} \qquad (9.10)$$

where:

$$\Delta = b^2 - a \cdot d$$
$$a = \frac{1}{\sigma^2}$$
$$b = \frac{\mu}{\sigma^2} + \lambda$$
$$d = \frac{\mu^2}{\sigma^2} - 2\log\left(\frac{C-A}{B-D} \cdot p \cdot \frac{1}{\lambda\sqrt{2\pi\sigma}}\right) + 2\lambda \cdot c$$

and A, B, C, and D are Utility function parameters (Equation 9.1).
For a given threshold th:

$$Recall = pZ(\frac{th - \mu}{\sigma})$$

$$Precision = \frac{p(1 - Z(\frac{th-\mu}{\sigma}))}{p(1 - Z(\frac{th-\mu}{\sigma})) + (1 - p)e^{-\lambda(th-c)}}$$

where:

$$Z(\alpha) = \int_{-\infty}^{\alpha} \frac{1}{\sqrt{2\pi}} exp(-x^2/2)dx$$

Since the F measure is a function of Precision and Recall (Equation 9.2), optimizing for it is also straightforward once μ, λ, c and p are known.

3.   The Non-Random Sampling Problem & Solution

Given a set of document scores, the basic parameter estimation method for normal and Exponential distributions is a simple calculation of the mean and variance over training data (Arampatzis and Hameren, 2001). One potential weakness with this simple approach is that it assumes that the training data accurately represents the distribution of relevant and non-relevant document scores. This assumption is not true in an adaptive filtering environment, because relevance information is obtained only for documents that are actually disseminated. Relevance information is not available for documents that have

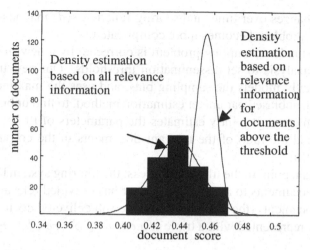

Figure 9.5. Estimation of parameters for the distribution of relevant document scores (OHSU Topic 3, OHSUMED collection). Parameters estimated without considering the sampling bias problem are overestimated.

scores below the threshold, so the training data is inherently biased. We call this the *non-random sampling problem*. Estimation of $(\mu, \sigma, \lambda, p)$ without considering this problem is incorrect. If the user profile is static and training data is restricted to scores above the threshold, the mean of the sample scores is likely to be higher than the real mean.

For example, the true mean and variance of the Gaussian distribution for OHSU Topic 3 (based on all relevant documents) are 0.4343 and 0.0169 (Figure 9.3). However, if training data is restricted to documents with scores above a dissemination threshold of 0.4435, the learned mean and variance are 0.4551 and 0.007 (Figure 9.5). This difference can lead to an inaccurate dissemination threshold.

Non-random sampling is inherent in the training data used for setting dissemination thresholds. Any generative method that assumes randomly sampled training data (e.g., generative analysis methods mentioned in Section 2, not just the basic method presented here (Arampatzis and Hameren, 2001)), must solve this problem.

3.1   A General Approach to Unbiased Estimation

In order to get an unbiased estimate of the distribution parameters, we must take into consideration the sampling constraint, which in a filtering environment is the dissemination threshold. In an *adaptive* filtering environment the threshold changes over time, and scoring function $s(d)$ may also change over time, so the problem becomes more complicated.

The non-random sampling problem is corrected by a new method of using generative analysis to set dissemination thresholds. Our new unbiased algorithm explicitly models the sampling bias, and uses the maximum likelihood principle, an unbiased parameter estimation method, to find unbiased estimates of the parameters. It jointly estimates the parameters of the two density distributions and the ratio of the relevant documents in the corpus (Zhang and Callan, 2001a).

At a certain point in the filtering process, the filtering system has already delivered N documents to a user and the user has provided relevance judgments for these documents (the training data). The i-th delivered document with user feedback is represented with a triple $(Feedback_i, Score_i, f_i)$, where:

$$Feedback_i = \begin{cases} R & \text{for a relevant document.} \\ NR & \text{for a non-relevant document.} \end{cases}$$

$Score_i :$ The score of document d_i.

$f_i :$ The function that delivered d_i. This contains information such as the relevance scoring function (s_i), and profile threshold (th_i) when d_i arrived. $f_i = s_i - th_i$.

$s_i :$ The scoring function used to measure relevancy when d_i arrived. Usually $Score_i$ represents $s_i(d_i)$.

$th_i :$ The threshold when d_i arrived.

Let θ represent the parameters for the generative model used to describe the density distribution of the scores. According to Bayes theorem, the most probable value of θ is:

$$\theta^* = \arg\max_{\theta} P(\theta|D)$$

$$= \arg\max_{\theta} \frac{P(D|\theta)P(\theta)}{P(D)}$$

For simplicity, we first assume that there is no prior knowledge of the distribution of θ and treat the prior probability of $P(\theta)$ as uniform.[2] Because $P(D)$ is a constant independent of H, it can be dropped. Thus the most probable θ is

---

[2]We will revisit and remove the assumption in Section 4.2 and use a conjugate prior of $P(\theta)$ for smoothing.

the one that maximizes the likelihood of the training data.

$$
\begin{aligned}
\theta^* &= \arg\max_\theta P(D|\theta) \\
&= \arg\max_\theta \prod_{i=1..N} P(d_i|\theta) \\
&= \arg\max_\theta \sum_{i=1..N} \log P(d_i|\theta) \\
&= \arg\max_\theta \sum_{i=1..N} \log P(Score_i, Feedback_i|\theta, f_i(d_i) > 0) \quad (9.11)
\end{aligned}
$$

The second step in Equation 9.11 is due to the assumption that each document is independent; the third step is due to the fact that maximizing a function is equivalent to maximizing its logarithm; and the last step indicates the sampling constraints for training data: $s_i(d_i) - th_i(d_i) > 0$. Notice that although the training data are not sampled randomly from the whole corpus, each individual training document is sampled randomly according to the conditional probability $P(Score = Score_i, R_i|\theta, f_i(d_i) > 0)$. So parameters estimated based on Equation 9.11 are unbiased.

3.2   Unbiased Estimation of Normal and Exponential Models

If we assume a Gaussian distribution for the scores of relevant documents and an Exponential distribution for the scores of non-relevant documents as in (Arampatzis and Hameren, 2001), and if the profile scoring function is not changing over time (revisited in Section 5.3), then $\theta = (\mu, \sigma, \lambda, p)$ and $f_i(d_i) > 0 \Leftrightarrow Score_i > th_i$. (The meaning of $(\mu, \sigma, \lambda, p)$ was described in Section 2.1.)

For each item inside the sum operation of Equation 9.11, we have:

$$
\begin{aligned}
&P(Score_i, Feedback_i|\theta, f_i(d_i) > 0) \\
&= \frac{P(Score_i, Feedback_i, Score_i > th_i|\theta)}{P(Score_i > th_i|\theta)} \\
&= \frac{P(Score_i, Score_i > th_i|\theta, Feedback_i)P(Feedback_i|\theta)}{P(Score_i > th_i|\theta)} \\
&= \frac{P(Score_i|\theta, Feedback_i)P(Feedback_i|\theta)}{P(Score_i > th_i|\theta)} \quad (9.12)
\end{aligned}
$$

The first step in Equation 9.12 is based on the definition of conditional probability; the second step is due to the chain rule of probability; and the last step is due to the fact that all training documents must have a score higher than the threshold.

For convenience, let $f_1(\mu, \sigma, th_i)$ represent the probability of a document getting a score above threshold th_i if it is relevant and $f_2(\lambda, th_i)$ be the probability of it getting a score above threshold th_i if it is non-relevant. The probability of getting a score above th_i can be calculated by integrating the density function from th_i to positive infinity. That is:

$$
\begin{aligned}
f_1(\mu, \sigma, th_i) &= P(Score > th_i | R) \\
&= \int_{th_i}^{+\infty} \frac{1}{\sqrt{2\pi}\sigma} e^{-\frac{(x-\mu)^2}{2\sigma^2}} \, dx.
\end{aligned}
\tag{9.13}
$$

$$
\begin{aligned}
f_2(\lambda, th_i) &= P(Score > th_i | NR) \\
&= \int_{th_i}^{+\infty} \lambda e^{-\lambda(x-c)} \, dx \\
&= e^{-\lambda(th_i - c)}
\end{aligned}
\tag{9.14}
$$

We use $g(\mu, \sigma, \lambda, p, th_i)$ to represent the probability of a document getting a score above threshold th.

$$
\begin{aligned}
g(\mu, \sigma, \lambda, p, th_i) &= P(Score > th_i | \theta) \\
&= P(R|\theta)P(Score > th_i | R, \theta) + \\
&\quad\ P(NR|\theta)P(Score > th_i | NR, \theta) \\
&= p f_1(\mu, \sigma, th_i) + (1-p) f_2(\lambda, th_i)
\end{aligned}
\tag{9.15}
$$

An intuitive explanation of Equations 9.13, 9.14, and and 9.15 is illustrated in Figure 9.6. If we assume the sum of areas under the Exponential and Gaussian curves is 1, then $p \cdot f_1(\mu, \sigma, th_i)$ corresponds to the area to the right of and below the normal distribution curve. $(1-p)f_2(\lambda, th_i)$ corresponds to the area to the right of and below the Exponential distribution curve.

From the previous equations derived in this section:

$$
(\mu^*, \sigma^*, \lambda^*, p^*) = \arg \max_{\mu, \sigma, \lambda, p} \sum_{i=1}^{N} LP_i
\tag{9.16}
$$

where for relevant documents:

$$
LP_i = -\frac{(Score_i - u)^2}{2\sigma^2} + \log(p/(\sigma g(\mu, \sigma, \lambda, p, th_i)))
$$

and for non-relevant documents:

$$
LP_i = -\lambda(Score_i - c) + \log((1-p)\lambda/g(\mu, \sigma, \lambda, p, th_i))
$$

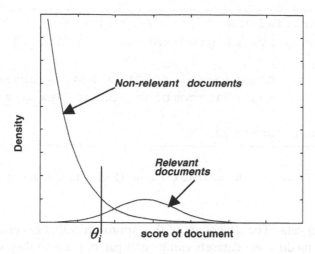

Figure 9.6. Distribution of scores of documents for a profile.

If the training data are random samples of the whole corpus (not true for filtering), $th_i = -\infty$ and thus $g(\mu, \sigma, \lambda, p, th_i) = 1$. If $g(\mu, \sigma, \lambda, p, th_i)$ in Equation 9.16 is replaced with 1, the optimal parameters will be the same as those used in the basic, biased method (Arampatzis and Hameren, 2001). In other words, the basic, biased method is a maximum likelihood estimation of the parameters if the training data are a random sample of the dataset. However, $g(\mu, \sigma, \lambda, p, th_i)$ is not equal to 1 because the sample is biased during filtering. Equation 9.16 must be used to find the unbiased parameters.

There is no closed form solution for Equation 9.16, so numerical methods can be used. One such method is conjugate gradient descent (CGD). CGD is a gradient based optimization procedure for a function (Press et al., 1992; MacKay, 2001). A brief sketch of the CGD algorithm is shown in Figure 9.7. At each step, x is the approximate solution, q is the search direction, and x is improved by searching for a better solution along direction q. When using CGD to estimate parameters for Normal and Exponential models, the derivative of the right side of Equation 9.16 is used for calculating the search direction q.

4. Experimental Methodology

The biased and unbiased generative methods of setting dissemination thresholds were evaluated in a series of experiments with TREC data. The experimental methodology for the TREC Filtering Track changes from year to year. The experiments reported here used the TREC-9 experimental methodology (Robertson and Hull, 2001) in experiments with TREC-8, TREC-9, and TREC-

```
x = initial guess for the minimum
q = negative of gradient at x (search direction)
do {
      x  =  the minimal point along direction q
      q  =  a linear combination of new gradient and
old q
   } until converge
```

Figure 9.7. Outline of the Conjugate Gradient Descent algorithm.

10 Filtering data. The advantage of this approach is that experimental results obtained with different datasets can be compared, because they were obtained with the same experimental methodology. However, a consequence is that the results reported here for TREC-8 and TREC-10 data are not directly comparable to results from systems participating in the TREC-8 and TREC-10 Filtering Tracks. The evaluation measures, datasets, and experimental methodology are described in more detail below.

4.1   Datasets

Three different text corpora were used in the experiments: the FT dataset used in the TREC-8 Filtering Track, the OHSUMED dataset used in the TREC-9 Filtering Track, and the Reuters 2001 dataset used in the TREC-10 Filtering Track. Each is discussed below.

4.1.1   FT Data.   The FT data is a collection of 210,158 articles from the 1991 to 1994 Financial Times. It was used by the TREC-8 Filtering Track (Hull and Robertson, 2000). TREC topics 351-400 were used to simulate user profiles. The relevance judgments were made by NIST on the basis of pooled output from several searches. For each profile, the system begins with two identified relevant documents and a natural language description of the information need, which is the title and description field of the corresponding TREC topic. The average number of relevant articles per profile in the testing data is 36.

4.1.2   OHSUMED Data.   The OHSUMED data is a collection from the US National Library of Medicine's bibliographic database (Hersh et al., 1994). It was used by the TREC-9 Filtering Track (Robertson and Hull, 2001). It consists of 348,566 articles from a subset of 270 journals covering the years 1987 to 1991. 63 OHSUMED queries and 500 MeSH headings were used to simulate user profiles. The relevance judgments for the OHSUMED queries were made by medical librarians and physicians based on the results of interactive searches. For the MeSH headings, assignment of a heading to a document by the National Library of Medicine is treated as equivalent to a positive relevance judgment. In the TREC-9 Filtering Track, it is assumed that the user profile descriptions arrive at the beginning of 1988, so the 54,709 articles from 1987 can be used to learn word occurrence (e.g., idf) statistics and corpus statistics (e.g., average document length). For each user, the system begins with a natural language description of the information need and 2 examples of relevant documents. The average numbers of relevant articles per profile in the testing data are 51 for the OHSUMED topics and 249 for the MeSH headings.

4.1.3   Reuters 2001 Data.   The Reuters 2001 data is a collection of about 810,000 Reuters English News stories from August 20, 1996 to August 19, 1997. It was used by the TREC-10 and TREC-11 Filtering Tracks (Robertson and Soboroff, 2002).

In TREC-10, 84 Reuters categories were used to simulate user profiles. For each profile, the system begins with two identified relevant documents and a natural language description of the information need, which is the title and description field of the corresponding topics provided by TREC-10. The average number of relevant articles in the testing data is about 9,795 documents per profile, which is much larger than the other two corpora.

4.2   Filtering Environment

The YFilter information filtering system (Zhang and Callan, 2001b) was used for the experiments reported here. It processes documents by first removing symbols such as punctuation and special characters, excluding the 418 highly frequent terms listed in the default INQUERY stop words list (Broglio et al., 1995), and then stemming using the Porter stemmer (Porter, 1980). Processed documents are compared to each profile using the INQUERY variant of BM25 tf.idf formula (Robertson et al., 1996; Callan, 1996) to measure the similarity of the document and user profile. For each topic, the filtering system created initial filtering profiles using terms from the TREC topic Title and Description fields, and set the initial threshold to allow the highest-scoring d documents in the training dataset to pass. For simplicity, the filtering profile term weights were not updated while filtering. Because the first two relevant documents given to the system were not sampled under the constraint that their scores must exceed the dissemination threshold, their probabilities were simply $P(d_i|\theta) = P(Score_i, Feedback_i|\theta)$, and the corresponding element of Equation 9.16 was changed to:

$$LP_i = -\frac{(Score_i - u)^2}{2\sigma^2} - \log(\sigma)$$

In Section 3.2, for simplicity we set the prior probability to be uniform. However, in the real filtering task, especially during the early stage of filtering when there is only a small number of samples, this may cause problems. For example, if only non-relevant documents are delivered, the estimate of p will be 0 without a prior. Or, if all the relevant documents have the same score, the variance will be 0. Smoothing using a prior of parameters can solve these problems. The prior needn't be very accurate, because as the amount of sample data increases, the influence of the prior decreases. In our experiments, we set the prior of p as a beta distribution[3]: $p^{\varepsilon_1} \cdot (1 - p)^{\varepsilon_2}$, which is equal to adding ε_1 relevant documents and ε_2 non-relevant documents sampled randomly for smoothing. The prior of σ^2 is set to be $e^{-\nu^2/(s\sigma^2)}$, which is equal to adding ν^2 to the sum of the square of the variance of relevant documents.[4] The value of $\varepsilon_1, \varepsilon_2$ and υ needn't to be very accurate and should be very small in order not to influence the final results. $\varepsilon_1, \varepsilon_2$ and υ were all set around 0.001-0.01 in our experiments.

4.3   Metrics

The effectiveness of the biased and unbiased generative methods of determining dissemination thresholds was measured using the linear utility function described in Section 1 with $(A, B, C, D) = (2, 1, 0, 0)$. The resulting utility measure is:

$$T9U' = 2R^+ - N^+$$

which is a slightly simplified variant of the T9U utility metric used in the TREC-9 Filtering Track. R^+ and N^- are the numbers of relevant and non-relevant documents disseminated. The corresponding delivery rule is:

$$\text{deliver if } P(Relevant|Score) > 0.33 \qquad (9.17)$$

Experiments were also conducted with other values of (A, B, C, D), to test the sensitivity of each method to specific parameter settings.

5.   Experimental Results

Three sets of experiments were conducted. The first set investigated the effectiveness of the biased and unbiased generative methods of determining dissemination thresholds when the target is a specific utility metric. The experiments also studied the effect of including a minimum delivery constraint. The second set of experiments investigated the two approaches using a wider range

---

[3]Because the beta distribution is a conjugate prior for the binomial distribution, we use it as a prior to simplify the calculations.
[4]This is a special case of inverse gamma distribution, which is the conjugate prior of the variance of the normal distribution.

	Biased (Run1)	Biased + Min. Delivery (Run2)	Unbiased (Run3)	Unbiased + Min. Delivery (Run4)
T9U'	1.84	3.25	2.70	8.17
Delivered docs per profile	3.83	9.65	5.73	18.40
Precision	0.37	0.29	0.36	0.32
Recall	0.04	0.08	0.05	0.14

Table 9.2. Comparison of the basic biased and unbiased Maximum Likelihood algorithms on the TREC-9 Filtering data. OHSUMED data, OHSU topics.

of utility metrics; the goal of these experiments was to identify any sensitivity to the evaluation metric. A third set of experiments investigated behavior when the underlying assumption about the distributions of relevant and non-relevant document scores is violated. These three sets of experiments are described below.

5.1   Biased vs. Unbiased Parameter Estimation

The first set of experiments investigated how well each method selects thresholds that optimize the $T9U'$ Utility metric, which is consistent with recent TREC Filtering Track evaluations. Optimizing Utility can lead to higher Precision or Recall as a side-effect, but is not guaranteed to do so. In some cases the best way to increase Utility is to increase Precision (higher threshold); in other cases the best way to increase Utility is to increase Recall (lower threshold). All three metrics are reported, to provide greater insight into the experimental results, but Utility, the metric being optimized, is the focus of the discussion.

Experiments were conducted on TREC-8 and TREC-9 Filtering Track data. Four runs were conducted using each dataset. The basic *biased* parameter estimation method (Arampatzis et al., 2001) served as the baseline method ("Run 1"). The *unbiased* run ("Run 3") used the unbiased maximum likelihood estimation. Both runs stopped delivering documents when Δ was negative.

It is especially common for Δ to be negative at the beginning of filtering; in these cases, no documents are disseminated, no user feedback is available, and no learning occurs. A minimum delivery constraint was introduced to avoid this problem. If a profile had not achieved the minimum delivery constraint, its threshold was decreased automatically. Runs 2 and 4 correspond to the biased

	Biased (Run1)	Biased + Min. Delivery (Run2)	Unbiased (Run3)	Unbiased + Min. Delivery (Run4)
T9U'	1.89	4.28	2.44	13.10
Delivered docs per profile	3.51	11.82	6.22	27.91
Precision	0.42	0.39	0.40	0.34
Recall	0.02	0.05	0.03	0.07

Table 9.3. Comparison of the basic biased and unbiased Maximum Likelihood algorithms on the TREC-9 Filtering data. OHSUMED data, MeSH topics.

and unbiased algorithms using a minimum delivery constraint that required an average of 10 documents to be disseminated to each profile.[5]

Neither algorithm worked well on the OHSUMED dataset without a minimum delivery constraint (Tables 9.2 and 9.3, columns 1 and 3). Especially at the early stage of filtering, with only about 2 documents delivered, it is very hard to estimate the score distribution correctly. When $\Delta < 0$ in Equation 9.9, the threshold is set too high to let any future documents be delivered, hence no learning takes place occurs. Introducing a minimum delivery constraint (i.e., forcing the system to deliver at least a certain percentage of documents) helps the system to recover automatically (Tables 9.2 and 9.3).

On the OHSUMED dataset, for both OHSU topics and MeSH topics, the unbiased maximum likelihood estimation plus a minimum delivery constraint achieved the best result. Although profile updating was disabled while filtering, all of the runs on this dataset received a positive average utility. The results for Run 4 on OHSU topics were above average compared with other filtering systems in the TREC-9 Adaptive Filtering Track (Robertson and Hull, 2001). This result indicates how effective the threshold-setting algorithm is, because the other filtering systems learned improved profiles while filtering, whereas all of our experiments used static filtering profiles.

All four algorithms performed equally well on FT data (Table 9.4). One difference between the FT dataset and the OHSUMED dataset is the average number of relevant documents per profile in the testing set. Most of the FT filtering profiles are not good profiles, which means it is almost impossible to find a threshold that achieves a positive utility without profile updating. Indeed, the biased method (Run 2) set thresholds so high for some profiles that no relevant documents were delivered, thus getting zero Precision and Recall on those profiles. The unbiased algorithm (Run 4) does not increase the threshold

---

[5]The goal is to restart profiles that stopped disseminating because their thresholds were mistakenly set too high, so the minimum delivery constraint does not need to be large. The 10 document constraint was chosen arbitrarily.

	Biased (Run1)	Biased + Min. Delivery (Run2)	Unbiased (Run3)	Unbiased + Min. Delivery (Run4)
T9U'	1.44	-0.200	0.65	0.84
Delivered docs per profile	9.58	10.44	9.05	12.27
Precision	0.20	0.17	0.22	0.26
Recall	0.16	0.17	0.15	0.19
Profiles with Precision=0.0	24	22	24	10

Table 9.4. Comparison of the basic biased and unbiased Maximum Likelihood algorithms on TREC-8 Filtering data.

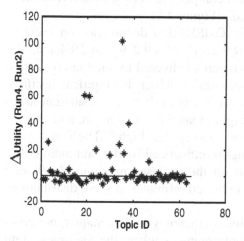
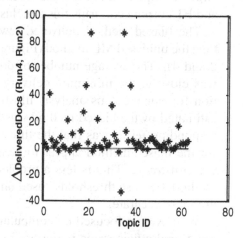

Figure 9.8. The improvement in utility of the unbiased method (Run 4) as compared with the biased method (Run 2). A minimum delivery constraint is used for both runs. Similar effectiveness is indicated by points near the horizontal line.

Figure 9.9. The improvement in the number of delivered documents for the unbiased method (Run 4) as compared with the biased method (Run 2). A minimum delivery constraint is used for both runs. Similar dissemination levels is indicated by points near the horizontal line.

much, which is why the biased and unbiased methods appear similar according to the utility metric yet different according to the Precision and Recall metrics. Indeed, this experiment demonstrates quite clearly that optimizing for utility is not guaranteed to improve Precision or Recall.

When we compared the utilities of each OHSU topic on Run 4 and Run 2 (Table 9.2), we found that the unbiased method are more likely to do well on some profiles where the score distribution of relevant documents and non-relevant documents match the model's assumptions. For other profiles, the difference between the unbiased ML method and the basic, biased algorithm is not

	Biased Estimation			Unbiased Estimation			Δ
(A, B)	Utility	Precision	Recall	Utility	Precision	Recall	Utility
(1,-1)	-3.09	0.22	0.16	-3.19	0.22	0.15	−3%
(2,-1)	-2.65	0.20	0.22	-2.58	0.20	0.20	+3%
(3,-1)	-1.65	0.18	0.24	-0.42	0.19	0.24	+75%
(4,-1)	2.19	0.16	0.27	5.60	0.18	0.26	+156%
(8,-1)	32.47	0.15	0.30	32.35	0.14	0.35	0%
(16,-1)	115.19	0.11	0.44	117.35	0.13	0.40	+2%

Table 9.5. Comparison of the basic biased and unbiased Maximum Likelihood algorithms on TREC-8 Filtering data, using different Utility metrics. FT data and topics. C=0 and D=0.

large. Comparison at the topic level and comparison between the OHSUMED and FT corpora confirms this conclusion (Figure 9.8).

The biased method delivered fewer OHSUMED documents, on average, than the unbiased ML method (Figure 9.9, and Tables 9.2, 9.3, and 9.4, columns 2 and 4). The average number of documents delivered by the biased method was close to the minimum delivery constraint, which is empirical justification for our previous analysis illustrated in Figure 9.5: The Gaussian mean estimated by the biased method was higher than the actual mean, and the corresponding result was that the threshold was set too high.[6] The final results for the biased method appear to be highly influenced by the minimum delivery constraint. This is less a problem for the unbiased maximum likelihood method, because thresholds based on unbiased estimates of score distributions are more accurate.

We have not focused on computational efficiency in this chapter, but computational efficiency is important in environments where the filtering system must keep pace with a high-speed document stream. Although the mathematics may look complex, the unbiased ML algorithm is computationally efficient. It took about 21 minutes ("wall-clock" time) to filter 4 years of OHSUMED data for 64 OHSU profiles (Table 9.2, Run 4) on a 500 MHz Intel Pentium III processor with 256 MB of memory. This time includes all aspects of document filtering, including the setting and updating of dissemination thresholds while filtering.

5.2   Varying the Utility Metric

The biased and unbiased algorithms can be compared using different utility metrics by varying the values of (A, B, C, D) in the linear utility function

---

[6]Theoretically the threshold set by the biased algorithm could be higher or lower than optimal. The sample bias problem will make the estimation of both the negative mean and the positive mean biased high, and the final threshold depends on both.

(A, B)	Biased Estimation			Unbiased Estimation			Δ
	Utility	*Precision*	*Recall*	*Utility*	*Precision*	*Recall*	*Utility*
(1,-1)	-1.40	0.27	0.11	-1.75	0.27	0.11	+25%
(2,-1)	3.55	0.26	0.18	6.38	0.27	0.17	+80%
(3,-1)	12.54	0.25	0.22	17.00	0.26	0.20	+36%
(4,-1)	25.70	0.24	0.24	29.63	0.25	0.22	+15%
(8,-1)	100.65	0.22	0.34	98.62	0.23	0.28	−2%
(16,-1)	287.71	0.18	0.42	285.83	0.20	0.38	−1%

Table 9.6. Comparison of the basic biased and unbiased Maximum Likelihood algorithms on TREC-9 Filtering data, using different Utility metrics. OHSUMED data and OHSU topics. C=0 and D=0.

(Equation 9.1). A second series of experiments was conducted that examined effectiveness when A was varied between 1 and 16, which corresponds to delivery rules "deliver if $P(Relevance|Score) > p$" with p varying from 50% ($A = 1$) to 5.9% ($A = 16$). Tables 9.5 and 9.6 summarize the experimental results.[7]

As the filtering goal was varied from "high Precision" (small A) to "high Recall" (large A), the value of unbiased estimation varied, too. The two algorithms were about equally effective when $A = 1$ ("high Precision") and $A \geq 8$ ("high Recall"). The unbiased Maximum Likelihood algorithm generally outperformed the basic, biased algorithm when $2 \leq A \leq 4$ ("medium Precision").

These results match our expectations. The filtering profiles were not sufficiently accurate for any dissemination threshold to satisfy the "high Precision" goal, leading to slightly negative utilities for both algorithms. The profiles were accurate enough to satisfy the "medium Precision" goal, and the unbiased algorithm generally made better use of its training data in these cases. Biased sampling is not a serious problem when dissemination thresholds are set low, as occurs when the goal is high Recall; in this case the biased and unbiased algorithms produced similar results.

5.3 Behavior When Assumptions Are Violated

This chapter presents a method of using unbiased generative analysis to set dissemination thresholds. Generative analysis makes strong assumptions about the underlying document score distributions, and these assumptions allow the algorithm to use training data very efficiently to discover the model parame-

---

[7]The results for $A = 2$ differ slightly from those reported in the previous section (Tables 9.2 and 9.4) because of changes to the software between the two experiments. The changes were primarily in how thresholds were lowered for profiles that did not satisfy the minimum delivery constraint, and in how thresholds were set when there was insufficient data to apply the generative method, e.g., during the early stage of filtering.

	Biased	Unbiased	Best System
T9U'	2458	2759	6799
T10SU	0.135	0.143	0.291
Precision	0.505	0.505	0.538
Recall	0.140	0.158	0.496

Table 9.7. Comparison of the basic biased algorithm, the unbiased Maximum Likelihood algorithm, and the best system in the TREC-10 evaluation. Reuters 2001 data and Reuters 2001 category profiles.

ters. However, when the model assumptions are wrong, i.e., when the actual distribution of document scores does not match the assumed distribution, the algorithm's behavior is undefined.

Two research groups participating in the TREC-10 Filtering track set dissemination thresholds using generative methods based on Normal and Exponential models (Arampatzis, 2002; Zhang and Callan, 2002). The utility scores were disappointing in both cases. Table 10 summarizes the TREC-10 results from Zhang and Callan, 2002 ("biased" and "unbiased") and from the best system participating in the track.[8],[9] The weak results for systems using generative models suggests that there might be problems with that approach to setting dissemination thresholds.

Closer inspection of the results revealed that the model assumption was wrong for some profiles, i.e., the distributions of relevant and/or non-relevant document scores did not match Gaussian and/or Exponential distributions. Two examples illustrate how the models failed to match the distribution of document scores, and suggest possible solutions.

Reuters 2001 profile 77 had a low utility score, so it was a candidate for deeper analysis. We used the final version of the learned profile (presumably a high quality set of query terms and weights) to re-score all of the documents in the corpus. Figure 9.10 shows the score density distribution of the relevant documents, which can be approximated by a normal distribution. Figure 9.11 shows the score density distribution for non-relevant documents that contain at least one profile term.

An Exponential model is not a completely accurate model of the probability density function of non-relevant documents for this profile. The inaccuracy is not a problem if the filtering goal is high or medium Precision because the training data is from the right side of the distribution, which matches an Ex-

---

[8] The best TREC-10 Filtering track result was run oraAU082201, which was submitted by Oracle (Robertson and Soboroff, 2002).

[9] TREC-10 used a scaled utility metric, defined as $T10SU = \frac{max(T9U, MinU) - MinU}{MaxU - MinU}$, where $MinU = -100$, $MaxU = 2 \cdot \text{TotalRelevant}$.

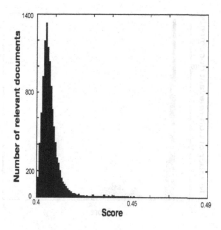

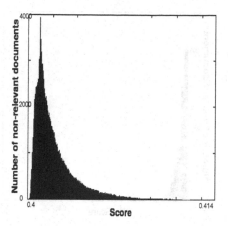

Figure 9.10. Score density distribution of relevant documents for profile 77. Reuters 2001 data.

Figure 9.11. Score density distribution of non-relevant documents for profile 77. Reuters 2001 data.

ponential model. If the filtering goal is high Recall, which includes training data from the left side of the distribution, a beta distribution would be a better fit. Since the Exponential distribution is a special case of the beta distribution, using a beta distribution would also cover cases where the Exponential distribution is the correct choice.

The maximum likelihood estimation method proposed in Equation 9.11 does not require any specific distribution; the beta distribution can be inserted into the general framework and the optimal parameters can be found. We did not implement the algorithm to find the optimal beta distribution parameters; we simply observe that it may be a better approximation function than the Exponential distribution proposed by (Arampatzis and Hameren, 2001; Manmatha et al., 2001) and used in our experiments. In fact this observation suggests that the type of model to use depends on the specific dataset and scoring algorithm. A more complicated model, such as the beta distribution, is likely to have less bias (making it more widely applicable) but more variance (requiring more training data).

Most of the TREC-10 filtering systems did poorly on Reuters 2001 profile 71, so it too was a candidate for deeper analysis. We used the final version of the learned profile (presumably a high quality set of query terms and weights) to re-score all of the documents in the corpus. Figure 9.12 shows the score density distribution for relevant documents.

The score density distribution for relevant documents looks initially more like an Exponential distribution than a Gaussian distribution (Figure 9.12). However, "zooming in" on the score density distribution of the top scoring

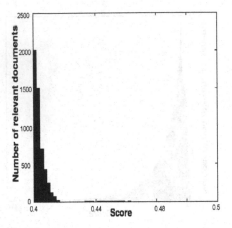 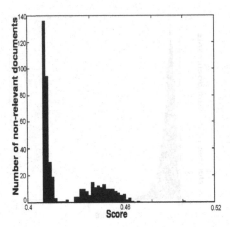

Figure 9.12. Score density distribution of relevant documents for profile 71. Reuters 2001 data.

Figure 9.13. Score density distribution of high score relevant documents for profile 71. Reuters 2001 data.

relevant documents shows that the distribution actually looks similar to a mixture of Exponential and Gaussian distributions (Figure 9.13).

The non-random sampling problem was identified in Section 3 as a cause of error in learning dissemination thresholds. However, it is also a cause of error in learning profiles, i.e., the terms and term weights that determine the score of a particular document. In our experiments, and indeed in most adaptive filtering research, the only relevant documents available to the profile learning algorithm are those that were disseminated. Thus the training data is a biased sample of the relevant documents.

The score density distribution of profile 71 is an extreme but real case that illustrates this problem. The information need described by profile 71 is a broad topic. With only two seed documents for training, the system tends to focus on a local area near the seed documents. The final learned profile, which is the function used to determine document scores, gives those documents and their close neighbors very high scores (corresponding to the normal area in Figure 9.13). The other relevant documents look to the profile just like non-relevant documents, hence they tend to get low scores (corresponding to the Exponential area in Figures 9.12 and 9.13).

Although this problem affects the profile-learning algorithm (e.g., Rocchio), the effect on the threshold-learning algorithm is very strong in some cases, as illustrated by this example.

This chapter proposed an algorithm to solve the sampling bias problem for setting dissemination thresholds *in isolation from the rest of the filtering system.* It didn't develop a solution to solve the sampling bias problem when terms, term weights, and thresholds are all being adjusted simultaneously. However, the bias problem for threshold learning and profile term updating are correlated and should really be solved together. One solution is to explicitly model the sampling bias while profile term weights and threshold are changing. One could begin with Equation 9.11 and model

$$P(Score_i, Feedback_i | \theta, f_i(d_i) > 0)$$

The solution would depend on what kind of scoring function and profile learning algorithm the filtering system uses. Another possible solution is to deliver interesting "near miss" documents, so that the learning software gets a broader view of the surrounding information landscape, thereby learning a less biased scoring function. Theories from other research areas, such as active learning and reinforcement learning, are also potentially useful considering the similarity of the tasks.

6. Conclusion

Generative modeling has received considerable attention recently. This chapter describes how it can be used to set dissemination thresholds for adaptive information filtering systems. Generative models embody strong assumptions about the distributions of relevant and non-relevant document scores, which enables an adaptive filtering system to learn dissemination thresholds from small amounts of training data.

A major problem for generative methods is the non-random sampling that affects adaptive filtering systems when the only source of training data is the set of documents the system disseminates. Non-random sampling causes the system to overestimate the mean scores of relevant and non-relevant documents, and to underestimate the variance. These systematic errors can produce suboptimal dissemination thresholds, especially when the goal is high Precision output.

The non-random sampling problem can be corrected by explicitly modeling and compensating for the bias inherent in the filtering environment, where training data consists only of documents with scores above a threshold that changes constantly. This chapter describes a general framework based on the maximum likelihood principle to estimate model parameters, using Normal and Exponential distributions as an example. An explicit solution based on this framework is provided to jointly estimate (i) the parameters of the density distributions for relevant and non-relevant document scores, and (ii) the ratios of relevant and non-relevant documents around the dissemination threshold. We believe this is the first research to explicitly model and compensate for the sample bias problem in an information filtering environment.

Non-random sampling is inherent in the adaptive filtering task scenario used in the TREC Filtering track evaluations, and it affects profile-learning as well as threshold-setting. It is common to treat the learning of profiles and dissemination thresholds as separate problems, but they are in fact highly related. Ignoring non-random sampling when learning profiles makes it more likely that the resulting document score distributions will be difficult for a threshold-setting algorithm to model.

The unbiased generative method of setting dissemination thresholds appears to offer the most advantage over alternatives when the filtering goal is "medium-to-high Precision". In these situations there is usually only a small amount of positive training data, and it is a very biased sample of the underlying distribution, so it is important to use an algorithm that compensates for the bias and uses training data efficiently. When the filtering goal is "high Recall", more training data is available, and it is a less biased sample, so the unbiased algorithm has less of an advantage.

The experimental results in this chapter demonstrate the strengths and weaknesses of using strong statistical models to set dissemination thresholds. When the model assumptions match the data, the unbiased generative method is quite effective; otherwise, its behavior is unpredictable. The unbiased generative framework presented here is more general than the Gaussian and Exponential models that were the focus of the chapter; a wide range of other models could be supported. Which models would be most general or most effective, or how one might determine during filtering which models best fit the data, are interesting topics for future research.

Acknowledgments

We thank Avi Arampatzis, R. Manmatha, Chengxiang Zhai, Wei Xu and Tom Minka for valuable discussions on some of the work in this chapter.

This material is based in part on work supported by Air Force Research Laboratory contract F30602-98-C-0110. Any opinions, findings, conclusions or recommendations expressed in this chapter are the authors', and do not necessarily reflect those of the sponsors.

References

Allan, J. (1996). Incremental relevance feedback for information filtering. In *Proceedings of the 19th Annual International ACM SIGIR Conference on Research and Development in Information Retrieval*, pages 270–278.

Arampatzis, A. (2002). Unbiased S-D threshold optimization, initial query degradation, decay, and incrementality for adaptive document filtering. In *Proceeding of the Tenth Text REtrieval Conference (TREC-10)*, pages 596–603. National Institute of Standards and Technology, special publication 500-250.

Arampatzis, A., Beney, J., Koster, C., and van der Weide., T. (2001). Incrementality, decay, and threshold optimization for adaptive filtering systems. In *Proceeding of Ninth Text REtrieval Conference (TREC-9)*, pages 589–600. National Institute of Standards and Technology, special publication 500-249.

Arampatzis, A. and Hameren, A. (2001). The score-distribution threshold optimization for adaptive binary classification task. In *Proceedings of the 24th Annual International ACM SIGIR Conference on Research and Development in Information Retrieval*, pages 285–293.

Ault, T. and Yang, Y. (2001). kNN at TREC-9: A failure analysis. In *Proceeding of Ninth Text REtrieval Conference (TREC-9)*, pages 127–134. National Institute of Standards and Technology, special publication 500-249.

Broglio, J., Callan, J., Croft, W., and Nachbar, D. (1995). Document retrieval and routing using the INQUERY system. In *Proceeding of Third Text REtrieval Conference (TREC-3)*, pages 29–38. National Institute of Standards and Technology,special publication 500-225.

Callan, J. (1996). Document filtering with inference networks. In *Proceedings of the Nineteenth Annual International ACM SIGIR Conference on Research and Development in Information Retrieval*, pages 262–269.

Hastie, T., Tibshirani, R., and Friedman, J. (2001). *Elements of Statistical Learning: Data Mining, Inference and Prediction*. Springer-Verlag.

Hersh, W., Buckley, C., J.Leone, T., and Hickam, D. (1994). OHSUMED: An interactive retrieval evaluation and new large test collection for research. In *Proceedings of the Seventeenth Annual International ACM SIGIR Conference on Research and Development in Information Retrieval*, pages 192–201.

Hull, D. A. and Robertson, S. (2000). The TREC-8 Filtering track final report. In *Proceeding of the Eighth Text REtrieval Conference (TREC-8)*, pages 35–56. National Institute of Standards and Technology, special publication 500-246.

Kim, Y., Hahn, S., and Zhang, B. (2000). Text filtering by boosting Naive Bayes classifiers. In *Proceedings of the 23rd Annual International ACM SIGIR Conference on Research and Development in Information Retrieval*, pages 168–175. ACM Press.

Kraaij, W., Pohlmann, R., and Hiemstra, D. (2000). Twenty-One at TREC-8: Using language technology for information retrieval. In *Proceedings of the Eighth Text REtrieval Conference (TREC-8)*, pages 285–300. National Institute of Standards and Technology, special publication 500-246.

MacKay, D. J. (2001). Macopt – a nippy wee optimizer. http://wol.ra.phy.cam.ac.uk/mackay/c/macopt.html.

Manmatha, R., Rath, T., and Feng, F. (2001). Modeling score distributions for combining the outputs of search engines. In *Proceedings of the 24th An-*

nual *International ACM SIGIR Conference on Research and Development in Information Retrieval*, pages 267–275.

Ng, A. Y. and Jordan., M. (2002). On discriminative vs. generative classifiers: A comparison of logistic regression and Naive Bayes. In *Proceeding of Fourteenth Neural Information Processing Systems*.

Porter, M. F. (1980). An algorithm for suffix stripping. *Program*, 14(3):130–137.

Press, W., Teukolsky, S., Vetterling, W., and Flannery, B. (1992). *Numerical Recipes in C: The Art of Scientific Computing*. Cambridge University Press.

Robertson, S. and Hull, D. (2001). The TREC-9 Filtering track report. In *The Ninth Text REtrieval Conference (TREC-9)*, pages 25–40. National Institute of Standards and Technology, special publication 500-249.

Robertson, S. and Soboroff, I. (2002). The TREC-10 Filtering track final report. In *Proceeding of the Tenth Text REtrieval Conference (TREC-10)*, pages 26–37. National Institute of Standards and Technology, special publication 500-250.

Robertson, S. and Walker, S. (2000). Threshold setting in adaptive filtering. *Journal of Documentation*, pages 312–331.

Robertson, S. and Walker, S. (2001). Microsoft Cambridge at TREC-9: Filtering track. In *Proceeding of Ninth Text REtrieval Conference (TREC-9)*, pages 361–368. National Institute of Standards and Technology, special publication 500-249.

Robertson, S., Walker, S., Beaulieu, M. M., Gatford, M., and Payne, A. (1996). Okapi at TREC-4. In *Proceeding of Fourth Text REtrieval Conference (TREC-4)*, pages 73–96. National Institute of Standards and Technology, special publication 500-236.

Rocchio, J. J. (1971). Relevance feedback in information retrieval. In *The SMART Retrieval System– Experiments in Automatic Document Processing*, pages 313–323. Prentice Hall.

Rubinstein, Y. D. and Hastie, T. (1997). Discriminative vs informative learning. In *Proceedings of the Third International Conference on Knowledge Discovery and Data Mining*, pages 49–53.

Schapire, R., Singer, Y., and Singhal, A. (1998). Boosting and Rocchio applied to text filtering. In *Proceedings of the 21st Annual International ACM SIGIR Conference on Research and Development in Information Retrieval*, pages 215–213.

Zhai, C., Jansen, P., Roma, N., Stoica, E., and Evans, D. (2000). Optimization in CLARIT adaptive filtering. In *Proceeding of Eighth Text REtrieval Conference (TREC-8)*, pages 253–258. National Institute of Standards and Technology 500-246.

Zhai, C., Jansen, P., and Stoica, E. (1999). Threshold calibration in CLARIT adaptive filtering. In *Proceeding of Seventh Text REtrieval Conference (TREC-*

7), pages 149–157. National Institute of Standards and Technology, special publication 500-242.

Zhang, Y. and Callan, J. (2001a). Maximum likelihood estimation for filtering thresholds. In *Proceedings of the 24th Annual International ACM SIGIR Conference on Research and Development in Information Retrieval*, pages 294–302.

Zhang, Y. and Callan, J. (2001b). Yfilter at TREC-9. In *Proceedings of the Ninth Text REtrieval Conference (TREC-9)*, pages 135–140. National Institute of Standards and Technology, special publication 500-249.

Zhang, Y. and Callan, J. (2002). The bias problem and language models in adaptive filtering. In *The Tenth Text REtrieval Conference (TREC-10)*, pages 78–83. National Institute of Standards and Technology, special publication 500-250.

Chapter 10

LANGUAGE MODELING EXPERIMENTS IN NON-EXTRACTIVE SUMMARIZATION

Vibhu O. Mittal*

Google

vibhu@mittal.net

Michael J. Witbrock[†]

Cycorp

witbrock@cyc.com

Abstract

Although most text summarization research to date has been applied to news articles, web pages are quite different in both structure and content. Instead of coherent text with a well-defined discourse structure, they are mostly a bag of phrases, links, graphics and formatting commands, thus providing few opportunities for extractive summarization methods. Extractive summarizers, moreover, are limited in their ability to produce very brief, headline-like, summaries where flexibility in lexical choice and phrasing are important. This paper discusses relatively simple statistical models for generating non-extractive summaries of web pages. It describes the datasets used to train these models, shows sample outputs, and discusses the results of some preliminary evaluations to assess the quality of the resulting summaries.

Keywords: summarization, text-processing

*Current address: 2400 Bayshore Parkway, Mountain View, CA 94043. This work was done while the author was employed at Just Research in Pittsburgh, PA.

[†]Current address: 3721 Executive Center Drive, Suite 100, Austin, TX 78731. Substantial portions of this work were performed while the author was at Just Research and Terra Lycos.

W.B. Croft and J. Lafferty (eds.), Language Modeling for Information Retrieval, 219–244.
© 2003 *Kluwer Academic Publishers.*

<HEADLINE> **U.S. Pushes for Mideast Peace** </HEADLINE>

President Clinton met with his top Mideast advisers, including Secretary of State Madeleine Albright and U.S. peace envoy Dennis Ross, in preparation for a session with Israel Prime Minister Benjamin Netanyahu tomorrow. Palestinian leader Yasser Arafat is to meet with Clinton later this week. Published reports in Israel say Netanyahu will warn Clinton that Israel can't withdraw from more than nine percent of the West Bank in its next scheduled pullback, although Clinton wants a 12-15 percent pullback.

Top Ranked Sentence in Story (32 words, or 41%)

President Clinton met with his top Mideast advisers, including Secretary of State Madeleine Albright and U.S. peace envoy Dennis Ross, in preparation for a session with Israel Prime Minister Benjamin Netanyahu tomorrow.

Second Ranked Sentence (35 words, or 45%)

Published reports in Israel say Netanyahu will warn Clinton that Israel can't withdraw from more than nine percent of the West Bank in its next scheduled pullback, although Clinton wants a 12-15 percent pullback.

Figure 10.1: Sample article with original headline and extraction-based summaries.

1.   Introduction

Generating effective summaries requires the ability to select, evaluate, order and aggregate items of information according to their relevance to a particular subject or for a particular purpose. This is, in general, AI-hard. It is not surprising, therefore, that most of the work to date on summarization has focused on *extractive summarization*: selecting text spans - either complete sentences or paragraphs – from the original document. These extracts are then arranged in a linear order, usually their order in the original document, to form a summary document. There are several drawbacks to this approach, including the inability of such a system to generate coherent summaries shorter than the smallest text-spans being considered, or using terms or phrasings not found in the source document. These are all severe shortcomings. For instance, in many situations, a short headline style indicative summary may be desirable, but highly ranked extracted sentences tend to be even longer than the average sentence in a document (Mittal et al., 1999).

Consider, for example, the short news story in Figure 10.1. The most important sentences in this story are the longer ones. While the original, manually generated headline summary of the article is only five words long, the relevant candidate sentences are six to seven times longer. To compound this problem, the defining information for a document is, in many cases, scattered across several of its passages. This is particularly likely for *non-linear content*, such as web pages and hyperlinked collections of web documents.

Typical state-of-the-art summarizers, such as the Maximal-Marginal Relevance[1] (MMR) models (Carbonell and Goldstein, 1998), usually generate very sub-optimal summaries for heavily hyperlinked documents because there is so little linear, self-contained text that can be used as is; web pages, for instance, by the very nature of their (intended) not-necessarily-linear perusal – via links to other pages or other objects on the same page – use of embedded HTML formatting instead of discourse cues, *etc.*, are difficult to summarize effectively using extraction. It is for this reason, amongst others, that none of the current web search engines attempt to actually summarize pages in the search results; lacking a human generated summary, they either display the first N characters from the page, or the text around the query terms, ignoring, for the most part, issues of readability or coherence.

In an effort to alleviate these problems, the approach taken in the work reported here was to experiment with designs for a system that could *synthesize* a summary, rather than extract one. The system relies on statistical models for both content selection (as a substitute for Natural Language Understanding) and surface realization (for Natural Language Generation). The models are built by training on large, representative collections of paired input-output documents: in our case pairs of original documents and corresponding summaries of the desired kind.

2. Related Work

The majority of previous work in automated summarization has focused on extractive summarization. Prior work here explored issues such as the utility of cue phrases (Luhn, 1958), positional indicators (Edmundson, 1964), lexical occurrence statistics (Mathis et al., 1973), and the use of implicit discourse structure (Marcu, 1997). Others explored the use of machine learning techniques to learn a linear combination function of some of these features (Kupiec et al., 1995; Hovy and Lin, 1997). However, all these efforts assumed that the source documents were a coherent stream of text with a logical discourse structure – an assumption that does not generally hold in web pages. Much closer in spirit to our current work is work on combining an initial information extraction phase with generation; embodied in, for instance, the frump system

---

[1] In recent ARPA evaluations of summarizers, the MMR – Maximizing Marginal Relevance – based summarizers were ranked in the top two in most categories.

(DeJong, 1982) and the Columbia system (McKeown and Radev, 1995), both of which were designed to generate summaries from multiple news stories.

More recently, there has also been work directly related to non-extractive summarization using learning approaches very similar to ours, though applied to conventional documents rather than to web pages. Marcu and Knight (Knight and Marcu, 2000), for example, learn parse tree transformations of source documents into summary documents. This has several advantages: it is capable of generating very fluent text; it can learn to maintain functional dependencies; and it is capable of making very fine grained decisions. It can, for instance, learn specific situations in which adjectives can or cannot be dropped. However, it also has some disadvantages compared to the model proposed here: it cannot currently combine information from multiple sentences or documents into the summary, it is limited in the amount of compression it is capable of, and it is constrained to use as tokens in the summary only those that are present in the source document. In future work, it may be possible to integrate the two approaches, or to combine the Knight-Marcu approach with an extraction based summarizer to find salient parts of several sentences and combine them together, thus yielding output similar in scope to that of the system described here.

Another related area of recent work is found in automatic translation of natural language, and served as a substantial source of inspiration for the work described here. The central idea of statistical machine translation is that, starting from a bilingual corpus of text, one can apply statistical machine learning algorithms to estimate maximum-likelihood parameter values for a model of translation between the two languages. For instance, the Candide system at IBM (Berger et al., 1994) used the proceedings of the Canadian parliament — maintained in parallel French and English versions — to learn an English-French translation model. In an entirely analogous way, we propose, in this work, to use Open Directory's "bilingual corpus" of web pages and their summaries to learn a mapping from the terms and syntactic patterns found in web pages to those found in their summaries. Probably the most fundamental difference between this work and natural language translation is its degree of difficulty: a satisfactory translation of a sentence must capture its entire meaning, while a satisfactory summary is actually *expected* to leave out most of the source document's content. A countervailing difference, though, is the relative scarcity of training data for the summarization problem. The work described here also somewhat resembles, in its use of probabilistic models for word relatedness, to some recent work in document retrieval (Berger and Lafferty, 1999).

3. Statistical Models of Gisting

We discuss three models for statistical summarization, or gisting, in this section. In practical implementations, each of these can be enhanced for specific tasks or document genres: for instance, in the case of web pages, we can incorporate a model of HTML: tags, anchors, structures such as lists and tables, formatting commands such as font-size and position, etc. However, for purposes of this paper, we shall focus on a minimal, simplified model and assume documents that are just collections of words. Parameter estimation for these models – using maximum-likelihood, and the Expectation-Maximization (EM) algorithm – is deferred to the next section.

3.1 Documents as bags of words

The weakest model of the three, this assumes that words in the gist are drawn in iid[2] fashion from the document according to some probability distribution ϕ over possible lengths. This model makes a strong independence assumption among the words in the input document, viewing them as an unordered collection.

3.2 Allowing for unseen words

The previous model is limited by the fact that the generated summaries can only contain words from the input document. This restriction can be relaxed as follows: draw a word from the input document, but allow the drawn word to be replaced by a related word before adding it to the gist.

To determine which word to substitute in place of the sampled word, we use a probability distribution $\sigma(\cdot \mid w)$: if u is a word very closely related to v, then we expect $\sigma(u \mid v)$ to be large. If the system recognizes W words, then the σ model is just a $W \times W$ stochastic matrix, the diagonal entries of which, corresponding to "self-similarity" probabilities, are likely to be large.) This algorithm, *expanded-lexicon gisting*, is similar to the IBM-style model of language translation (Brown et al., 1993), since the lexicon of candidate words for a summary of $\mathbf{d}$ is no longer just the set of words in $\mathbf{d}$. In this case, the probability of generating a specific gist $\mathbf{g} = \{g_1, g_2, \ldots g_n\}$ for a document d

---

[2]iid: independently and identically distributed random trials

---

BOW gisting:	**Expanded-lexicon gisting**
Input: Document **d** with word distribution $\lambda(\cdot \mid \mathbf{d})$;	*Input:* Document **d** with word distribution $\lambda(\cdot \mid \mathbf{d})$;
Distribution ϕ over gist lengths;	Distribution ϕ over gist lengths;
Output: Gist **g** of **d**	Word-similarity model $\sigma(\cdot \mid u)$ for all words w
	Output: Gist **g** of **d**
1. Select a length n for the gist: $n \sim \phi$	
	1. Select a length for the gist: $n \sim \phi$
2. Do for $i = 1$ to n	
	2. Do for $i = 1$ to n
3. Pick a word from the document: $w \sim \lambda(\cdot \mid \mathbf{d})$	
	3. Pick a word from the document: $u \sim \lambda(\cdot \mid \mathbf{d})$
4. Set $g_i \leftarrow w$	
	4. Pick a replacement for that word: $v \sim \sigma(\cdot \mid w)$
	5. Set $\mathbf{g}_i \leftarrow v$

Figure 10.2: Two models for selecting summary content

---

containing m words, $\{d_1, d_2, \ldots d_m\}$, is:

$$p(\mathbf{g} \mid \mathbf{d}) \;=\; \phi(n) \prod_{i=1}^{n} p(g_i \mid \mathbf{d}) \tag{10.1}$$

$$=\; \phi(n) \prod_{i=1}^{n} \frac{1}{m} \sum_{j=1}^{m} \sigma(g_i \mid d_j)$$

3.3 Coherent gisting

Recall, though, that the intent of this work is to produce a model that exhibits both *fidelity* and *readability*. The expanded-lexicon gisting model, above, allows for the possibility of faithfully representing the content of the source document, perhaps in other terms, but it says nothing about the order in which this content should be prevented in the summary. It cannot contribute to readability. In this section, the model is extended by scoring candidate gists not only on how well they capture the essence of the content of the original document, but also on how coherent they are as a string of English words.

The coherence or readability of an n-word string $\mathbf{g} = \{g_1, g_2, \ldots g_n\}$ comprising a candidate gist is modeled as the *a priori* probability of seeing that string of words in text, which we write as $p(\mathbf{g})$.[3] One can factor $p(\mathbf{g})$ into a product of conditional probabilities as

$$p(\mathbf{g}) = \prod_{i=1}^{n} p(g_i \mid g_1, g_2 \cdots g_{i-1})$$

In practice, we use a *trigram* model for $p(\mathbf{g})$, meaning that

$$p(g_i \mid g_1, g_2 \cdots g_{i-1}) \approx p(g_i \mid g_{i-2}g_{i-1}) \tag{10.2}$$

Although n-gram models of language make a strong, and clearly false, locality assumption about text, they have nonetheless proven successful in many human language technologies, including speech and optical character recognition (Jelinek, 1997; Nathan et al., 1995).

To devise a formal model of gisting which accounts for both readability and fidelity to the source document, we apply Bayes' Rule:

$$\mathbf{g}^{\star} \;=\; \mathrm{argmax}_{\mathbf{g}} p(\mathbf{g} \mid \mathbf{d})$$

$$=\; \mathrm{argmax}_{\mathbf{g}} p(\mathbf{d} \mid \mathbf{g})\, p(\mathbf{g}). \tag{10.3}$$

---

[3] We are overloading the term p to refer to multiple probability distributions, as well as values assigned by those distributions, but hope that the proper meaning is clear from context.

Algorithm 3: *Coherent gists*

Input: Document **d** with word distribution $\lambda(\cdot \mid \mathbf{d})$;

   Distribution ϕ over gist lengths;

   Word-similarity model $\sigma(\cdot \mid w)$ for all words w

   Trigram language model $p(\mathbf{g})$ for gists

Output: Gist **g** of **d**

   1. Select a length n for the gist: $n \sim \phi$

   2. Find, by searching, the sequence $\mathbf{g} = \{g_1, g_2, \ldots g_n\}$ which maximizes $p(\mathbf{d} \mid \mathbf{g})p(\mathbf{g})$

According to (10.3), the optimal gist is the product of two terms: first, a fidelity term $p(\mathbf{d} \mid \mathbf{g})$, measuring how closely **d** and **g** match in content, and a readability term $p(\mathbf{g})$, measuring the *a priori* coherence of the gist **g**.

For the readability term we can use the language model (10.2). For the content proximity model $p(\mathbf{d} \mid \mathbf{g})$, we can simply reverse the direction of (10.1):

$$p(\mathbf{d} \mid \mathbf{g}) = \hat{\phi}(m) \prod_{i=1}^{m} p(d_i \mid \mathbf{g}) \qquad (10.4)$$

$$= \hat{\phi}(m) \prod_{i=1}^{m} \frac{1}{n} \sum_{j=1}^{n} \sigma(d_i \mid g_j)$$

Here $\hat{\phi}$ is a length distribution on *documents*.[4].

One can think of $p(\mathbf{g})$ as a prior distribution on candidate gists, and $p(\mathbf{d} \mid \mathbf{g})$ as the probability that the document **d** would arise from the gist **g**.

4.   Training the Models

4.1   Datasets

Each of the previous three models requires, as input, various model parameters. These parameters can be empirically estimated for different situations and

---

[4]The system's task is to find the best gist of a document, and the $\hat{\phi}$ term will contribute equally to every candidate gist. We can therefore ignore this term from now on.

tasks given suitable datasets. In the present case, we trained on two different training sets: (1) news articles: approximately 650,000 news articles from various leading newspapers, with articles from 1997 through 1999, and (2) Web Pages from the Open Directory Project: a directory of web pages compiled and maintained by volunteers. The Open Directory is an excellent testbed for applying machine learning techniques in summarization because each web site in the Open Directory has an accompanying, manually generated, summary. As of January 2000, when a copy was downloaded for experiments, the Open Directory contained 868, 227 descriptions of web pages.

Both of these datasets were normalized by: (i) removing punctuation, converting all text to lowercase; replacing numbers by the symbol NUM; removing stop-words (in this case, simply the 100 most common words, over all), (ii) removing all html links, images, and meta-information from the web pages, (iii) removing explicitly pornographic pages (iv) removing HTML markup information from the pages; (v) removing pages containing html frames; (vi) removing pages when their lengths were too small—including fewer than 400 and 60 characters for pages and gists, respectively. (vii) partitioning the remaining set of pairs into a training set (99%) and a test set (1%).

After this normalization, we were left with 103, 064 summaries and links in the training set, and 1046 in the test set. After processing, the average length of the summaries was 13.6 words, and the average length of the documents was 211.1 words.

4.2 Parameter Estimation

4.2.1 Related Word Models.

If there are W_g different recognized words in gists and W_p different recognized words in web pages, then calculating the parameters of the individual σ models for the third gisting algorithm is equivalent to filling in the entries of a $W_g \times W_p$ stochastic matrix. Brown et al (1993) discuss algorithms for estimating maximum-likelihood values for the entries of this matrix. For estimating the σ parameters, we introduce, following this previous work, the notion of an *alignment* a between sequences of words, which, here, captures how words in gists produce the words in a web page. We'll also make use of an artificial NULL added to position zero of every gist, whose purpose is to generate those words in the web page not strongly correlated with any other word in the gist.

Using a, we can decompose $p(\mathbf{d} \mid \mathbf{g})$ as

$$p(\mathbf{d} \mid \mathbf{g}) = \sum_{\mathbf{a}} p(\mathbf{d}, \mathbf{a} \mid \mathbf{g}) = \sum_{\mathbf{a}} p(\mathbf{d} \mid \mathbf{a}, \mathbf{g}) p(\mathbf{a} \mid \mathbf{g}) \qquad (10.5)$$

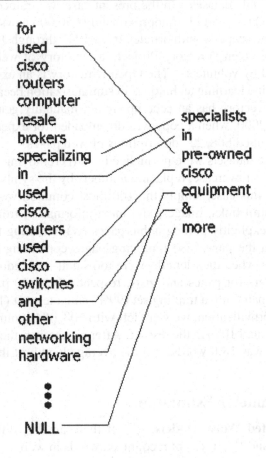

Figure 10.3: One of the exponentially many alignments between this imaginary document/gist pair. Calculating the score $p(\mathbf{d} \mid \mathbf{g})$ of a document/gist pair involves, implicitly, a sum over *all* possible ways of aligning the words.

Making the simplifying assumption that to each word in **d** corresponds to exactly one "parent" word in **g** (possibly the null word), we can write

$$p(\mathbf{d} \mid \mathbf{a}, \mathbf{g}) = \prod_{i=1}^{m} \sigma(d_i \mid g_{a_i}) \qquad (10.6)$$

Here g_{a_i} is the gist word aligned with the ith web page word. Figure 10.3 illustrates a sample alignment between a small web page and its summary.

If **d** contains m words and **g** contains $n+1$ words (including the null word), there are $(n+1)^m$ alignments between **g** and **d**. By assuming that all these alignments are equally likely, we can write

$$p(\mathbf{d} \mid \mathbf{g}) = \frac{p(m \mid \mathbf{g})}{(n+1)^m} \sum_{A} \prod_{i=1}^{m} \sigma(d_i \mid g_{a_i}) \qquad (10.7)$$

We view the Open Directory dataset as a collection of web pages and their summaries,

$$\mathcal{C} = \{(\mathbf{d}_1, \mathbf{g}_1), (\mathbf{d}_2, \mathbf{g}_2), (\mathbf{d}_3, \mathbf{g}_3) \ldots$$

The likelihood method suggests that one should adjust the parameters of (10.7) in such a way that the model assigns as high a probability as possible to $\mathcal{C}$. This maximization must be performed, of course, subject to the constraints $\sum_d \sigma(d \mid g) = 1$ for all words g. Using Lagrange multipliers,

$$\sigma(d \mid g) = Z \sum_{\mathbf{a}} p(\mathbf{d}, \mathbf{a} \mid \mathbf{g}) \sum_{j=1}^{m} \delta(d, d_j) \delta(g, g_{a_j}), \qquad (10.8)$$

where Z is a normalizing factor and δ is the Kronecker delta function.[5]

The parameter $\sigma(d \mid g)$ appears explicitly in the left-hand side of (10.8), and implicitly in the right. By repeatedly solving this equation for all pairs d, g (using the EM algorithm), one eventually reaches a stationary point of the likelihood.

Equation (10.8) contains a sum over alignments, which is exponential and suggests that the computing the parameters in this way is infeasible. In fact, this is not the case, since

$$\sum_{\mathbf{a}} \prod_{i=1}^{m} \sigma(d_i \mid g_{a_i}) = \prod_{i=1}^{m} \sum_{j=0}^{n} \sigma(d_i \mid g_j) \qquad (10.9)$$

This rearranging means that computing $\sum_{\mathbf{a}} p(\mathbf{d}, \mathbf{a} \mid \mathbf{g})$ requires only $\Theta(mn)$ work, rather than $\Theta(n^m)$.

Figure 10.4 shows the progress of the perplexity of the Open Directory training data during the six iterations of training. For the EM training, we used $103,064$ gist/web page pairs in the training set, totaling $24,231,164$ words in the web page data and $1,922,393$ words in the summaries. The vocabularies were constructed from the top 65535 words appearing at least twice; all other words were mapped to the symbol OOV (for "out of vocabulary"). Table 10.1 shows the top entries for a few selected words.

---

[5]the Kronecker delta function, $\delta(i, j)$ is defined simply as a function whose value is 1 if $i = j$ and 0 if $i \neq j$

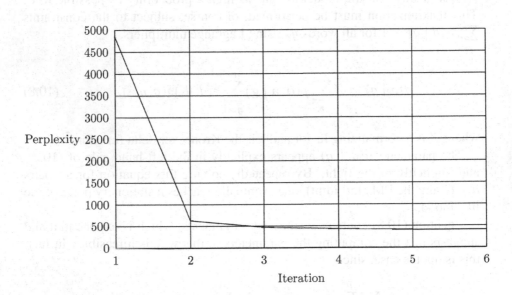

Figure 10.4: Progress of the EM algorithm, measured in training set perplexity, during six iterations.

job	job 0.194	jobs 0.098	career 0.028
wilderness	wilderness 0.123	the 0.061	national 0.032
associations	associations 0.083	association 0.063	oov 0.020
ibm	ibm 0.130	business 0.035	solutions 0.019
camera	camera 0.137	cameras 0.045	photo 0.020
investments	investments 0.049	investment 0.046	fund 0.033
contractor	contractor 0.080	contractors 0.030	construction 0.027
quilts	quilts 0.141	quilt 0.074	i 0.036
exhibitions	exhibitions 0.059	oov 0.056	art 0.048
ranches	ranches 0.089	springs 0.034	colorado 0.032

Table 10.1: Word-relatedness models $\sigma(\cdot \mid w)$ for selected words w, computed in an unsupervised manner from the Open Directory training data.

4.2.2   Estimating a Language Model.   The system uses a trigram language model to model the linear structure of the surface language form. For a W-word vocabulary, such a model is characterized by W^3 parameters: $p(w \mid u, v)$ is the probability that the word w follows the bigram u, v. We computed $p(w \mid u, v)$ values from both the $868, 227$ Open Directory gists, as well as the news articles. Note that this model can be built from a corpus of any text that resembles the desired output. Building the language model consisted of the following steps: (i) constructing an active vocabulary of words appearing at least twice ($37, 863$ words), (ii) building a trigram word model from this data using maximum-likelihood estimation, and (iii)"smoothing" this model (assign some probability mass to unseen trigrams) using the Good-Turing estimate (Good, 1953). For the final two steps we used the publicly-available CMU-Cambridge Language Modelling Toolkit (Clarkson and Rosenfeld, 1997).

5.   Output and Evaluation

We have already seen that extraction based summarizers, even state-of-the-art ones, usually designed for news articles, may not work well with web pages because of the differences between linear, written text and non-linear, hyper-linked documents. For instance, consider how non-extractive models might do on the article in figure 10.1. Figure 10.5 shows the output of our system using a few different statistical models on the same news story. The generated summaries are, indeed, significantly better in terms of information density than any of the sentences in the story itself. This advantage comes, however, at some cost: some of the summaries amount to no more than keyword lists, and some, (e.g. C4) are factually false.[6] As these models are improved, both (i) in terms of having better parameter estimates for content selection and better realization models than simple trigram probabilities, and (ii) in terms of making use of additional structural information about the text being summarized, we believe that both quality and content of the summaries being generated can be substantially improved.

For non-linear text, such as web pages, non-extractive models are even more essential to investigate. Figures 10.6 and 10.7 show the output of the system on two typical web pages.

5.1   Evaluation

Evaluating the intrinsic quality of a summary is harder than evaluating the quality of a text passage: not only must the evaluator consider issues such as coherence, lexical choice, style, etc., but also issues such as fidelity, implications that arise from dropping content, re-ordering sentences, etc., as well as the trade-offs between conciseness and completeness, summary-information redundancy and source-document emphasis, etc. Thus, previous efforts in summary evaluation have focused on extrinsic quality, which measures how well a summary might fare as a replacement for the original document in the context of a specific task (Hand, 1997; Tipster, 1998; Jing et al., 1998; Goldstein et al., 1999).

For this paper, we conducted a user-based evaluation of extrinsic summary quality. Since this must, of necessity, be small, we also conducted some, rather perfunctory, studies of intrinsic summary quality to get some idea of how feasible this might be. We describe the intrinsic evaluation very briefly before discussing the extrinsic one.

Content Models: Measuring Intrinsic Summary Quality.   We attempted to measure intrinsic summary quality in the simplest way possible: using a measure of word overlap between system generated summaries and a gold standard for two different datasets: headlines for news articles from the Reuters data set, and manually generated summaries for the Open Directory web sites.[7] The numbers are shown in Table 10.2. For each document, the maximum overlap between the "standard" summary and the generated summary was noted; the length at which this overlap was maximal was also taken into account for

---

[6]In the case of these factual errors, the verisimilitude provided by the language model might be regarded as harmful. A keyword list does not suggest roles.

[7]We recognize that a lexical overlap evaluation is problematic in many ways. For instance, a hypothesized gist may be as good as the real gist, yet share very few words with it. Conversely, a hypothesized summary may contain exactly the same words as the true summary, but arranged nonsensically.

<HEADLINE> **U.S. Pushes for Mideast Peace** </HEADLINE>

President Clinton met with his top Mideast advisers, including Secretary of State Madeleine Albright and U.S. peace envoy Dennis Ross, in preparation for a session with Israel Prime Minister Benjamin Netanyahu tomorrow. Palestinian leader Yasser Arafat is to meet with Clinton later this week. Published reports in Israel say Netanyahu will warn Clinton that Israel can't withdraw from more than nine percent of the West Bank in its next scheduled pullback, although Clinton wants a 12-15 percent pullback.

4:	clinton to meet albright	-105.5
5:	clinton in israel for albright	-129.9
6:	clinton in israel to meet albright	-158.57

(a) System generated output using a lexical + POS model.

2:	clinton mideast	-12.53
3:	clinton netanyahu arafat	-17.66
4:	clinton netanyahu arafat israel	-23.1
5:	clinton to meet netanyahu arafat	-28.8

(b) System generated output using a lexical + positional model.

3:	clinton in israel	- 58.13
4:	clinton meeting in israel	-78.47
5:	clinton to meet with israel	-87.08
6:	clinton to meet with netanyahu arafat	-107.44

(c) System generated output using a lexical + positional model + POS models.

Figure 10.5: Non-extractive summaries generated by the system using augmented gisting models. Numbers to the right are log probabilities of the generated strings under the generation model.

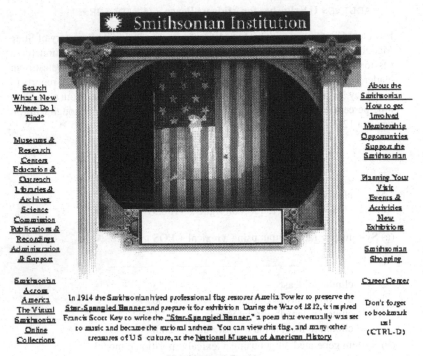

Open Directory Summary: Composed of sixteen museums and galleries, the National Zoo, and numerous research facilities in the ...

System Summary: research and education museum with the star-spangled-banner

Figure 10.6: The Smithsonian Museums web page with summaries.

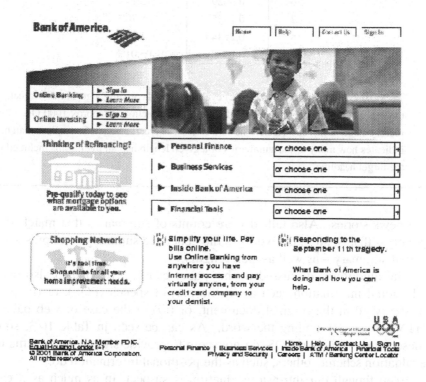

Open Directory Summary: Created from the merger of BankAmerica and NationsBank, Bank of America provides full-service banking ...

System Summary: business financial services and investing

Figure 10.7: The web page for the Bank of America with human and system generated summaries.

gist len	Word overlap	% age exact match
4	0.4116	19.71%
5	0.3489	14.10%
6	0.3029	12.14%
7	0.2745	08.70%
8	0.2544	11.90%
9	0.2353	05.01%

Table 10.2: One possible (simplistic) evaluation of the gisting algorithm. Evaluating the use of the simplest lexical model for content selection on approx 1000 Open Directory Pages and 1000 Reuters news articles. The percentage of complete matches indicates how many of the summaries of a given length had all their terms included in the target headline.

the news stories. Also tallied were counts of summaries that matched completely – that is, all of the words in the generated summary were present in the actual summary – as well as their lengths.

The algorithms discussed in this paper can be extended to also consider additional information such as (i) the part of speech (POS), or (ii) position of the word in the original document, or (iii) in the case of web pages, the HTML tags surrounding the word. As can be seen in Table 10.3, some of these sources, such as POS, do not seem to provide significant benefits in our evaluation scheme, others, such as the positional information do.

Even though our intrinsic evaluation is suspect, in as much as it cannot, even in principle, evaluate the ordering effect of the language model,[8] there are insights – about both summarization and evaluation – that can be gained from this effort; Even extremely simple statistical models can be very effective at summarization, given sufficient training data. While the outputs of a non-extraction based summarizer (on news stories) may not look as good as the output from an extraction based summarization system (on news stories), they are qualitatively different, and in cases where extractive summaries are not suitable, worth considering seriously. The weaknesses of this sort of evaluation are not all favorable to the summaries: Table 10.4 shows some legitimate alternate summary phrasings that the system produced, but that were counted as errors.

---

[8]But it could, in principle, detect LM-derived improvements in lexical coherence.

L	Lex	+Position	+POS	+Posn.+POS
1	0.37414	0.39888	0.30522	0.40538
2	0.24818	0.26923	0.27246	0.27838
3	0.21831	0.24612	0.20388	0.25048
4	0.21404	0.24011	0.18721	0.25741
5	0.20272	0.21685	0.18447	0.21947
6	0.20804	0.19886	0.17593	0.21168

Overlap with (news) headlines

L	Lex	+Position	+POS	+Posn.+POS
1	0.61589	0.70787	0.64919	0.67741
2	0.57447	0.63905	0.57831	0.63315
3	0.55251	0.63760	0.55610	0.62726
4	0.56167	0.65819	0.52982	0.61099
5	0.55099	0.63371	0.53578	0.58584
6	0.55817	0.60511	0.51466	0.58802

Overlap with top summary sentences

Table 10.3: Overlap between terms in the generated headlines and in the original headlines and the top extracted summary sentences, respectively, of the article. The extracted summary sentence was extracted using a modified version of Kupiec et al's machine learning approach to summarization (Kupiec *et al*, 1995). Using Part of Speech (POS) and information about a token's location in the source document, in addition to the lexical information, helps improve performance on the Reuters' test set.

Original	Generated
Nations Top Judge	Rehnquist
Kaczynski	Unabomber Suspect
ER	Top-Rated Hospital Drama
Drugs	Cocaine
Wall Street Stocks Decline	Dow Jones index lower
49ers Roll Over Vikings 38-22	49ers to nfc title game
Corn, Wheat Prices Fall	grain prices lower
Many Hopeful on N. Ireland Accord	britain ireland hopeful of irish peace

Table 10.4: Some pairs of target headline and generated summary terms that were counted as errors by the evaluation, but which are semantically equivalent, together with some "equally good" generated headlines that were counted as wrong in the evaluation.

Coherence Models: Evaluating the Syntactic Language Model.   Since the system uses both a language model and a word-relatedness model to calculate a gist of a web page, isolating the contribution of the language model to the performance of the system is a difficult task. Work in speech recognition suggests measuring language model quality by testing how well it might predict a previously-unseen collection G of actual summaries. Specifically, we can calculate the probability which the language model assigns to a set of unseen Open Directory gists; the higher the probability, the better the model.

The log-likelihood assigned by λ to an n-word collection G is

$$\log p(G) = \sum_{i=1}^{n} \log p(g_i \mid g_{i-2}g_{i-1})$$

The *perplexity* of G according to the trigram model is related to $\log p(G)$ by

$$\Pi(G) = \exp\left\{-\left(\frac{1}{n}\right)\sum_{i=1}^{n}\log p(g_i \mid g_{i-2}g_{i-1})\right\}$$

Perplexity can be thought of as the average number of guesses the language model must make to identify the next word in a string of text comprising a gist drawn from the test data. An upper bound in this case is $\mid W \mid = 37,863$: the number of different words which could appear in any single position in a gist. To the test collection of 1046 gists consisting of 20,775 words, the language model assigned a perplexity of 362. This is to be compared with the perplexity of the same text as measured by the weaker bigram and unigram models: 536 and 2185, respectively.

5.2   Extrinsic Evaluation

For an extrinsic evaluation, we considered the task of document classification as a proxy for summary quality. For this, we used a set of 629 randomly collected web pages, along with their human-generated summaries, from the Open Directory project. The pages were distributed across the following categories:

Sports/Martial Arts	Society/Philosophy
Sports/Motorsports	Society/Military
Sports/Equestrian	Home/Gardens

For each page, we generated six different "views": (i) the text of the web page, (ii) the title of the page, (iii) the automatically-generated summary of the page , (iv) the Open Directory-provided human summary of the page, (v) a set of words, equal in size to the automatically-generated summary, selected uniformly at random from the words in the original document, and (vi) the leading sequence of words in the page, equal in size to the automatically-generated summary.

Taking an information theoretic perspective, one could imagine each different view as the result of passing the original document through a different noisy channel. The question addressed in this user study is how much information is lost through each of these filters. To assess the information quality of a view, we ask a user to try to guess the proper classification of the original page, using only the information in that view.

For concreteness, Table 10.6 displays a single entry from among the 629 records used in the study. Only very minor text normalization was performed: lowercasing all words, removing filenames and mapping numbers containing two or more digits to the canonical token [num].

Table 10.5 contains the results of the user study. The results consist of six different users, each of whom classified approximately 120 views. The records assigned to each user were selected uniformly at random from the full collection of records, and the view for each record was randomly selected from among the six possible views.

Perhaps the most intriguing aspect of these results was the fact that the human-provided summary was actually *more* useful to the users, on average, than the actual web page. This may be explained by the fact that human summaries, of the sort found in the Open Directory project, often tend to bring in extra knowledge about the page, other closely related pages, the topic in general, and abstract away from the specifics to a more useful level where the infor-

information source	samples	correct	accuracy
Words in original page	131	108	0.824
Open Directory summary	109	94	0.862
Title of page	112	80	0.714
Synthesized summary	**115**	**80**	**0.695**
Words randomly-selected from page	122	76	0.622
First n words in page	98	75	0.765

Table 10.5: Results of an extrinsic user study to assess the quality of the automatically-generated web page summaries.

TOPIC: MOTORSPORTS

full page: davidcoulthard com david coulthard driving the [num] mclaren mercedes benz formula 1 racing car click here to enter copyright [num] [num] davidcoulthard com all rights reserved privacy policy davidcoulthard com is not affiliated with david coulthard or mclaren

title: david coulthard

Open Directory human summary: website on mclaren david coulthard the scottish formula 1 racing driver includes a biography

automatically-generated summary: racing formula 1 automobiles issues shift crash teams mercedes benz car driver click photos

Randomly-selected words: davidcoulthard policy click david mclaren driving to [num] com reserved with [num] copyright or

Leading words: davidcoulthard com david coulthard driving the [num] mclaren mercedes benz formula 1 racing car

Table 10.6: A single record from the user study, containing the six different views of a single web page.

mation density is higher. The system generated summary performed almost as well as the title of the page, and significantly better than a randomly-generated summary. However, it was clearly inferior to both the actual page and the human-generated summary, which is also understandable, because the system generated summary was limited to the information available on the page itself. Unfortunately, in our study, the generated summary was also somewhat worse than simply extracting the first few words from the page, which may be particularly effective for web pages which, typically, start with labeling headers.

6. Conclusion

Extractive summarization algorithms seem to work very well in most cases, especially news stories, where the writing style can be exploited to rank sentences. However, as more and more people start generating text that is meant to be read on a computer screen, rather than on paper, non-linear documents such as web pages, are beginning to proliferate. Summarization of these document genres will be an important task in browsing such document collections. Non-extractive summarization systems, even though they are substantially more computationally expensive, offer one possible approach to quickly skimming such documents. Another advantage of this approach, even for traditional, linear documents, is the potential to achieve substantially greater compression than extractive approaches.

This paper presents a machine learning approach; this has several advantages, and some disadvantages compared with more analytical approaches. For instance, a summarizer trained on a specific data set can generate summaries that reflect the underlying style, both in terms of content selection and exposition. Whereas the statistical models discussed in this paper are quite straightforward, they can be easily augmented with additional features of the source documents.

This paper has reported on very preliminary studies about the effectiveness of non-extractive summarization for generating summaries of web pages. Since web pages are often disjointed collections of links, formatting commands, graphics and incomplete sentences, this approach works fairly well on this application, which has been problematic for more traditional extractive approaches. This was mildly surprising, because our system, for practical reasons, did not take account of additional information, such as font-size, color, indentation, adjacent graphics, and linked or related pages, any of which could possibly be used to generate a better summary.

Despite this show of initial promise, it is clear that there remains a lot of work to be done before such algorithms can be used in a production setting, for instance, at a search engine site. These needs include better content selection and surface realization models. It is clearly desirable to make the models sensitive to the kinds of functional dependencies addressed by the Knight and Marcu model. An n-gram model of language, and a selection model insensitive to relative position, clearly do not even begin to capture some of the most essential relationships in language.

One intriguing possibility for inexpensively improving the credibility of these summaries lies in over-generating summaries, and then using other knowledge sources to invalidate or validate their content. These sources might include a detailed syntactic analysis of only those sections of the source document that have contributed to the summary, use predicate argument constraints from a knowledge base such as Cyc, or use statistical information, for instance, from Web sources, for lexical collocations similar to the generated summary.

Given the potential advantages of a data-based approach to learning summarization, exciting opportunities lie ahead for summarization researchers: with appropriate data, models like these can, in principle, be trained to perform cross-lingual summarization, where the words in the summary are picked from a different language. Even cross-modal summarization does not seem entirely out of the question. Each of these tasks will require addressing different sets of modeling concerns, and finding ways to take best advantage of existing training sets. Undoubtedly, as these issues are pursued, there will be new insights on many of the issues we have discussed in this paper, leading to increasingly better summaries.

Acknowledgments

The authors wish to acknowledge the support of Just System Corporation and Clairvoyance Corporation in this work. We are indebted to Adam Berger of Carnegie Mellon University and Eizel Technologies for numerous discussions, arguments and experiments regarding these ideas, including the user study mentioned here. However, the views expressed in this paper do not necessarily reflect either those of our sponsors or our collaborators, past, present, or future.

References

Berger, A., P. Brown, S. Della Pietra, V. Della Pietra, J. Gillett, J. Lafferty, H. Printz, and L. Ures. 1994. The Candide system for machine translation. In *Proceedings of the ARPA Human Language Technology Workshop*.

Berger, A. and J. Lafferty. 1999. The Weaver system for document retrieval. In *Proc. of the Eighth Text REtrieval Conference (TREC-8)*.

Brown, P., S. Della Pietra, V. Della Pietra, and R. Mercer. 1993. The mathematics of statistical machine translation: Parameter estimation. *Computational Linguistics*, 19(2):263–311.

Carbonell, Jaime and Jade Goldstein. 1998. MMR and diversity-based reranking for reodering documents and producing summaries. In *Proceedings of the 21st meeting of International ACM SIGIR Conference*, pages 335–336, Melbourne, Australia, August.

Clarkson, P. and R. Rosenfeld. 1997. Statistical language modeling using the CMU-Cambridge toolkit. In *Proceedings of Eurospeech '97*.

DeJong, Gerald F. 1982. An overview of the FRUMP system. In Wendy G. Lehnert and Martin H. Ringle, editors, *Strategies for Natural Language Processing*. Lawrence Erlbaum Associates, pages 149–176.

Edmundson, H. P. 1964. Problems in automatic extracting. *Communications of the ACM*, 7:259–263.

Goldstein, Jade, Mark Kantrowitz, Vibhu O. Mittal, and Jaime Carbonell. 1999. Summarizing Text Documents: Sentence Selection and Evaluation Metrics. In *Proceedings of the 22nd International ACM SIGIR Conference on Research and Development in Information Retrieval (SIGIR-99)*, pages 121–128, Berkeley, CA.

Good, I. 1953. The population frequencies of species and the estimation of population parameters. *Biometrika*, 40.

Hand, T. F. 1997. A proposal for task-based evaluation of text summarization systems. In *ACL/EACL-97 Workshop on Intelligent Scalable Text Summarization*, pages 31–36, July.

Hovy, E. and C. Y. Lin. 1997. Automated text summarization in SUMMARIST. In *ACL/EACL-97 Workshop on Intelligent Scalable Text Summarization*, pages 18–24, Madrid, Spain, July.

Jelinek, F. 1997. *Statistical methods for speech recognition*. MIT Press.

Jing, H., R. Barzilay, K. McKeown, and M. Elhadad. 1998. Summarization evaluation methods experiments and analysis. In *AAAI Intelligent Text Summarization Workshop*, pages 60–68, March.

Knight, Kevin and Daniel Marcu. 2000. Statistics-based summarization - step one: Sentence compression. In *Proceedings of the Seventeenth National Conference on Artificial Intelligence (AAAI-00)*, Austin, TX, August. AAAI.

Kupiec, J. M., J. Pedersen, and F. Chen. 1995. A trainable document summarizer. In *Proceedings of the 18th Annual Int. ACM/SIGIR Conference on Research and Development in IR*, pages 68–73, July.

Luhn, P. H. 1958. Automatic creation of literature abstracts. *IBM Journal*, pages 159–165.

Marcu, Daniel. 1997. From discourse structures to text summaries. In *Proceedings of the ACL'97/EACL'97 Workshop on Intelligent Scalable Text Summarization*, pages 82–88.

Mathis, B. A., J. E. Rush, and C. E. Young. 1973. Improvement of automatic abstracts by the use of structural analysis. *Journal of the American Society for Information Science*, 24:101–109.

McKeown, Kathleen K. and Dragomir R. Radev. 1995. Generating summaries of multiple news articles. In *Proceedings of ACM/SIGIR 1995*, pages 74–82. ACM.

Mittal, Vibhu O., Mark Kantrowitz, Jade Goldstein, and Jaime Carbonell. 1999. Selecting Text Spans for Document Summaries: Heuristics and Metrics. In *Proceedings of the Sixteenth National Conference on Artificial Intelligence (AAAI-99)*, pages 467–473, Orlando, FL, July. AAAI.

Nathan, K., H. Beigi, J. Subrahmonia, G. Clary, and H. Maruyama. 1995. Real-time on-line unconstrained handwriting recognition using statistical methods. In *Proceedings of the IEEE Conference on Acoustics, Speech and Signal Processing (ICASSP)*.

Tipster. 1998. Tipster text phase III 18-month workshop notes, May. Fairfax, VA.

Index